# Mathematics …

Colin Rowe's *Mathematics of the Ideal Villa* in 1947 marked a mo.
reconnection between Renaissance and Modernist beliefs in mathematical ordering
systems. Comparing Palladio's Villa Foscari (Malcontenta) with Le Corbusier's
Villa Stein at Garches, Rowe notes a similarity between the two villas, despite their
different "moods." Both architects, he writes, "share a common standard,
a mathematical one."[1]

The apparent bemoaning of the loss of adherence to rules that concludes
*Mathematics* becomes a call for just that in *Collage City*, more than 20 years later.
Summarized as "an appeal for order and disorder, for the simple and the complex,
for the joint existence of permanent reference and random happening,"[2] the text
calls for a malleability of form that is responsive to context.

At around the same time, the discipline of mathematics was experiencing
radical changes itself. The 20th century had already witnessed two mathematical
revolutions, which had destabilized the principles of Newtonian physics:
relativity and quantum mechanics. Finally, in the 1970s, chaos theory developed
the discipline's ability to describe apparent randomness and complexity through
nonlinear mathematics. This shift emerged in part from an engagement with
observed phenomena, in which many natural systems were shown to behave with
both stability and unpredictability.

Given the established relationship between the two disciplines, it is perhaps
inevitable that the consequences of this schism should have reverberated strongly
in architecture. Greg Lynn, himself educated in the Rowian tradition, proposed
an alternative to his predecessor's "mathematical, exact, geometric, and analytical"
practices with other techniques that were instead "anexact, multiplicitous, temporal,
supple, fluid, disproportionate and monstrous spatial bodies" resisting any reductions
to ideal form.[3] Lynn's provocations, both written and designed, instigated a final
resurgence of mathematics in architecture. In the past 20 years, conversations of
algorithms, topology, data analysis, and periodicity became commonplace in the
education of an architect, producing an architecture where variation, proliferation,
adaptability, and formal complexity have dominated.

In the hangover that follows this initial frenzy of chaotic geometrical profi-
ciency, architecture is now beginning to interpret mathematics differently: as script
versus form, as instructions versus object, as recursive, reactive, and responsive
systems. No longer is mathematics used as an aesthetic tool for ordering a set of
givens; it has become a generative tool or input yielding architecture that has the
potential to be uncontrolled.

This issue of the *Cornell Journal of Architecture*, in exploring our discipline's
obsessions with mathematics, oscillates between two extremes: the Ideal,
mathematics understood as order, proportion, symmetry, part-to-whole relationships;
and the Uncertain, mathematics understood as probability, fuzziness, recursion,
games, and randomness. While this issue engages with contemporary interpretations
of mathematics in architecture, it also projects beyond current practices and tries
to understand how the contemporary mathematics of uncertainty and disorder can
be embraced and incorporated into our thinking and making of architecture.

The Editors of the *Cornell Journal of Architecture*

# ... From the Ideal to the Uncertain

Consider the Greek letter φ, a symbol for the Golden Ratio that has been used over the ages—from Vitruvius, to da Vinci, to Le Corbusier, among many others—to ensure a certain harmonious aesthetic in the design of building facades, plans, and structural elements. And, perhaps for good measure, to reflect a mystical connection between the order of the universe and human proportions.

In mathematics, φ is at once a symbol for a simply written irrational fraction and an endless decimal number 1.61803398874989484820458683436563811772..., which is, paradoxically perhaps, infinitely precise in its imprecision or uncertainty. φ, then, can be understood to represent a condition that is common to the disciplines of Architecture and Mathematics: the simultaneous comfort and security of certain long-held physical and conceptual rules, contrasted with more open-ended methods for solving contemporary problems. Euclidian geometry and Modulor-based methods come to mind on the one hand; fractal dimensions and parametric design approaches on the other.

Issue 9 of the *Cornell Journal of Architecture*, which in a sense can be considered as a literal reflection, or an examination of such multiple meanings of φ, places side-by-side these two disciplines that have been engaged in a long-standing relationship. Their association has often been characterized by a mutual fascination for the other's seemingly incomprehensible and mysterious ways and also, at least in the case of Architecture toward Mathematics, by an uncomfortable yet nonetheless critical dependency. This disciplinary pairing is clearly advantageous in the present context in that it permits a strategic section to be cut through the diverse interests of our faculty and guests, as well as our global network, from those whose concerns include proportion to those focused more on digital matters, from theory and aesthetics to building, and from systems analysis to moods.

Mathematics. Architecture. The Ideal. The Uncertain. Considered individually, each is a vastly expansive topic of perhaps unfathomable depths; when considered all at once, the interconnections become infinitely rich in possibility and yield dialogues that are fundamental to the architectural processes of conceptualization and production.

Mark Cruvellier,
*Chair, Department of Architecture, Cornell University*

**Endnotes**

1  Colin Rowe, *Mathematics of the Ideal Villa* in "Mathematics of the Ideal Villa and Other Essays" (Cambridge, MA: MIT Press, 1976), pp. 1–27. Originally, "The Mathematics of the Ideal Villa: Palladio and Le Corbusier Compared," *Architectural Review* (March 1947): 101–104.

2  Colin Rowe and Fred Koetter, *Collage City* (Cambridge, MA: MIT Press), 8.

3  Greg Lynn, *New Variations on the Rowe Complex*, in "Folds, Bodies, Blobs: Collected Essays," La Lettre Volée, 1998, 201.

# Contents

## Tom Fecht

*is an artist and guest lecturer at the Royal College of Art and Imperial College, London. He was a visiting lecturer at Cornell University in 2004 and 2005, where he taught experimental photography studios in the Departments of Art and Architecture, including Listening with the Eyes —Artistic Strategies of Inversion; a Soup Kitchen on photo theory; and the seminars Broken Vision, with John Zissovici, and It Might Just Work, with Chris Wise. He still contributes to Cornell's Rome program. Current research focuses on photography as a design tool and heuristic toy.*

# Refocusing the Euclidian Horizon

*Σημεῖόν ἐστιν οὗ μέρος οὐθέν. (Semeion estin ou meros outhen.):*
*The Sign is that which has no parts.*
Euclid, *Elements*

The common Latin translation *Punctum est cuius pars non est*, which surfaces in all modern languages as *the point is that which has no parts*, contains a jarring inaccuracy. It uses the pre-Euclidean term στιγμή (*Stigmé*) for point and not σημεῖον (*Semeion*) for sign. According to Wolfgang Schaeffner, a cultural historian at Humboldt University Berlin, Euclid's use of *Semeion* is not accidental, and further, its meaning was significantly expanded as a referential operation throughout the fourth and third centuries B.C.[1]

This sets the historic stage for a geometrical zero with surprising entities. We are no longer looking at a pre-Euclidean point-unity but a limit that is nothing; it starts and stops as it connects and interrupts. This point-sign is separated from anything rooted in numbers,[2] not an abstract principle but a multitasking character and operational mode: a sign that *is* and simultaneously *is not*, no longer an object but a relation, a geometric agent with the powerful mission to divide, and "more fundamental than the unit, the 1."[3]

The true essence of Euclid's sign, the genesis of zero, the establishment of a conceptual and numeric horizon, and all related geometric operations have the critical capacity to open the gateway from the realm of the undividable into the divided, border-lining from the ideal into the material, moving continuously back and forth between the concrete and the abstract—or, in today's terms, between the real and the virtual world. It is precisely at this gateway where projection moves in as a transitional operation mode, sharing its material-immaterial stage with fantasy—and in particular with imagination.[4]

By establishing Euclid's point-sign and its operational options as the universal mediator between imagination and creation, Schaeffner's completed analysis[5] might challenge the theory of design and the discourse of analog image theory. The possible impact becomes even more evident in considering that an expanded understanding of "Euclid's sign" also applies to non-Euclidean geometry. In mathematics, non-Euclidean geometry refers only to elliptic and hyperbolic geometry, both of which imply an essentially different concept of the nature of parallel lines.[6] The denial of Euclid's notorious fifth *parallel postulate* neither fundamentally alters nor questions the remaining four postulates and their respective common notions and definitions. Thus, a deeper understanding of Euclid's *Sign* may well reinspire future practice of Euclidean and non-Euclidean geometry.[7]

Habit has generated a certain blindness for the material "stage" that most design performances require: from stone to dry skin to paper, wood, canvas, and film, to the omnipresent screen and the virtual horizon—in any case, a flat two-dimensional surface, which does not exist as such in nature. Yet the projection surface is a primary tool that visualizes operations and materializes the outcome in a technical memory. Thus, a flat table may be regarded as a basic representation of such a material-immaterial stage. Fusing nature with the abstract, it assembles skyward grown wood with the horizontality of geometric lines.

**Finis Terrae**, 1997/2007. (See note at end of essay.)

Once a spirit level positions the table in perfect tune with the gravitational lines of the natural horizon, its surface transforms into an artificial horizon, a doppelgänger flattened out for an expanding gaze at human scale.[8] A design in mind—still to be developed but not yet there—can now be divided into single operations while morphing into something that stretches out "before the hand"[9]—in Vilèm Flusser's terms. Projected onto the pale blankness of the surface, the innocence of the two-dimensional interface gives birth to whatever becomes the project, by "staging" it. Powered by projection, we may conclude, imagination generates horizons always greater than ourselves, pointing beyond our current knowledge base.

The inspiring momentum of *the sign which has no parts* remained surprisingly hidden until early Renaissance and into the end of the 16th century under the dominant pre-Euclidean discourse of geometry represented by Aristotle's *Physics*, which considered the arithmetic of the Pythagoreans as being more fundamental than geometry.[10] Here the dormant potency of the analog code finally explodes.

The algorithms that allow for any drawing or painting, letter or book, and the processing of all calculations could be only generated and processed by the geometric code. Euclid's *Sign* operates at the foundations of the three cultural key techniques; the *Elements* become their common operational system. Since antiquity, the analog code generated a set of universal tools for measurement, like the gnomon, the quadrant, and the astrolabe, followed by the sector for calculation in the 16th century. These instruments implement geometric operations that become the foundation for numerous sciences, the arts, and innovative engineering, transmitting the geometric code independently from the treatises.[11]

With Alberti, Filippo Brunelleschi, Leonardo da Vinci, Albrecht Dürer, Biagio Pelacani, Lorenzo Ghiberti, Piero della Francesca, and many others,[12] operations of point and lines become the fundamental code for the construction of images, and "those who do not follow these rules will not even be considered a mediocre painter."[13] Most of this is well known and has been widely published, but reading the Renaissance's technical and visual revolution as an outcome of geometric tooling gives us a different starting point and generates a deeper picture of the era.

*Florence & Bagdhad* by art historian Hans Belting is a key contribution.[14] His West-Eastern history of the human gaze distinguishes two visual cultures, "one without pictures or imitations of the visible world, and the other centered on the need to think in pictures in order to explain the world."[15] His research unfolds a double history of perspective originating in Baghdad and the Middle East as a visual theory primarily founded on geometrical abstraction combined with an early anatomic understanding of the human ocular system. Developed by the Muslim polymath Ibn al-Haytham (965–1039/1040), it resurfaced in Renaissance Florence. There, it transformed into a pictorial theory of perspective art to construct images and paint horizons that adopted the focal point of the human gaze. Thus, the common notion of '*being-in-the-world*' transforms into '*gazing-at-the-world,*' as much as the "perspective painting became a symbolic mirror in which the gaze depicted itself."[16] Nature's visible horizon that once moved with the viewer can now be reconstructed. The new viewer, liberated from nature's constructive limits, may now choose his position in front of different horizons;[17] the multiple aspects of the world—still an essential ingredient of new media.

Siegfried Zielinski, a founding figure innovating *Media Archaeology*, introduced the interaction of imagination with the long—and often accidental— history of media technology into this new epistemological field. Inspired by Michel Foucault, Zielinski's *Deep Time of the Media: Toward an Archaeology of Hearing and Seeing by Technical Means* broke established conventions of progressive genealogies and implemented his creative definition of media "as spaces of action for constructed attempts to connect what is separated."[18]

More recently, Zielinski's long-term *Variantology*[19] project compiled the research of an international network of scholars into five volumes with a profound insight *On Deep Time Relations of Arts, Sciences and Technologies*. *Variantology 4*[20] sets the focus on the *Arabic-Islamic World and Beyond* and includes mathematics, sound, music, clock making, and the relations between image and text. In *How One Sees: A Short Genealogy on the Variation of a Model*, he traces the scientific concepts of the human ocular system against the evolutionary backdrop of the *camera obscura* as a master-concept, revealing the archeological layers of our knowledge base on vision, optics, and visual perception.[21] The genealogic overview spans from the optical canon of the Chinese Mohists in the fourth century B.C.E. to Shen Kuo and Ibn al-Haytham[22] as early protagonists of geometrical optics into current research on how sight can be restored for the blind. He concludes: "Here, the organ of vision is no longer required as a medium. Machines, which simulate optical stimuli for the brain, replace it. Visual perception functions by direct connection to the visual capabilities of the brain. Physically, we are capable of getting out of the cave (Plato's), but are we capable of leaving it metaphysically, without divine assistance?"[23]

This conclusion reflects, in many ways, the thinking of the Czech-born media-philosopher Vilèm Flusser and recalls in particular his concept of *null dimension.* Design, in Flusser's terms, embraces projection and implies a new form of imagination powered by technology (*Einbildungskraft*). Here Euclid's *Sign* resurfaces finally as a technological power to implement an image by means of abstraction: passing again through the gateway of the point-sign with zero dimension, becoming the gateway of computation and symbolic numbers.[24]

In a recent lecture, Zielinski developed the dialectics of his concept of *deep time* (*Tiefenzeit*) further by fusing the opposition of two philosophical signatures into one creative option, which elegantly connects the past with the future in a double movement: the prospective concept of *design* (*Entwerfen*) as promoted by Vilém Flusser and the retrospective idea of *revealing* (*Entbergen*) by Martin Heidegger.[25] His updated proposal makes deep time a melancholia-free twin-application that implements *Face Time* with current media tooling and practice: a forward- and rear-facing zoom that allows us to refocus the long-lasting relationships between imagination and projection folded into the media practice of the present and the past while anticipating future options.

Applied to the ever-changing horizons of design and artistic practice, this twin-application reminds us of the Italian philosopher Giorgio Agamben revealing the profound ambiguities of contemporaneity.[26] The preferred media-horizon in Zielinski's research becomes the experimental interface between artifacts and systems and their users. Here, "as so often before, the tension between calculation and imagination, between uncertainty and unpredictability, proved to be an inexhaustible fount of discussion about cultural techniques and technological culture." For the media-archeologist, it amounted to "a debate where no consensus is possible, and any dogmatic opting for one side or the other can lead only to stasis."[27] The horizon, conceptually, is a natural border-phenomenon on which the human eye can hardly focus. Thus, it can be read as a perfect image of uncertainty.

What then is the significance of the fundamental sign that has no parts? The multilayered principles of geometric creation in Proclus's commentary resonate a similar magic vision when he mirrors Euclid's point-zero as a "creative force that brings into existence all which is divided."[28] In the respective passage, Proclus establishes a genetic relationship between point, line, and circle by expanding the center point into that which becomes the circle. But the point does not remain ideal, its power is real: as the center of planetary rotation the point's *creative force* becomes a material reality and a source of never-ending movements in the universe, gravity.

Here Proclus's neo-Platonic view recalls in particular the *formless void* in the first lines of the Book of Genesis, where the world's horizon is switched on from a zero's zero by a divine operation, *separating the light from the darkness,*[29] a founding act that still resonates in the cosmological model of the Big Bang theory. This shortcut reveals Euclid's sign again as a doppelgänger[30] of the divine—and creation.

The separation of light and darkness, however, remains a key operation of creation—not only in photography. The synonym, knowing and not knowing, still determines the fundamental setup of scientific experiment and makes uncertainty a creative institution that belongs to the foundations of science.[31] Here the power of the analog code becomes particularly apparent in the ultimate identity of a continuous code with its representation. Code and representation fuse into one unique expression, 1:1. The horizon, like no other part of the natural landscape, still attracts imagination and emits such a high degree of persistent abstractness. The vanishing point performs as a line, separating the dividable finite from undividable infinity. Its powers recall the point's operational options, while gravity stages day, night, and the seasons for us, as well as the desire to move on into the open.

The stage seems to be an archetype that is as material as it is immaterial. The natural horizon at the open sea fuses with a magnetic attraction that draws fantasy to the straightest of nature's longest and oldest lines. Once bent by gravitational forces, the horizon's curved line became the birthmark of the planet, making it an imperfect sphere and a perfect stage for us—beyond our scale.[32] The infinite sky arched over an open sea already incarnates the key features of the ancient proscenium theater; most of them survived in the still-classic canon of contemporary practice and still determine the signature-architecture of the world's leading theaters today.[33]

*Deep Time of the Media* reconnects us in multiple ways with the long shadow of human imagination. Projecting three dimensions onto a flat surface already makes technical images an explicit construction of Euclidean geometry. Equally, capturing an image requires tools rooted in optical geometry, and requires a set of repetitive operations still close to geometry: pointing, framing, the choice of a standpoint, changing perspective, reframing, focusing, metering, and setting the aperture for depth of field, and so on. Embedded in lens-based media, like photography, however, is imagination, a human gesture from inside the body, with the option to turn the rules of geometry inside out; such a risk-option is of "crucial importance for engaging with media."[34] The shadow-geometry of imagination seemingly adopts the planet as its universal media: governed by the rules of separation, it carries the critical potency to reconnect what had to be divided to become.[35]

In Euclidean space there seems to be no geometrical end—in practice and in theory.[36] Like the still-expanding universe, *The Sign*, geometry's master-tool, maintains the potency to expand again and further beyond its own horizon toward the open, into no-man's-land. Landscape means *framed nature*; its scale can be determined by the distance to paradise, the innocent desire to be naked under new stars again. It is time for *The Sign* to break the wall, unframing the world instead of reframing it.

*Pages 4–9:* Electric Cinema V, VIII, and IX, *Tom Fecht, 2011. All photographs courtesy of the artist,* © *Tom Fecht, 2012. The image on page 11 is part of Fecht's project* Movement into the Open. *Tom Fecht and Dietmar Kamper (eds.),* Umzug ins Offene: Vier Versuche über den Raum (Movement into the Open: Four Experiments on Space) *(Vienna and New York: Springer Verlag,*

*2000). The title refers to Martin Heidegger's concept of "Das Offene" (The Open). Ute Guzzoni, former assista of Martin Heidegger at the University of Freiburg, contributed an analysis of the image for this project. An English translation is available at <http://www. tomfecht.com/photography/guzzoni.pdf>.*

## Endnotes

1 Wolfgang Schaeffner, "Die Macht des Punktes: Euklid MIT Proklos (The Power of the Point: Euclid with Proclus)." The paper was presented at the annual *eikones* convention *Imagination. Suchen und Finden*, Schaulager Basel, November 18, 2010, pp. 3–4 of the still unpublished manuscript. Schaeffner's current research focuses on the theory of structures and geometric operations, the architecture of scientific knowledge, interdisciplinary designs of science, and material epistemology.

2 The *Elements* literally turned the pre-Euclidean hierarchy upside down. Line, circle, square, and all successive elements are rooted in Euclid's point-sign; only Book 7 finally introduces the arithmetical unit as the origin of numbers.

3 Extracted from Wolfgang Schaeffner: "The Sign of Euclid: The Genesis of the Analog Code in Early Modern Europe." The paper is an earlier version of *The Power of the Point* and was presented at the University of Konstanz (Germany) in June 2008. Only the German version of the manuscript has been published on the H-Net information network for art history as "Euklids Zeichen: Zur Genese des analogen Codes in der Frühen Neuzeit," *Bildwelten des Wissens* 7, no. 2, November 30, 2010: *Mathematische Forme(l)n*, Kunsthistorisches Jahrbuch für Bildkritik, Horst Bredekamp, Matthias Bruhn, and Gabriele Werner (eds.); <http://arthist. net/archive/575>. The German and the English versions differ considerably, making exact citations difficult.

4 So far, my brief summary of Schaeffner's findings draws—with kind permission of the author—from all of the above sources.

5 Wolfgang Schaeffner, *Punkt 0.1 Zur Genese des analogen Codes in der Frühen Neuzeit* (Berlin/ Zürich: Diaphanes Verlag) announced for October 2012 as one of three volumes compiling an analysis and documentation of the point-sign as Euclid's main element.

6 Euclid's fifth postulate defines *parallels* as lines that remain at constant distance from each other, even if extended to infinity, whereas the *ultra-parallels* of *hyperbolic geometry* curve away from each other with increasing distance from the points of intersection with the common perpendicular. In *elliptic geometry*, by contrast, the lines curve toward each other with the option to eventually intersect.

7 This includes the non-Euclidean concepts of *absolute* or *neutral geometry* (János Bolyai, 1832), *Affine* and *Projective Geometry* (Felix Klein's *Erlangen Program*, 1872), *Incidence Geometry* (relations of incidence between geometrical objects like point, lines, curves, or planes), and *Ordered Geometry* (Moritz Pasch's concept of *betweenness*, omitting the basic notion of measurement, 1882). Compare also endnote 36.

8 Also compare: Tom Fecht and Dietmar Kamper (eds.), *Umzug ins Offene: Vier Versuche über den Raum (Movement into the Open: Four Experiments on Space)* (Vienna and New York: Springer Verlag, 2000). The title refers to Martin Heidegger's concept of "Das Offene" (The Open). Ute Guzzoni, former assistant of Martin Heidegger at the University of Freiburg, contributed an analysis of the cover-image, the iconic Leitmotiv of the project. An English translation and the image (Finis Terrae, 1997) is available at <http://www.tomfecht.com/ photography/guzzoni.pdf>

9 Vilèm Flusser in a letter to his cousin David Flusser in Jerusalem, from November 25, 1990 (written in German), where he mentions his plan for "an essay on projection (design) in opposition to subjectivity (obsequiousness)"; Flusser died a year later. Letter number 56 of Flusser's archived correspondence at the Vilèm_Flusser_Archive, Berlin. A facsimile has been recently published by S. Zielinki (see endnote 24).

10 Schaeffner, "The Sign of Euclid," extracted from the unpublished English manuscript, p. 3 (see endnote 3).

11 Ibid., pp. 7–8. Pointing to M. Serres, Schaeffner references the Gnomon as the material equivalent of Euclid's point-sign (see endnote 1, pp. 5–6).

12 Schaeffner mentions in particular the Florence artist and engineer Leon Battista Alberti, who resurrects with *Elimenti di pittura* (1435) Euclid's far-reaching vision. In *Ludi mathematici* (1448), he finally realizes calculation with geometric operations (compare also H. Belting, endnote 14).

13 L.B. Alberti, *Elementa picturae* (1436), 336, as quoted by Schaeffner in "The Sign of Euclid," p. 6 (see endnote 3).

14 Hans Belting, *Florence and Baghdad: Renaissance Art and Arab Science*, translated from the German edition (2008) by Deborah Lucas Schneider (Cambridge, MA: Harvard University Press, 2008), 146–149. Belting's detailed overview of the key contributors to the art of perspective adds the mathematician and philosopher Biagio Pelacani da Parma (ca. 1347–1416) as a key figure when it comes to the implementation of mathematical space.

15 Hans Belting, "Afterthoughts on Alhazen's Visual Theory and Its Presence in the Pictorial Theory of Western Perspective," in *Variantology 4—On Deep Time Relations of Arts, Sciences and Technologies in the Arabic-Islamic World and Beyond* (Cologne: Walther König, 2010), 43–52 (see endnote 20).

16 H. Belting, *Florence and Baghdad*, pp. 162–163.

17 Belting dedicates a full chapter of *Florence and Baghdad* to the "Horizon and the View Through a Window," two metaphors that "sum up the new visual culture of perspective" (238–252).

18 Siegfried Zielinski, *Deep Time of the Media— Toward an Archaeology of Hearing and Seeing by Technical Means*, Gloria Custance (trans.); foreword by Timothy Druckrey (Cambridge, MA: MIT Press, 2006).

19 The project includes five international conferences and their respective publications (Cologne: Walther König), 2005–2010. The approach reflects in many

ways Michel Foucault's concept of genealogy, which draws from Nietzsche's understanding of morality as a historical and social construction; <http://variantology.com/>.

20 Siegfried Zielinski and Eckhard Fürlus (ed.), *Variantology 4—On Deep Time Relations of Arts, Sciences and Technologies in the Arabic-Islamic World and Beyond* (Cologne: Walther König, 2010).

21 Siegfried Zielinski and Franziska Latell, "How One Sees—A Short Genealogy on the Variation of a Model," in *Variantology 4*, 413–442.

22 Arab polymath known in the West as Alhazens or Alhacen. He was among the first geometers who attempted to challenge Euclid's parallel postulate to be a theorem from the other four by *proof of contradiction*.

23 S. Zielinski, in *Variantology 4*, 442.

24 Siegfried Zielinski, "Designing and Revealing— Some Aspects of a Genealogy of Projection," in M. Blassnigg (ed.), *Light, Image, Imagination: The Spectrum Beyond Reality and Illusion* (Amsterdam: Amsterdam University Press, 2011). Extracted from the original German edition: *Entwerfen und Entbergen—Aspekte einer Genealogie der Projektion*, published as part of the *International Flusser Lectures* series by the Vilém_Flusser_ Archive, Berlin (Cologne: Walther König 2010), 7. <http://www.flusser-archive.org/>.

25 Ibid., 50–53.

26 Giorgio Agamben, "What Is the Contemporary?" in David Kishik and Stefan Pedatella (trans.) *What Is an Apparatus?* (Palo Alto, CA: Stanford University Press, 2009), 39–55.

27 S. Zielinski, *Deep Time of the Media*, Introduction, 10.

28 W. Schaeffner, "Die Macht des Punktes," extracted from the manuscript (see endnote 1, 9–10), and the Euclid comment by Proclus Lycaeus (412–485 B.C., in particular, his definitions of the circle).

29 New American Standard Bible, *The Creation*.

30 Double-character that lives on in current software like *Second Life* and its *Avatars*.

31 In quantum mechanics, established as Heisenberg's Uncertainty Principle (1927).

32 Created an estimated 4.54 billion years ago, with a mean radius of 6,371 kilometers, equal to approximately 3,959 miles. Here the concepts of *Deep Time* in geology and media seem to mirror each other on an open stage, where the mind seems "to grow giddy by looking so far into the abyss of time." Concepts similar to the geologic term of *Deep Time* were already recognized by the Persian geologist and polymath Ibn Sina, known as Avicenna (973–1037), and the Chinese naturalist and polymath Shen Kuo, also known as Shen Kua (1031–1095).

33 This includes, for example, a generous *proscenium arch* with a high *flyspace, backstage, offstage*, or the *wings*, once granted by the spherical bent. The *thrust stage* once spanned like a gigantic *apron* from the *prospect* of the horizon to the feet of the audience. The shore morphed into today's *house* with a *limited audience* while the darkness—once separating the ancients from nature's *stage* at night—morphed into the *dark front curtain*. *Archetype* seems to be an appropriate term, since nobody—except for the gods—was ever authorized to *break the fourth wall*, that imaginary barrier at the front of the stage separating the audience from the performance on (horizon's) stage.

34 S. Zielinski, *Deep Time of the Media*, 10.

35 Giorgio Agamben approaches man as the outcome and simultaneously as the very watershed of ongoing divisions and caesuras by expanding Heidegger's concept of "Das Offene," in *The Open: Man and Animal*, translated from the Italian (2002) by Kevin Attell (Palo Alto, CA: Stanford University Press, 2004).

36 Jorge R. Dantas, "The End of Euclidean Geometry or Its Alternate Uses in Computer Design," in *Poéticas de la Disrupcion* (Open Conference System at the University of São Paulo, 2010), 161–164. Download at <http://cumincades.scix.net/data/works/att/sigradi2010_161.content.pdf>.

37 *Electrical Cinema* includes a series of 10 Piezo-Pigment prints, 87 × 229 cm and has been photographed in Ireland (2007), Italy (2008), and France (2011). A complete view is available at <http://www.tomfecht.com/>.

## Bernard Cache

*developed the concept of nonstandard architecture in his book* Earth Moves, *published by MIT Press in 1995. This concept was given the name "objectile" by Gilles Deleuze in his book* Leibniz: The Fold. *In 1996, Bernard Cache founded the company Objectile in order to conceive and manufacture nonstandard architecture components. He teaches nomadically at many universities and currently at Cornell University Department of Architecture.*

# Instruments of Thought: Another Classical Tradition

**The Antiquities of Athens**, James Stuart and Nicholas Revett. Elevation with sundial lines and plan

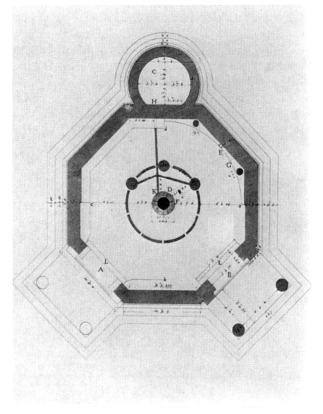

Parametric design and mechanics are not new in architecture: they were actually there from the very beginning of the written sources of our discipline. To understand this, we must return to classics such as works by Euclid, Plato, and Vitruvius. A renewed reading of those classics has the potential to bring contemporary architecture back into a historical tradition. In order to demonstrate this, I will mainly rely on an intermediary character between our time and antiquity: Albrecht Dürer, the great artist of the German Renaissance, who lived at the turn of the 16th century.

Instead of discussing his paintings, however, I will mainly focus on his treatise of geometry, *Underweysung der Messung* or *Instruction in Measurement*. It is a rather unique case in the history of mathematics, since it is written by a non-mathematician for non-mathematicians. Rather than showing geometrical figures, Dürer often shows mechanical instruments that are intended to be used to draw curves. These instruments take on so much importance that sometimes the curves themselves are not even represented. Thus, in order to read this classical text, we can use CAD/CAM software, which enables us to establish parametric relations between elements in the figures, model the mechanical instruments, and simulate their movements in order to generate their trajectory.

Mechanics has been part of architecture since antiquity. Vitruvius's second definition of architecture in *De Architectura*[1] consists of three parts: the construction of buildings (*aedificatio*), the construction of solar clocks (*gnomonica*), and the construction of machines (*machinatio*). The first building mentioned in this treatise is the Tower of the Winds.

While this looks like a building, it is actually a masterpiece of *gnomonica* and of *machinatio*, designed by a master clockmaker. There was a sundial on each wall of this octagonal tower, the lines of which were clearly indicated by Stuart and Revett in their book *The Antiquities of Athens*.[2] Unfortunately, the tower is empty today, but there are traces of a mechanism on the ground. American archaeologists discovered that the cylindrical tower at the rear of the building was a water tank, from which water spilled into another tank. There, a float lifted a cable which, in turn, wound a rope around an axis to cause a large bronze disk to rotate.

The disk was a stereographic projection of the celestial sphere, being used as a clock in the Tower of the Winds. The problem was that the water was spilling at a constant rate, but in antiquity, hours did not have a constant duration. The day was divided into 12 hours, both in summer and in winter, so the hours of each day varied. Thus, to measure a varying time with a mechanism rotating at a constant speed, a network of conversion curves was built.

The heavy black line is the stereographic projection of the horizon. Above this horizon circle are the hours of the day, and underneath are the hours of the night. The curves divide the arcs into 12 equal and varying parts along the year. This was one of the first clocks to enable the time to be known during the night or when there was no sun.

Thus, this Tower of the Winds incarnates quite well the three parts of the Vitruvian definition of architecture: it is a building (*aedificatio*), it has at least eight planar sundials (*gnomonica*), and, above all, it is a machine (*machinatio*). It was a machine that produced information; what we today would call a computer, from the Latin verb *computare*, or *to calculate*.

Dürer inscribes himself within this antique tradition of variation, both parametric and mechanical, by proposing to us a variety of instruments. Since he is the first to write a treatise in German, he has no scientific vocabulary at his disposal. He invents names for his drawing instruments by taking names of animals: the snail, the spider, and the snake. Besides the drawing instruments, he also proposes calculating instruments that provide solutions to complex mathematical problems.

The snail line (*schneckenlinie*) comes directly from Vitruvius's description of the ionical volute in *De Architectura*, book III. However, this particular chapter of Vitruvius's text is very difficult to understand, if only because the ten figures at the end of the treatise have disappeared. As a result, Dürer turned toward Alberti's interpretation, which is based on the same principle but is slightly different from Vitruvius's.

The device that Vitruvius described could be generated by winding a thread around four nails positioned on the corners of a square inscribed within the oculus of the ionic volute.

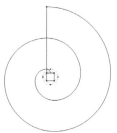

A thread is rotated around four nails. While rotating, each time the thread is intercepted by one of the nails, the moving section is shortened by the distance between two of the nails. Hence, the free end of the thread traces a spiral with a diminishing radius. This is typically what mathematicians call a "thread construction" (the nail holes are actually visible on a number of ionical capitals such as those from the "teatro maritime" of the Villa Hadriana at Tivoli).

The solution proposed by Alberti was with two nails, vertically placed, rather than four. This is only the first of the many snails Dürer will propose. Having completed this one, he writes: "Now, I will draw another spiral by a different method which can be put to many uses and is very useful. Much can be learned from it, and it can be used instead of the one described before."[3]

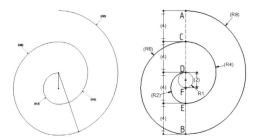

Actually, we can take this as a general principle in Dürer's geometry: *There is nothing asserted in a figure that cannot be submitted to variation in a subsequent figure.*

The next spiral is that of Archimedes. At the time, there was no device with which to draw this spiral.[4]

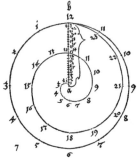

So, in order to draw the Archimedes spiral, Dürer took the radius of a circle and divided it into 24 equal parts. Then, he divided the circle into 12 equal angles, and he associated an angle with a length on the radius. This gave points around the circle and enabled him to draw interpolation curves between the points in order to draw this spiral.[5]

These interpolation curves are the ancestors of NURBS and B-spline used in CAD software. Dürer introduces the third snail as follows: "Now I shall alter this previously made spiral once more. … But if you want to increase the spaces between the outer lines of the spiral even more and make those closer to the center narrower, then incline the vertical line *ab* at its upper end toward point *c*."[6]

Dürer starts by drawing a varying diagram. It is an arc of a circle that is divided into equal parts that project from the vertex *g* onto the vertical line *ab* into varying segments, instead of the equal segments we had before with the Archimedes spiral. Then, not only is the aperture angle a variable parameter, but the line *ab* can also be slanted in order to get a different projection. We understand where this variable diagram comes from when we switch to the drawing of a tower with a written inscription in book III of *Underweysung der Messung*.

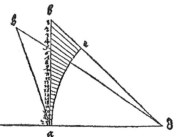

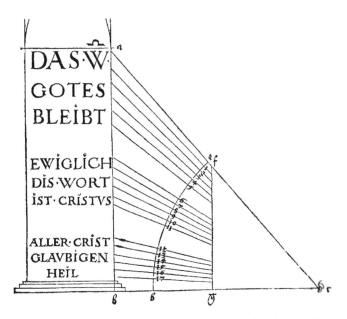

In this inscription,[7] the letters have a varying height in order to appear at
an equal angle from point *c*. This brings us back to the optics of antiquity. Plato's
*Sophist*[8] explains that artists are perfectly entitled to deform the proportions of
a statue that is placed at the top of a column in order that when seen from below,
the statue appears to have the correct proportions. Dürer was among one of the
first theoreticians of perspective but, interestingly enough, he resisted this new
technique, even though he had invented the first mechanical imaging device that
did not require a human eye.

In all previous perspectival devices, the eye of the observer played a fundamental role. In this particular one,[9] the "eye" is actually a nail in the wall from which
you pull a string toward an arbitrary point in the object. The person on the right
then marks the coordinate of the intersection of the string through the perspectival
window. The person on the left turns back the sheet of paper and places a point
onto the drawing. If these people were blind, it would work all the same. This is the
first computer image in history.

It is important to understand that Dürer also uses this antique optical diagram
for curves that he develops in 3D.[10] This leads directly to architectural applications.
The diagram with equal arcs that project into varying segments reappears[11] where
it is used to generate the spiraling fluting on the vertical shaft of the column. Three
figures later, Dürer puts into variation everything proposed above, and makes the
column itself spiral.[12]

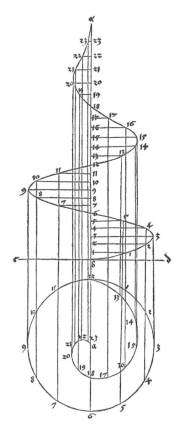

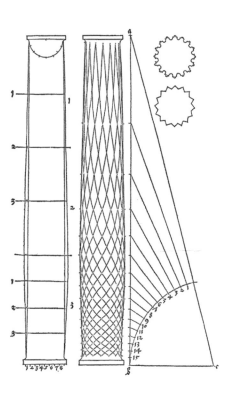

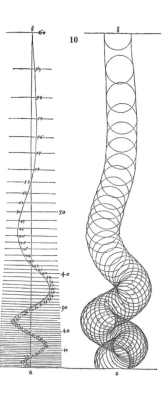

Now we have reached the limit of the snail, and we come to the spider. We understand this image better[13] if we remember that Dürer was interested in simulating the movements of the human body. In the *Codex Huygens*,[14] we find drawings by Carlo Urbino di Crema, where the body movements are based on the a diagram of epicyclic circles similar to those generated by Dürer's instrument.[15]

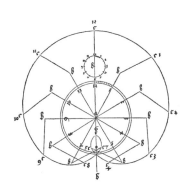 

The parameters of the instrument vary, making the joints of the arm rotate at different speeds to get many kinds of curves:

| Dürer's configuration = one single retrogradation loop: | Inversion of the rotations = eccentric circle: | Generation of an ellipse as an epicyclic curve: | Barocco curve generated by Dürer's spider instrument: |
|---|---|---|---|

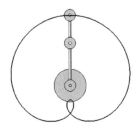 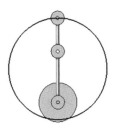  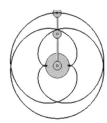

Copernicus's ideas circulated in Germany and Poland much before the astronomer published *De Revolutionibus Coperinicus: De Revolutionibus*.[16] Dürer was, thus, perfectly aware of the many uses of the curves that could generate this instrument in astronomy. For instance, the eccentric circle could be used to explain the varying duration of the seasons. Looped curves could be used to simulate the apparent retrogradation of the planets. Thus, in the Renaissance, the same principles were applied to simulate the movements of the human body as for the celestial bodies. Does this same principle of motion necessarily lead to a conception of harmony between the microcosm and the macrocosm? I am doubtful.

Let us look at the very famous "Vitruvian Man" that lies behind the magnificent drawing of Carlo Urbino di Crema. If we look closely, we realize that there is nothing that coincides in this drawing.

There is no particular relationship that would stipulate that there should be, at the hands, a small corner going outside the circle, and, at the feet, a large corner. The center of the square and the circle do not coincide. The latter is on the navel,

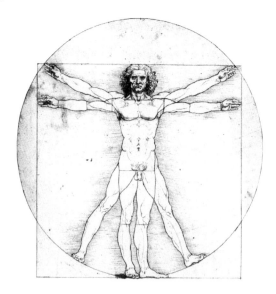

while the previous is on the genitalia. Leonardo da Vinci knew how to draw, so if he had wanted to do it another way, he would have. Instead, he made a montage between two consecutive paragraphs of Vitruvius's *De Architectura*, where Vitruvius describes first the human body lying on the ground, inscribed in the circle, the center of which is the navel. In the other paragraph, he speaks of the body standing up, which is inscribed in a square. He describes two different figures, one horizontal and one vertical. Leonardo combines the two to make us realize that *nothing* coincides in the body. There is a varying center: a discordance within the human body just as in the sky. The heliocentric conceptions of the Pythagoreans and then of Aristarchus of Samos were never totally eclipsed by the prevailing geocentric view,[17] and even without considering the persistence of the heliocentric system, we can find several instances of a discordant conception of both the celestial and human bodies.

An interesting example is that of Varro, an important writer and political figure, who lived slightly before Vitruvius. In the section VII of his book *De Lingua Latina*,[18] Varro states that the situation is similar for celestial and human bodies. The apparent center of the Earth would be Delphi (a religious center at the time), whereas the effective center is deep in the center of the sphere. In the human body, the apparent center would be the navel, whereas the effective center is "the organ that makes the difference between man and woman."[19] Hence, the correspondence of human and celestial bodies lies on the fact that neither of those bodies is organized around one unique center.

Returning to Dürer, it is important to remember that his main purpose is to write a treatise on painting. His ambition is that his treatise would be a new *De Pictura* (Alberti), but, finally he splits his project into several books. Besides *Underweysung* (1525), he publishes a treatise on fortifications (1527), and one on human proportions (1528).

In the treatise on human proportions, Dürer rejects the idea of one single perfect system of proportions. There are differences between men and women, between adults and children, and also between different temperaments. For Dürer, there is only a system of variation. Besides static topological deformations, there are deformations of the human body with motion. In order to show this, he needs an instrument that generates lines in 3D space. This is our third animal —the snake or the serpentine line.

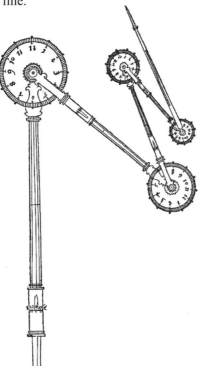

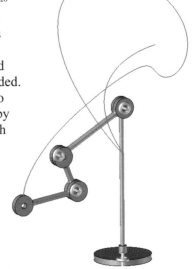

This is the only picture that Dürer provides that is related to the serpentine.[20] Strangely enough, he does not provide any drawing of the line itself. We have to use contemporary software in order to visualize it. Below are only two examples of the infinite variety of curves that can be generated with such an instrument.

This is described by Dürer in a parametric way: "The rods shall be arranged in a manner that they can be advanced by degrees and can be shortened or extended. The instrument should also be made with few or many dials or rods, according to the intended applications. The rods can be pulled apart or pushed together, also by degree, so that they become shorter or longer."[21] This is perfectly compatible with what we can do with mechanical software today.

It is also interesting that Dürer rejects all systems of perfect harmony, but he still uses proportion as a tool to control the variety of objects that he can generate. At that time, proportions were the horizon of mathematical knowledge. People were using proportions to study phenomena that were not proportional, and this only changed much later with Newton and Leibniz. The problem is that when those new mathematical tools were invented, artists were not able to understand them. They took Newton as an excuse to reject proportions. To be clear: I am not advocating a discourse in favor of proportions; I am advocating being able to use the mathematical tools at our disposal in order to control what we are doing in design.

As we have seen, the classical is not necessarily classic: it is not necessarily invariable, symmetrical, ideal, abstract, or harmonic. More precisely, there is a plurality of traditions in antiquity. Andronikos's Tower of the Winds was already an information machine. Additionally, Vitruvius's catapult was a war machine, the main parameter of which depended on a complex mathematical formula with a cubic root which, in its turn, needed another machine in order to be calculated. Dürer precisely focuses on the instrument enabling the calculation of cubic roots, one of which was falsely attributed to none other than Plato. Hence, parametric design is not new, and mechanics were already an essential part of architecture in antiquity. It is precisely on these grounds—parametric design and numerical instruments— that we can think of inscribing contemporary architecture within this other classical tradition.

This text is an abbreviated version of the lecture "Instruments of Thought" by Bernard Cache, presented in March 2012, following the workshop *Underweysung der Messung: Instructions for Measurement* with students and faculty from the Department of Architecture.

### Endnotes

1   Vitruvius, De Architectura I, 3, 1.
2   James Stuart and Nicholas Revett, *The Antiquities of Athens*, Vol. I, London, 1762.
3   Albrecht Dürer, *Underweysung der Messung*, (1525), bk. I, fig. 7.
4   Huygens had invented such a device in 1630 and had discussed it with Descartes while Descartes was writing his own geometry treatise, but Dürer was not aware of this.
5   Albrecht Dürer, *Underweysung der Messung*, bk. I, fig. 6b.
6   Albrecht Dürer, Underweysung der Messung, bk. I, fig. 7.
7   Albrecht Dürer, *Underweysung der Messung*, bk. III, after 27.
8   Plato, Sophist, 360 B.C., 235e–236a
9   Albrecht Dürer, *Underweysung der Messung*, bk. IV, last image of the 1525 edition.
10  Albrecht Dürer, *Underweysung der Messung*, bk. I, fig. 15.
11  Albrecht Dürer, *Underweysung der Messung*, bk. III, fig. 7.
12  Albrecht Dürer, *Underweysung der Messung*, bk. III, fig. 10.
13  Albrecht Dürer, *Underweysung der Messung*, bk. I, fig. 40.
14  To be found in Erwin Panofsky, *The Codex Huygens and Leonardo da Vinci's Art Theory*. The Pierpont Morgan Library Codex M.A. 1139. London, The Warburg Institute, 1940.
15  Carlo Urbino di Crema, Codex Huygens (c. 1570) Folio 6 (right) and 12 (left).
16  Nicolaus Copernicus, *De Revolutionibus*, Nuremberg 1543. One of the people he sent his manuscript to was Johannes Werner, who was Dürer's mathematics teacher.
17  As we can see in Theon of Smyrna's *Mathematical Knowledge Useful for Reading Plato (2nd Century A.D.)* (120).
18  This is mentioned in *De Architectura.*
19  Marcus Varro, *De Lingua Latina*, (1474), VII, 7.
20  Albrecht Dürer, *Underweysung der Messung*, bk. I, fig. 42.
21  Albrecht Dürer, *Underweysung der Messung*, bk. I, fig. 41.

## Val Warke

*is an associate professor at Cornell University's Department of
Architecture, and a partner in Simitch + Warke Architecture. His teaching
and research focus is on criticism and genre theory, including issues of
fashion, formalism, populism, reception, and relations to literary theory.*

# The Grotesque Body and the Post-Humanist Subject

**Venus of Willendorf**. © Naturhistorisches Museum Wien.
Photo: Alice Schumacher.

Human fascination with the figuration of bodies seems to have taken a variety of forms, to varying degrees, at various times. Inevitably, these fascinations have had effects on modes of artistic—and therefore, architectural—production.

These interests appear to have been derived from five renditions of the body: there is the continually theorized and periodically eroticized fascination with the *ideal* body (with notions of the "ideal" differing, of course, from culture to culture, time to time); the probably instinctive and possibly totemic fascination with the *hypertrophically fertile* human body; the ostensibly anthropological and occasionally theological fascination with the *amalgamous* marvelous/monstrous body; the socially ignoble but probably equally instinctive fascination with the *anomalous* body; and the relatively recent horrific and enchanting fascination with the *otherworldly* body.

Vitruvius is one of the earliest proponents of the analogs that might be developed between the *ideal* human figure and ideal proportions in architecture. There are enthusiastic iterations of these Vitruvian constructions throughout much of architectural history, from the Renaissance onward through certain strains of 20th-century modernism. One finds that, beginning in the Renaissance, the geometrized body appears in both the theoretical architecture of treatises as well as among the Western world's foremost constructed works. Ideal bodies appear in everything from the component: (columns [where proportions might even be gendered in relation to their orders], capital details, doors, windows, moldings, and so on) to the overall building formation (plans, sections, and elevations) to the city plan. In the Renaissance, for instance, one need only look at the proportioned drawings of Francesco di Giorgio—of his cornices, capitals, columns, and cathedrals—to find bodies everywhere. In the 20th century one has Le Corbusier's Modulor.[1]

In most of these earlier instances, the translation of the ideal human body's proportions to two- and three-dimensional figures generally employed ratios in establishing proportions: bottom-of-feet-to-navel by feet-to-top-of-head, for instance. Scale per se was not as significant as proportion, in that proportion was considered to be a fundamental element of perspective construction and, therefore, of the spatial developments that followed from theories of perspective:[2] the repetition of an identifiable rectangular figure can imply depth in two dimensions, a technique frequently utilized in facade compositions from the Renaissance onward.[3] Also, since the human body as an ideal condition was essentially both a translation (ostensibly, of the image of God) and a microcosm (of the universe), the scalar

1  In this abridged exposition of the relevance of the ideal body, I apologize for what some might construe as reductiveness, others as evasiveness, many as unnecessary. (But one might take heart: while I am, for example, omitting the delightful physiognomic experiments of Lequeu, that contemporary of Ledoux and Boulée who used self-portraits in various emotional and even transgendered modes to represent potential façade compositions in their relationships to various functional requirements, one can be thankful that this allows me to also omit Schultze-Naumburg, one of the Third Reich's architects and a proponent of Aryan physical perfection). Everyone may be correct: I simply hope that we mostly know this concept already, and that it needs only a cursory mention.

2  Direct scalar relationships emerge most frequently in those treatises concerned with rhetoric and artificial memory, with the memory loci units of theoreticians such as Peter of Ravenna (1491), Johannes Romberch (1533), and Agostino del Riccio (1595); see, for instance, Frances Yates, *The Art of Memory* (Chicago: University of Chicago Press, 1966). Not until the 20th century do we find renewed fascination with body scale: with Oskar Schlemmer's locus-defining Bauhaus costumes and the above-mentioned Modulor of Le Corbusier, a system that uses the scale of the ideal body—specifically, in its second iteration, that of the traditional English detective—as the basis of a more expansive proportioning system.

3  See my "The Plight of the Object," in *Cornell Journal of Architecture*, No. 3 (New York: Rizzoli, 1987), 78–95.

aspects of the body were clearly subordinated to their more abstract geometric attributes.

Furthermore, just as architecture already from the time of Vitruvius has used incorporations and representations of "nature" and "the natural" to justify the validity of its fundamental precepts, the "discovery" of certain of architecture's "ideal" ratios and proportions throughout nature—in leaves, shells, and other botanical and biological figures—has served to reinforce the notion that there is a singular, harmonic geometry that unites the ideal body/building with the remainder of the natural world. For the first of the five renditions of the body mentioned above, mathematics has served as the cohesive mechanism for uniting conceptions of the ideal in nature to the presumptive ideal in architecture, for embedding notions of the ideal man and his god within the forms of the ideal building and city.

But, as mentioned above, the *ideal* body is only one of five configurations that have piqued human interest. The other four non-ideal types—the hypertrophically fertile, the amalgamous, the anomalous, and the otherworldly—might be generally described as variations of what, for the sake of brevity, one might refer to as the "grotesque body."[4]

The *grotesque* body is grotesque to the degree that it appears to deviate from normative conceptions of the body. The key words here are *appears* and *normative*: one must necessarily define the grotesque body as it is measured against a preconceived understanding of the normative body, which is essentially an imagined average of all known bodies. Paradoxically, then, "normative" or "typical" bodies can only very rarely exist, based as they are on the norm of a presumptive set of vaguely ascertained measures; and, of course, these measures as well as the concomitant techniques for measurement have changed from period to period, society to society. Furthermore, left to their own devices, cultures inevitably desire the ideal to be a subset of the normative, whereas the actual "typical" might more likely be found migrating toward the category of the grotesque. And while the concept of "appearance" is not only intensely individual—and, as conceived by the individual, "appearance" is also always momentary and contextual—the grotesque body inevitably transcends simple "appearance," generally operating on more than one level of apprehension, frequently incorporating a sense of the alien.[5]

In other words, both the ideal and the grotesque body are always a latent aspect of the normative. As Ernst Gombrich has pointed out in an essay considering Leonardo da Vinci's "Grotesque Heads":

*In fact anyone who studies these drawings for any length of time will tend to see them suddenly spring to life among the crowds of our cities. The reason must be that we are too much disposed to call a 'monstrosity' in art what is rather commonplace ugliness in reality. Those of us who are not professional painters, at any rate, are easily inclined to think of the typical human face in terms of the traditional 'conceptual' image and not to notice the frequent*

4   While I am stretching its meaning here, I use the term fundamentally as it was developed by Mikhael Bakhtin in his *Rabelais and His World*, trans. Hélène Iswolsky (Cambridge, MA: MIT Press, 1968; original 1940). As with Bakhtin, I am more interested in the external, public, and social aspects of the grotesque than with its internal, psychological modes.

5   For more on this, see Caroline O'Donnell, in "Fugly," *Log* 22 (Spring/Summer 2011), who provides an outline of the changeability as well as the integrative aspects of various concepts of ugliness in their relationships to architecture and art.

*deviations, such as asymmetry and distortions, unless we meet with them unexpectedly within the context of art.*[6]

Gombrich convincingly demonstrates that Leonardo's fascination with the production of the "grotesque heads" is an essential step in his construction of the ideal, Vitruvian man.

The *hypertrophically fertile* body is perhaps the most elemental of all of the grotesque configurations, and is the subject of some of the earliest representations on record. Consider the Woman of Willendorf, dated to between 24,000 and 22,000 B.C.E., or her earlier ancestor, the Woman of Hohle Fels, dated to between 38,000 and 32,000 B.C.E.

Art historians and museum curators have commonly named both of these figurines "Venus," after the Roman goddess of fertility, despite any possible deistic connection. The name is in recognition of the figures' exaggerated breasts, abdomens, and detailed vulvae, and quite probably it is a means of entitling the theory that these early representations functioned as some sort of totems. An alternative theory—that the figurines are actually self-portraits, and that the facial omissions and proportional distortions are the effects of self-observation[7]—is perhaps even more suggestive: grotesque hypertrophy is possibly rooted in an attempt at representing the normative, a form of self-portraiture.

Interestingly, in the same cave in Hohle Fels where the ancient woman was discovered, a polished stone phallus of approximately the same age was also pieced together. Just as representations of exaggeratedly fertile female figures have proliferated since prehistory, exaggeratedly endowed male figures—or at least metonymic elements of such endowment—have also found their way into the artifacts of most early cultures. In classic cultures, hypertrophic fertility is prized (if not admired), and so it was inevitable that gods would evolve that would be endowed with these characteristics; one thinks of Priapus, especially popular in Pompeii, and Diana of Ephesus, who enjoyed enthusiastic esteem well into the 17th century, not least of all as a frequent garden ornament.

This is perhaps because, as cultures developed into more complex societies, this particular body form—the hypertrophically fertile—seems to have become a fundamental element of the various carnival cultures that developed. The bulbous protrusions that represented the distinguishing characteristics of each gender were replicated not only as an emblematic presence within carnivals, but also as a basic characteristic of the costumed appearance of many carnival participants. As has been well documented, these public celebrations of the grotesque body were gradually suppressed in most societies, allowed to erupt only in the occasional literary and artistic work, in the forms of various psychological neuroses, and in infrequent but sanctioned events.[8]

6  Ernst Gombrich, "The Grotesque Heads," in *The Heritage of Apelles: Studies in the Art of the Renaissance* (Ithaca: Cornell University Press, 1976), 58–59.

7  LeRoy McDermott, "Self-Representation in Upper Paleolithic Female Figurines," *Current Anthropology* 37, no. 2 (April 1996).

8  This is most effectively introduced by M.M. Bakhtin in his *Problems in the Work of Dostoevsky* (the later version, published as *Problems of Dostoevsky's Poetics*, translated by Caryl Emerson, is more broadly known) and in his *Rabelais and His World*, cited above; and with further, more specific analysis by others, including Allon White, "Hysteria and the End of Carnival: Festivity and Bourgeois Neurosis," in *The Violence of Representation: Literature and the History of Violence*, ed. Armstrong and Tennenhouse (New York: Routledge, 1989) 157ff; Terry Castle's *Masquerade and Civilization* (Stanford: Stanford University Press, 1986), and Barbara Ehrenreich's *Dancing in the Streets: A History of Collective Joy* (New York: Henry Holt and Company, 2006).

By the 16th century, even the most romantic depictions of the pagan gods with their occasional and fearful gigantism—physical transmogrifications that were central to so many origin myths—were almost completely eradicated by the predominant religious beliefs of the Western world. What we find instead is the comic and grotesque gigantism of literary characters such as Rabelais's Gargantua and his son, Pantagruel, where the enormity of the subjects has its repercussions in terms of appetite and various explicit body functions. Meanwhile, the public recitation of songs and rhymes, and even the exaggerated miming of these functions—intercourse, urination, defecation, regurgitation, and so on—formed an important part of carnival activities. In other words, at the same time that ideal man was seen as model or microcosm of the entirety of the known world, carnivalized hypertrophic man (or woman) was understood to literally *become* that world. As Bakhtin has pointed out, "the grotesque body is cosmic and universal.... This body can merge with various natural phenomena, with mountains, rivers, seas, islands, and continents. It can fill the entire universe."[9]

If, beginning in the 13th century, and especially in the Renaissance, architecture and the arts provided the principal venues for the ideal body, and literature and carnival seems to have been the predominant sites of the hypertrophic body, it seems that during this same period the *amalgamous* body found its greatest exposure in religious and scientific works.

By the amalgamous body, I refer to the semihuman, compound bodies that incorporated certain human elements, but with parts that were either rearranged or combined with the anatomies of other animals. Amalgamous bodies occupied much of folklore and, with Pliny's accounts of some of these "monstrous races," were given a certain verisimilitude as they were incorporated into countless anthropological, ethnological, and theological studies. St. Augustine, for example, while not asserting their existence, incorporated these "races" in one of his treatises, arguing that they were undoubtedly descended from the children of Noah. As a result of this validation, Rudolf Wittkower has demonstrated that these "creatures" could be found in most of the more exhaustive encyclopedias of the 12th and 13th centuries.[10] Amalgamous bodies ranged from those with extremely long ears, sciapods (with their singular large leg), antipodes (with reversed feet), and cyclopeans, to acephalons (with their heads subsumed within their chests), cynocephali (with the heads of dogs), crane-headed men, manticores, and so on. As Wittkower pointed out, various illustrated "bestiaries" were published in the 13th century—and with considerable popular appeal—giving these "creatures" certain metaphorical and symbolic moral values, such as humility, pride, and so on.[11] Inevitably, by the late 13th century, and once these metaphorical values were established, satirical versions were substituted for the more virtuous ones. The dog-headed beings, for example, were depicted as representing calumny, and the headless people represented lawyers who overcharged.[12]

"Scientific" literature on the amalgamous body as an ethnographic phenomenon was perpetuated and validated in that it reinforced the limitless expanse of the

9 Bakhtin, *Rabelais*, 218.
10 Rudolf Wittkower, "Marvels of the East: A Study in the History of Monsters," in *Allegory and the Migration of Symbols* (London: Thames and Hudson, 1977), 50.
11 Ibid., 56.
12 Ibid., 56–57.

unknown world. That there were unknown and wondrous species—witness
the fantastic renderings of the first rhinoceroses, alligators, and so on, as late as
the 17th century—was taken as a matter of fact.

The concept of the amalgamous body provided considerable inspiration
to Hieronymous Bosch, who seems to have taken to heart the Augustinian
arguments regarding the lost offspring of Noah, as he combined humans with
birds, fish, and even plants, especially in his paintings depicting the *Temptation
of St. Anthony* and the *World in the Days of Noah* (right hand panel).[13]

**The Garden of Earthly Delights (The World in the Days
of Noah)**, Hieronymous Bosch, Museo Nacional del Prado.

His tree-man, for example, reappeared in a number of paintings, etchings, and
drawings, and has clearly stirred the fantasy of a number of other artists as well
as architects. In the Noah triptych, this character appears to be a rather benevolent
figure hosting a pub inside his body cavity and a promenade deck on his head,
with his trunklike legs rooted in two large boats. The image seems to be a direct
inspiration for a number of Hermann Finsterlin's designs from 1919 to 1924,
for Frederick Kiesler's famous Endless House model for the Museum of Modern
Art Exhibition of 1958–59, and quite possibly of J. Mayer H.'s Metropol Parasol
in Seville of 2011.

13  Gombrich's arguments are quite compelling regarding the notion that Bosch's *Garden of Earthly Delights* should more properly be called *Sicut erat in Diebus Noe*, "As it was in the Days of Noah," or "The Lesson of the Flood," and I see no reason to doubt him. E.H. Gombrich, "Jerome Bosch's 'Garden of Earthly Delight,'" in *The Heritage of Apelles: Studies in the Art of the Renaissance* (Ithaca, NY: Cornell University Press, 1976), 90.

Nevertheless, despite the inventiveness of artists such as Bosch, it seems that most of these amalgamous, semihuman species as depicted in popular and "scientific" literature were based upon some initial observation, probably of someone with serious birth *anomalies*, and that this initial observation was ultimately conveyed with the same degree of hyperbole with which previously unknown animal species were described. These birth conditions could be as minor as albinism, as moderate as various skin conditions (hence, the birdlike or reptilian analogs—the Bird Men and Alligator Boys—so popular with the sideshows of the 20th century), or as major as acute birth irregularities (such as conjoined twins) and other forms of severe physical deformity.

Additionally, by the start of the 16th century, threats of conquest from non-Christian powers to the east, the forceful consolidation of certain religious and political states, and the development of Protestantism, led to numerous invasions, civil disruptions, reformations, and counterreformations. There was a ubiquitous fear of the unknown that amplified superstitious beliefs. Inevitably, disruptions of the status quo were linked with the recording of abnormal births, since both events were being noted and publicized with increased frequency.

The observation of abnormal births was most often noted in various nonhuman species. Albrecht Dürer's *Monstrous Sow of Landser*, for instance,

**The Monstrous Sow of Landser**, Albrecht Dürer, 1496

is based upon the description and rough woodcut of a partially twin-bodied pig that appeared in a pamphlet by Sebastian Brant.[14] Despite the fact that this pig, born in Alsace in 1496, lived for only one day, Dürer's elegant and realistic depiction—a

14  Giulia Bartrum, *Albrecht Dürer and His Legacy*, exhibition catalog no. 43 (London: The British Museum Press, 2002).

relatively healthy pig seems to be blissfully grazing on the grounds of a romanticized Landser castle—provides the description with the ultimate credence one can achieve only through the verisimilitude of graphic representation. The sow's birth was interpreted, alternately, as foreshadowing a Turkish invasion, as the end of Christendom, and as the coming of the antichrist.

   Slowly and eventually, Augustine's charitable theory of these "monsters" as having been descended from Noah was rejected in favor of claims that such births were instead omens of some imminent evil.[15] We find increased occurrences when the nonstandard body—previously called "monstrous" (as in "demonstrative"), "marvelous," and "prodigious," and generally understood to be a wonder of creation—was broadly vilified, not just occasionally but universally. The case of the Monster of Ravenna is clearly such an instance.

**The Monster of Ravenna, from De Monstrorum Caussis**. Courtesy of the Division of Rare and Manuscript Collections, Cornell University Library.

   In the 16th century, a pharmacist published a description of a drawing he had seen that depicted an abnormal birth in Ravenna:

15   Ibid., 64. Wittkower cites publications, including those of Jobus Fincelius, Johannes Wolf, as well as an omen reported by Martin Luther himself and involving two abnormal births. Luther and

Philip Malancthon published illustrations of such anomalies in pamphlets that were widely distributed, usually linking them to antipapal auguries.

*We had heard that a monster had been born at Ravenna, of which a drawing was sent here; it had a horn on its head, straight up like a sword, and instead of arms it had two wings like a bat's, and the height of its breasts it had a fio [Y-shaped mark] on one side and a cross on the other, and lower down at the waist, two serpents, and it was a hermaphrodite, and on the right knee it had an eye, and its left foot was like an eagle. I saw it painted, and anyone who wished could see this painting in Florence.*[16]

The description uses imagery that is already related to religious and military symbolism in describing an unknown phenomenon. Naturally, such a description—already several times removed from the original ("a drawing was sent here ... I saw it painted")—can lead only to more vividly imagined images, and more exaggerated graphic representations of these descriptions. The besiegement of Ravenna 18 days after the reputed birth seemed an inevitability to the pharmacist.

While current science tends to see in the description either a case of Roberts Syndrome or a group of clustered birth anomalies,[17] popular imagination ran wild with the description and a series of increasingly exaggerated illustrations followed. See, for example, the illustration in Fortunio Liceti's *De Monstrorum Natura, Caussis, et Differentiis*, a 17th-century text that advocated that we should embrace these anomalies as wondrous examples of nature's flexibility. By the time of Liceti, who also attempted to offer scientific explanations for the anomalies, the wings had become more avian (and angelic) and the legs had merged into one, reminiscent of the early sciapods.

While texts such as Liceti's were still being consulted for their scientific value well into the 19th century,[18] and a fascination with teratology remains a simultaneous form of distaste and delight for most people, the 20th century brought on a new form of the grotesque in terms of the *otherworldly* body.

Distinctly nonhuman bodies made their first major appearance in the late 1890s, in H. G. Wells's *War of the Worlds*,[19] although they were most likely substituting for others of a very human type. As with the earlier prognostications associated with abnormal births, Wells's Invaders foretold of a new form of invasion, one that was threatening the world in the years leading up to World War I. The Invaders from Mars in the Wells novel are described as somewhat octopoid—with a single large head, two eyes, and eight tentacular appendages encircling a beaked mouth—although the text suggests that they were perhaps evolved from humanoid stock, a brain and partial neural and circulatory systems without any digestive organs, they were essentially organs without a body.

Perhaps it is to be expected that descriptions of such bodies are often metaphorically constructed. Nonhuman bodies from other worlds tended to be described in either anthropomorphic or zoomorphic terms (such as insectoid, lizardlike, and

16  Luca Landucci, in March 1512, quoted in Armand Marie Leroi, *Mutants: On Genetic Variety and the Human Body* (New York: Viking, 2003), 3.

17  María-Luisa Martínez-Frías, "Another Way to Interpret the Description of the Monster of Ravenna of the Sixteenth Century," *American Journal of Medical Genetics* 93, no. 3 (February 1994): 362, for example, argues that the child could have had "cyclopia with forehead probiscus and sirenomelia."

18  Dan Knapp, "Rare 17th-Century Book Examines Anatomical Anomalies," *USC Chronicle*, October 18, 2011, http://dotsx.usc.edu/newsblog/index.php/main/comments/rare_17th-century_book_examines_anatomical_anomalies/.

19  Some of the very earliest space aliens, those from Sirius and Saturn in Voltaire's "Micromégas" of 1752, differed from humans primarily in scale (about 120,000 feet tall) rather than form. The text was fundamentally a critique of myopically human-centric studies and of theological interpretations of astronomy.

so on), with the occasional ominous vegetable. Not until the 1950s, when film had almost completely supplanted texts as the preferred medium of science fiction and the *descriptive* was replaced by the *shown*, does one begin to discover relatively feature-less monsters (such as the eponymous Blob from filmdom) as well as a spate of aliens that are fully imitative of humans or that have parasitic mind-controlling capabilities.[20] If the former were propelled at least in part by the fears of nuclear invasion, the latter seem to predict the effects of ideological invasions.[21] By the 1980s, we find other types of intrinsically featureless, but chameleonic entities (the 1982 Thing and the 1991 T-1000 Terminator, for example), suggesting that one should reserve the most fear for the bodies that look the most like us. Ultimately, as with a Leonardo drawing, the grotesque body merges with the real.[22]

As Bakhtin had discussed in connection to Rabelais's construction of the grotesque body—a construction rooted in the persistence of carnival culture—the carnivalized grotesque body is perhaps best characterized by its exaggerated features, its excessive bodily functions, and its general profanation of the sacred world in which it is (temporarily and provisionally) located, a world from which it is banished and to which it inevitably returns. "The grotesque body ... is a body in the act of becoming. It is never finished, never completed; it is continuously built, created, and builds and creates another body."[23] He continues, "The grotesque body has no façade, no impenetrable surface, neither has it any expressive features.... It swallows and generates, gives and takes. Such a body, composed of fertile depths and procreative convexities is never clearly differentiated from the world but it is transferred, merged, and fused with it."[24]

While this description of the grotesque body, based primarily on early conceptions of the grotesque and carnival, could apply equally to many of the later versions,[25] the societal function of the grotesque, especially in its relationship to fear, has varied considerably through time. The grotesque monsters of the medieval and Renaissance times were primarily comic, representative of terrors that could be dissolved through laughter.[26] However, "[t]he world of Romantic grotesque is to a certain extent a terrifying world, alien to man. All that is ordinary, commonplace, belonging to everyday life, and recognized by all suddenly becomes meaningless, dubious, and hostile. Our own world becomes an alien world. Something frightening is revealed in that which was habitual and secure."[27]

One might argue that, beginning in the latter 20th century and as an extension of the Romantic world, the aliens were manifestly and literally alien, and that fear

20 One assumes that the initial impetus for human-as-alien was largely budgetary: it's more economical to have humans play at being monsters than for a film production to simulate convincing alien monsters. The full implications of the alien/human were probably understood only later.

21 During the 1950s there was also a subset of science fiction/horror films involving gigantic animals, the "big bug" films. These films were very inexpensive to make, requiring simple camera effects, and their messages were invariably warnings of the instability of post-nuclear biology.

22 For this reason, one notes that among the science fiction films of the 1950s, the hubris of humanity is frequently cast as the monstrous entity, and that today a considerable number of horror films deal with characters who posses severe levels of psychopathology; cf., Ruth Goldberg, "'In the church of the poison mind,'" in *Monstrous Adaptations*, ed. Richard J. Hand and Jay McRoy (New York: Manchester University Press, 2007).

23 M.M. Bakhtin, *Rabelais and His World*, trans. Hélène Iswolsky (Cambridge, MA: MIT Press, 1968), 317.

24 Ibid., 339.

25 In some ways, Bakhtin could, for example, have been describing the Blob.

26 One finds a compressed, modern version of the medieval carnivalesque in J.J. Rawlings's Harry Potter novels with the "Boggart-banishing spell," whereby a fearful entity is transformed by proxy into one that can be ridiculed.

and terror were hypothetically deferred by the production of these aliens made obvious. Concomitantly, beginning with the Romantic grotesque, "bodily life, such as eating, drinking, copulation, defecation, almost entirely lost their regenerating power and were turned into 'vulgarities.'"[28] One of the more terrifying traits of the Romantic grotesque, found in Victor Hugo and Mary Shelley, is a version of the anomalous body—incomplete metamorphosis—whereby the constant evolution of the carnival grotesque and its promises of continuous renewal is suddenly frozen in a stunted state.[29] This is a form of the grotesque that cannot be shed from daily life; it is always present in the inchoate, in the irresolute.

Until the late 20th century, architects have traditionally employed mathematics for at least three reasons. There are the quantitative mathematics that are in service of structural formulas and used for describing spatial enclosures such as domes, vaults, and gables. There are the cultural mathematics that shape a work by means of symbolic or ritualized geometries meant to transfer allegorical meanings (such as is the case with star-shaped churches, pyramidal tombs, and so on). And there are the mathematics that attempt to imbue a work with some qualitative notion of the ideal, often by associating the proportions of the body to the proportions of a building. It is a version of this latter role of mathematics as a series of harmonic ratios that Rudolf Wittkower invokes, in his *Architectural Principles in the Age of Humanism*, in an attempt to demonstrate the Renaissance amalgamation of the arts into a singular humanist project.

The preeminence of this final form of mathematics is undoubtedly derived from the ancient belief in geometry as an underlying explicator of nature,[30] and nature has provided the fundamental verisimilitude for most architectural theories, at least until the 20th century, when certain technological and industrial metaphors began to challenge nature as architecture's principal measure.

Nevertheless, at least one architect, Le Corbusier, inherited and developed a sense of mathematics that was fundamentally based in the Renaissance, with 19th-century overtones. In *The Modulor*, he invokes the microcosmic conception of proportions when he says, "Mathematics is the majestic structure conceived by man to grant him comprehension of the universe. It holds both the absolute and the infinite, the understandable and the forever elusive."[31]

Le Corbusier's attitude toward proportion is undoubtedly descended from that of Owen Jones, whose *The Grammar of Ornament*, originally published in 1856,

27 Bakhtin, 39. This aspect of the grotesque should not be confused with that of the uncanny. As Rosemary Jackson pointed out, the grotesque is essentially a structure of "the estranged world, our world, which has been transformed," whereas the uncanny is without a structure, the "real" emptied of "meaning." (See Rosemary Jackson, *Fantasy: The Literature of Subversion* [London, Methuen, 1981], 68.)

28 Ibid.

29 David K. Danow, *The Spirit of Carnival: Magical Realism and the Grotesque* (Lexington: The University Press of Kentucky, 1995), 35.

30 As D'Arcy Thompson had written in 1917: "The mathematical definition of 'form' has a quality of precision[:] … it is expressed in few words or still briefer symbols, and these words or symbols are so pregnant with meaning that thought itself is economised; we are brought by means of it in touch with Galileo's aphorism (as old as Plato, as old as Pythagoras, as old perhaps as the wisdom of the Egyptians), that 'the Book of Nature is written in characters of Geometry.'" D'Arcy Wentworth Thompson, *On Growth and Form* (Cambridge, UK: Cambridge University Press, 1961), 269.

31 Le Corbusier, *The Modulor: A Harmonious Measure to the Human Scale Universally Applicable to Architecture and Mathematics*, trans. Peter de Francia and Anna Bostock (Cambridge, MA: MIT. Press, 1968), 71.

was probably the closest to a design textbook the young Charles-Édouard Jeanneret ever possessed.[32] In that, Jones enumerates a series of "General Principles in the Arrangement of Form and Colour, in Architecture and the Decorative Arts, Which Are Advocated Throughout This Work" that include:

> *Proposition 1: The Decorative Arts arise from, and should properly be attendant upon, Architecture.*
> . . .
> *Proposition 3: As Architecture, so all works of the Decorative Arts, should possess fitness, proportion, harmony, the result of all which is repose.*
> . . .
> *Proposition 8: All ornament should be based upon a geometrical construction.*
> *Proposition 9: As in every perfect work of Architecture a true proportion will be found to reign between all the members which compose it, so throughout the Decorative Arts every assemblage of forms should be arranged on certain definite proportions; the whole and each particular member should be a multiple of some simple unit. Those proportions will be the most beautiful which it will be most difficult for the eye to detect. Thus the proportion of a double square, or 4 to 8, will be less beautiful than the more subtle ratio of 5 to 8; 3 to 6, than 3 to 7; 3 to 9, than 3 to 8; 3 to 4, than 3 to 5.*[33]

Still, while he was dedicated to the virtues of regulating lines and the principles of similar triangles, Le Corbusier retained a certain ambivalence toward geometry, especially when it was used as a form of occult association (as in the case of the "cultural mathematics" mentioned above) and divorced from the science of vision and rules of perception. He felt that Renaissance architects became bedazzled by mathematics, and as a result, [t]heir architecture was devised with the compass on paper, star-shaped; the humanist geometricians had arrived at the star-shaped icosahedron and dodecahedron, forcing the mind to a philosophizing interpretation, worlds removed, in so far as building is concerned, from the basic premise of the problem: the eye's vision. Their system was erected outside the medium of visual perception.[34]

And then, in an amazingly prescient statement, and one not without a bizarre surrealist inflection, he warns that "[t]he human eye is not the eye of a fly, placed within the heart of a polyhedron."[35]

But also during the 20th century, both before and after Le Corbusier's search for the ideal, there were architects who were distinctly attracted by the appeal of the grotesque. While much of Antonio Gaudí's work achieves its curvilinear exuberance

32  Charles Jencks, *Le Corbusier and the Tragic View of Architecture* (Cambridge: Harvard University Press, 1973), 20.

33  Owen Jones, *The Grammar of Ornament* (New York: Portland House, 1986), 5–6. Note that, throughout the text, Jones's more refined proportions are frequently derived from the Fibonacci series, also the basis for Le Corbusier's *Modulor* proportions.

34  Le Corbusier, *The Modulor*, 72. At the same time, it is not beyond belief that Le Corbusier's *Modulor*

of 1954 was at least in some small way provoked by Rowe's "Mathematics of the Ideal Villa" from 1947, with its comparisons of Palladio's Villa Malcontenta to Le Corbusier's Villa Garches, and of the Villa Rotonda to Villa Savoye (see below). While Le Corbusier was constantly placing himself alongside Michelangelo, especially in his *Vers Une Architecture*, the opportunity to propagate a comparison with one of the iconic architects of the Renaissance would not have been passed up.

35  Ibid., 73.

by utilizing the rigors of ruled surfaces, we see in his work an early understanding of architecture's capacity to propose a grotesque, deformed corporeality. His understanding of the gothic, for example, is clearly grounded in Romantic notions of the grotesque, incompletely transformed body:

> *Gothic art is imperfect, only half resolved; it is a style created by the compasses, a formulaic industrial repetition. Its stability depends on constant propping up by the buttresses: it is a defective body held up on crutches .... The proof that Gothic works are of deficient plasticity is that they produce their greatest emotional effect when they are mutilated, covered in ivy and lit by the moon.*[36]

Similarly, I have already mentioned the work of Finsterlin and Kiesler. One could also mention Rudolf Steiner, Hugo Häring, Hans Scharoun, and possibly even Bertrand Goldberg, among others: while eschewing the perceived delimitations of the right angle, these architects appear to have found a certain inspiration in architecture's capacity to evoke versions of the anomalous grotesque body, arriving at the development of forms through the organic externalization of ostensibly internal, programmatic phenomena. At other times, Robert Venturi and Denise Scott Brown, and on occasion the later work of Charles Moore and the latest of Michael Graves, have been among those infatuated with architecture's hypertrophic

**Exterior view of the Endless House model, Frederick Kiesler, 1958/9.** Gelatin silver print. Architecture & Design, Study Center, photograph by George Barrows. Digital Image © The Museum of Modern Art/Licensed by SCALA/Art Resource, New York. © Austrian Frederick and Lillian Kiesler Private Foundation, Vienna.

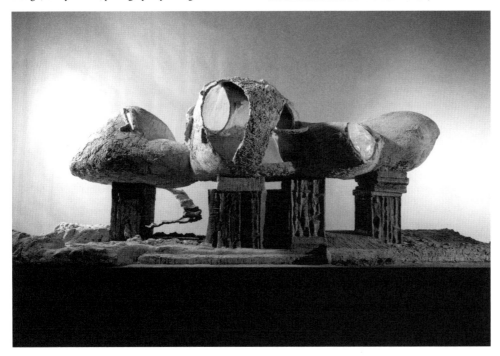

36  Quoted in Carlos Flores, *Les lliçons de Gaudí*, trans. Glòria Bohigas (Barcelona: Empúries, 2002), 89.

grotesque, with the frequent hyperbolic inflation of selective motifs in the
exploitation of a zaftig, hypervoluptuous architecture.[37]

With each of its various incarnations, the grotesque body evolves further from
human mimesis, although occasionally retaining a type of human absorption. At
the same time, mathematics has moved from ratios and geometry to calculus and
beyond. Indeed, there is even a complex mathematics that is more or less buried
within the scripts of contemporary graphic programs that enables—occasionally
insists upon—certain relational formulae and the almost automatic generation of
unpredicted formal attributes. These may be highly advantageous in meteorological
and aeronautic applications, in modeling fluid dynamics and biological mutations;
but their values in architectural design have been largely metaphorical and allegorical when in the best hands, and at other times, they have facilitated potentially
tedious iterations of an often superficial formal inventiveness.

There has been a parallel relationship—though somewhat lagging and not
thoroughly considered—between the developments of the computer-generated
imagery one finds within the hybrid sci-fi/horror genres of film and the developments
of certain "calculus-based" architectures. While the latter are theoretically spawned
from hyperfunctional aspirations founded on certain programmatic determinants,
both the cinematic and the architectural graphic proceed with a good deal of decorative frippery. As a result, there seems to be an intimate association between the
production of many contemporary architects and the designed monsters of cinema,
and these monsters—as well as their constructions (spaceships, satellites, and
occasional inhabitations)—have increasingly been represented as exaggeratedly
biomorphic.[38]

Perhaps one of the most notable representatives of contemporary architecture's
fascination with anomalous and otherworldy bodies, a fascination supported by

37  The theme even runs throughout the Venturi, Scott Brown, and occasionally Izenour productions. One thinks, for example, of the revised edition of Robert Venturi, Denise Scott Brown, and Steven Izenour, *Learning from Las Vegas* (Cambridge, MA: MIT Press, 1977), with its cover featuring a billboard featuring a woman in a bikini, and text with matrices that appear at first to be methodically filled, but that, on closer inspection, include repetitive images of a man in a white suit and a woman in very low-cut bathing attire (*Learning from Las Vegas*, 43–44). One also thinks of Venturi and Scott Brown's more subtly full-figured "ironic column" at Allen Memorial Art Museum at Oberlin.

38  For example, whereas the constructions left behind by the ancient, intellectually advanced alien Krell civilization in the 1956 film *Forbidden Planet* were based on very primary solids (principally cubes and spheres), in 1958's *The Blob*, the eponymous alien life-form that seems devoted exclusively to acts of ingestion, was fully shapeless and, to a certain extent, even scaleless, changing size throughout the film. It seems that angular, geometric forms typi-cally signify highly intelligent yet often aggressive aliens that tend to develop elaborate strategies for domination. (Think also of the spherical, moonlike Death Stars of the Star Wars series.) The more bulbous, biomorphic types of aliens and their constructions often signify aliens that are also mostly aggressive, but for whom domination is more instinctive than strategized. While *Star Trek*'s Klingons, for example, tend toward lots of sharp angles mixed with avian references, and the Borgs toward platonic solids—cubes and spheres, with lots of nurnies and greebles—we find that most of the nonhumanoid aliens move about in bulbous, organlike vessels that appear to have been manu-factured using a process of secretion or excretion. (Interestingly, even in his famous designs for vari-ous alien environments, such as in *Alien* and *Aliens*, H.R. Giger frequently implies horizontally stacked masonry and metal panels shaped into curvilinear objects and voids that generally evoke biomorphic forms. Perhaps the signification of construction as a technological endeavor or as a scale-giving technique, trumps any desire for liquidity.) One might assume that art directors choose such forms to either signal a tendency for alien species to replicate their own physiques—often insectoid or lizardlike—as if there were an extraterrestrial Vitruvius posing an alienist iteration of the ideal alien body as design determinant. Or the art direc-tors may be attempting to demonstrate the nature of constructions that might be generated by species lacking opposable thumbs.

arguments insisting on a calculus-based architecture, can be found in the intriguing writings and works of the architect Greg Lynn. While Lynn confesses an interest in the monsters of sci-fi/horror films, he continues to use "nature" as a model. Nevertheless, he rejects the concept of the ideal as well as that of the holistic body, and claims to be more interested in obscure or irregular natures, for which he finds considerable material and support in William Bateson's *Materials for the Study of Variation Treated with Especial Regard to Discontinuity for the Origin of Species* of 1894, which proposes the concept of "minor symmetry" in the abnormal replication of anomalous limbs, vertebrae, and organs.[39]

In terms eerily reminiscent of the values proposed within the treatises of early modernism, Lynn equates a holistic model of the body with a "static" condition, whereas "dynamism" is ideal.[40] But it would be a mistake to associate dynamism with the fragmentation of the body: despite his antiholistic concepts, fragmentation of any ilk is equally condemned. Throughout his writings there is a search for a new "whole," a monstrous whole, founded on notions of anomalous bodies, with an occasional dose of the amalgamous, which he in turn names the "composite body." He states that "[q]uestions of composite bodies seem intimately related to questions of urban and architectural composition."[41] Actually, there is an attractive prospect in the notion that urbanism is related to issues of the "composite body" (and less so in terms of architecture at the scale of the building). In a sense, despite Lynn's denials, such a notion parallels that at the core of Rowe and Koetter's *Collage City* text. These denials, the subject of Lynn's frequent confrontations of this and other writings by

39  It seems that *minor*, however, is the operative term, in that Bateson demonstrates such replication when there are extra-secondary appendages (for example, a secondary thumb is generated from within the original thumb, rendered in a curvature in opposition to the primary thumb), though these replications are rarely symmetrical when considering the entire animal. (Rowe and Slutzky, and Hoesli in their various essays in *Transparency* would have referred to these as "local symmetries," a significant aspect of the center/recenter mantra that dominated much of their façade analysis and design techniques, and is most evident in certain palazzi throughout the Veneto, in the paintings of Cezanne, and in the occasional Corbusian elevation. Similarly, one could note here Barry Maitland's "The Grid," which is an extension of Rowe's "Mathematics of the Ideal Villa" arguments and deals with the almost Batesonian deformations of the grid in certain of Le Corbusier's designs, most notably in the Villa Savoye and the Porte Molitor apartment building. See Barry Maitland, "The Grid," *Oppositions* 15/16 [Winter/Spring 1979]: 90–117.) More often than not, as Bateson illustrates, the larger effect is that of asymmetrical development, as with extra nipples on humans and bulldogs (Chapter VIII; the engraving of suit-cuffed male hands lifting the breasts of a nude female, taken from F. L. Von Neugebauer, was possibly an early version of the bikini-matrix diagram in Venturi, Scott Brown, and Izenour's *Learning from Las Vegas*) or of roebuck horns (chapter XI).

See William Bateson, *Materials for the Study of Variation Treated with Especial Regard to Discontinuity for the Origin of Species* (New York: MacMillan and Co., 1894).

Strangely, this concept of symmetry becomes major in Lynn's work. One need only look at the bathroom Lynn designed for the Bloom House (described in terms of the hypertrophic grotesque by *New York Times* critic Nicolai Ouroussoff: "luxury" and "voluptuous white surfaces decorated with mirrors," he enthuses in his article [Nicolai Ouroussoff, "Ahead of the Curve," *New York Times Magazine*, April 19, 2009, M276]). The bathroom could have provided an ideal proof of the capacity of a calculus-based architecture to transcend the illusive ideal and prototypical in favor of the individual and nonstandard. Instead, its double vanity ignores the opportunity of accommodating the variable distinctions of two personalities, ergonomics, use patterns, genders, and so on. The vanity and its mirroring mirror (it replicates the sinks' fascia) become a symmetrically swollen confection in service to the Corian company, more reminiscent of a Botero than the Blob. As is often the case, the messy process of construction—and possibly of sponsorship—seems to grate against theoretical constructs.

40  Greg Lynn, *Folds, Bodies, & Blobs* (Brussels: La Lettre Volée, 2004), 135–136, 167 n2.

41  Ibid., 136. This essay, "Body Matters," was originally published in *Journal of Philosophy and the Visual Arts: The Body*, 1993.

Colin Rowe,[42] seem ultimately centered on a conflation of "urban and architectural composition."

Similarly, the terminology that surrounds Venturi—most notably "complexity and contradiction"—and Scott Brown seems to swirl about Lynn's work, as does his recurrent associations between Rowe and Venturi/Scott Brown. This process of conflation may be central to his design methodology, but it leads to a series of potential misdirections when he conflates terminologies and references, and then employs definitions derived from select scientific disciplines. For example, in his "The Folded, the Pliant and the Supple," Lynn merges Venturi's "complexity" with his "contradiction," while subtly folding Rowe and Koetter's *Collage City* into the mix.[43] He goes on to define "complication" in its biological sense in order to counter Venturi's construction of "complexity."[44] Later, Lynn counters Venturi's construction of "complexity and contradiction" by measuring his use of the concepts against their geometric and mathematical definitions, derived from Deleuze and Guattari in their *A Thousand Plateaus: Capitalism and Schizophrenia*.[45] This is a fundamentally flawed project in that Venturi's use of "complexity and contradiction" is never intended in its mathematical sense, and is instead profoundly *literary* in its inception.[46] Accompanying this is Lynn's regular association of Venturi with Rowe, especially in regard to their formal strategies and concepts of complexity, which again are founded on distinctly nonmathematic characteristics.[47]

42  See, for example, the essays originally first published as "Multiplicitous and Inorganic Bodies," *Assemblage* 19 (1992); "Architectural Curvilinearity: The Folded, the Pliant, and the Supple," *Architectural Design* 102 (March/April 1993); "New Variations on the Rowe Complex," *ANY Magazine* 7/8 (1994); and "Charles Gwathmey: A Physique Out of Proportion," *ANY Magazine* 11 (1995). All are republished in his *Folds, Bodies, & Blobs* collection cited above.

43  Lynn, *Folds, Bodies, & Blobs*, 109–110 ff.

44  Ibid., 120. Specifically, Lynn's definition is borrowed from the process whereby an embryo folds in on itself.

45  Paradoxically, the use of mathematic concepts—in particular as derived from Deleuze and Guattari (D&G)—to interpret a literary dichotomy is in some ways a reversal of certain critiques of D&G (for example, Alan Sokal and Jean Bricmont's critique in *Fashionable Nonsense*, suggesting that D&G's mathematics are actually literary tropes in disguise).

46  Ibid., 162.
    See the notes in Robert Venturi, *Complexity and Contradiction in Architecture* (New York: Museum of Modern Art, 1966), 134–135. Venturi's text is essentially an exercise in finding an architectural application for the literary theories associated with American New Criticism, an analytical/critical movement of sorts, to which he was undoubtedly exposed at Princeton (possibly through the programs established by R. P. Blackmur) and perhaps more intensively at the University of Pennsylvania. Venturi's notes are a virtual reading list of the poets and critics central to New Criticism: T. S. Eliot, Cleanth Brooks, Stanley Edgar Hyman, Kenneth Burke (who was heavily influenced by New Critics Robert Penn Warren and Allen Tate), and William Empson (who, while not directly associated with the group, supplied theories of ambiguity that were readily incorporated into their analytic projects). Very few others not associated with the movement are cited.

Strangely, Robert Penn Warren is one of the few New Critics to have been omitted from Venturi's text—even from citation—despite the fact that he clearly supplied the text's title and principle formal arguments in his famous essay "Pure and Impure Poetry." The essay was taken from one of the Mesures Lectures Warren delivered at Princeton in 1942, just as Venturi arrived on campus, and following such New Critical luminaries as Cleanth Brooks and Allen Tate. (Needless to say, Warren comes down on the side of "impure" poetry: complex, occasionally contradictory, full of ironies and ambiguities, tensions and turbulence.) Specifically, Warren writes: "The saint proves his vision by stepping cheerfully into the fires. The poet, somewhat less spectacularly, proves his vision by submitting it to the fires of irony—to the drama of his structure—in the hope that the fires will refine it. In other words, the poet wishes to indicate that his vision has been earned, that it can survive reference to the complexities and contradictions of experience. And irony is one such device of reference." (Robert Penn Warren, "Pure and Impure Poetry," *The Kenyon Review* 5, no. 2 [Spring 1943], 252.) Both Warren and Allen Tate were visitors at the American Academy in Rome in 1955, when Venturi was a fellow. (Arnold Rampersad, *Ralph Ellison: A Biograpy* [New York: Knopf, 2007], 317.)

Lynn also expresses what seems to be a sense among certain academics, that Rowe and Koetter's *Collage City*, published in 1978, represents a retraction of Rowe's 1947 "The Mathematics of the Ideal Villa," and that Rowe's interest in proportions was supplanted by the messier process of collage composition in some sort of postmodern epiphany. Lynn writes, "It was the faulty assumption that mathematics could only be used to describe an ideal villa that led Rowe to jettison analytic formalism in favor of collage aesthetics."[48] Furthermore, the false dichotomy here is suggestive: that a "collage aesthetics" cannot also subscribe at some level to an "analytic formalism."[49]

47 If Venturi's concepts of "complexity" and "contradiction" are steeped in New Criticism's techniques of poetic analysis, Rowe's tend toward a more critically based, art historical process that measure texts, drawings, and buildings against each other. Here he relates these concepts to Le Corbusier: In other words, *publicly*, he upheld a structure which he could then, *privately*, proceed to contradict. For contradiction does imply something valuable and known in that which is contradicted; and, just as Le Corbusier's complexities are located in simplicity, so his contradictions assert a situation conceived to be public. (Colin Rowe, "Robert Venturi and the Yale Mathematics Building," *Oppositions* 6 [Fall 1976]: 13.)
   Clearly, Rowe shows little tolerance for the New Critical manifestation of ambiguity through the ordinary, and for Venturi's employment of it: "And, apart from all this, it might be suggested that the cult of ambiguity *could* become an excuse for irresolution, that the cult of the "ordinary" *might* become an alibi for non-performance. *Am I being fastidious or am I being careless?* One sees already where the question leads. Blatant failures can become explained as ironies and total lack of distinction may become exonerated by asserting the ideal of the average." (Rowe, *Oppositions* 6: 18–19.)
   Rowe's definition of complexity—used primarily in the earlier *Transparency* text of 1955, coauthored with Robert Slutzky—seems to have been based on that supplied by Gyorgy Kepes in his *The Language of Vision*.
48 Greg Lynn, *Folds, Bodies, & Blobs: Collected Essays*, 201; essay originally published as "New Variations on the Rowe Complex," *Any Magazine* 7/8 (1994).
49 There are at least five responses to the observation that Rowe's later work represents a retraction of his position on "mathematics." First, the difference in emphasis is largely a shift in subject matter: "The Mathematics of the Ideal Villa" is about *villas*, and *Collage City* is about *cities*. Whereas villas—even more than other buildings—are intrinsically free-standing, often isolated, and traditionally utopian in their aspirations, cities tend to be consequential, contingent, occasionally utilitarian, often accidental, and generally sporadic in their formation. It is rare that a city would be composed of villas, except in cases of suburban sprawl, building exhibitions,

or of "surgically" bombed postwarfare cities. The notion that villas might be different from cities could be unacceptable only to those who believe in some form of unified theory of architecture.
   Second, both of the texts have at their centers a critique of formulaic modernism. "Mathematics of the Ideal Villa" concludes with an admonition regarding the vacuousness of derivative architectures of both the Palladian and Corbusian brands:
   *Corbusier is in some ways the most ingenious of eclectics. The orders, the Roman allusion, are the apparatus of authority, customary, and in a sense universal forms. It is hard for the modern architect to be quite so emphatic about any particular civilisation; and with Corbusier there is always present an element of wit, suggesting that the historical reference has remained a quotation between inverted commas, possessing always the double value of the quotation, the associations of both old and new context ....*
Allusion is dissipated at Garches, concentrated at the Malcontenta; within the one cube the performance is mixed, within the other; Roman; Corbusier selects the irrelevant and the particular, the fortuitously picturesque and the incidentally significant forms of mechanics, as the objects of his virtuosity .... Unlike Palladio's forms there is nothing final about their relationship: their rapprochement would seem to be affected by the artificial emptying of the cube, when the senses are confounded by the apparent arbitrariness, and the intellect more than convinced by the intuitive knowledge, that here in spite of all to the contrary, there is order and there are rules.
   Corbusier has become the source of fervent pastiches, and witty exhibition techniques: the neo-Palladian villa became the picturesque object in the English park .... It is the magnificently realisable quality of the originals which one fails to find in the works of neo-Palladians and exponents of "*le style Corbu.*" The difference is that between the universal, and the decorative or merely competent; perhaps in both cases it is the adherence to rules which has lapsed. (Colin Rowe, "The Mathematics of the Ideal Villa: Palladio and Le Corbusier Compared," *The Architectural Review* [March 1947]: 104.) Which brings us to the observation that, while mathematics is the ostensible subject of the essay, the vocabulary of the article's conclusion—words like

Ultimately, what Lynn proposes is a version of Deleuze and Guattari's "body without organs" that exploits aspects of their concept of "two-fold deterritorialization," with its continuous redefinition—by means of diffusion and fusion—of inside and outside. He sees that this "logic of continuous differentiation constructs a fluid semipermeable boundary between interior and exterior."[50] The goal is apparently the development of an inclusiveness that avoids any of the reductiveness necessarily associated with typological categorization, averaging, material specialization, or of the identification of "ideals." Linearity is believed to be intrinsically reductive. Because "[g]estures are always intensely curvilinear"[51] (specifically as recorded by Etienne-Jules Marey in the late 19th century), reducing them "to ideal average lines would evacuate them of their particular content."[52]

Given, then, that the curvilinear is considered to be superior to the linear— for example, as artists have frequently demonstrated, a simple egg can be perceived

**Eggs**. Images by Daniel Marino.

 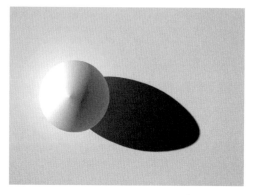

*wit, reference, quotation, context, allusion*, and so on—clearly situates the object of the essay outside of mathematics. Both texts ultimately argue against invention as a type of functionalist myth, suggesting that historical referents might be requisite foundations for the development of architecture and urban design. (Compare Colin Rowe and Fred Koetter, *Collage City* [Cambridge, MA: MIT Press, 1978].)

Third, in the later version of the "Mathematics" essay, published in 1976, there is an addendum written in 1973, while the Collage City arguments were being formulated, that rather than *retracting* the original arguments, *expands* them to include Le Corbusier's later works. This version also contains minor modifications to the original text and considerably more illustrations. (Colin Rowe, *Mathematics of the Ideal Villa and Other Essays* [Cambridge: MIT Press, 1976], 1–28.) One can even imagine further mathematical engagements of Le Corbusier's last works: it is possible to see D'Arcy Thompson's explanation of the evolution of diverse species by means of distorted matrices as a plausible explanation for Ronchamp's evolution from a basic cubic volume.

Fourth, Rowe's "Lockhart, Texas," written in 1955, and with contributions by John Hejduk (who

states that the text was by Rowe [John Hejduk, *Mask of Medusa* (New York: Rizzoli, 1985), 460]) already lays the groundwork for a mediate position between the "Mathematics" and *Collage* texts in its enthusiasm for the gridded courthouse cities of the West, along with the modest monumentality expressed through iconographically charged set pieces. (See Colin Rowe and John Hejduk, "Lockhart, Texas," *Architectural Record* 121, no. 3 [March 1957], 201–206.)

And finally, it seems that Rowe never lost his fascination with mathematics, especially insofar as it promised pleasant proportions. In all of his teaching, at Cornell and elsewhere, the mathematics of organization and proportion was always brought to the foreground, from the arrangement of the components of a collaged urbanism to the ratios of baseboard to wainscot to wall.

50  Lynn, 143. Deleuze and Guattari's "body without organs" proposition, from their *A Thousand Plateaus*, is in some ways the inverse of Wells's Martian Invaders—organs without bodies—as described above.

51  Ibid., 149.

52  Ibid., 152–153.

as a virtually infinite number of figures, from a sphere to a stretched ovoid—an object traced by the three-dimensional movement of a continuously morphing spline might be considered even more superior. The irregular, infinitely variable form is theoretically infinitely adaptable to environments. Its liquid, indefinite shape is considered an asset, and is generally accompanied by a smooth external contour.[53] Again, Lynn finds much to advocate in the malleable, inclusive characteristics of gelatinous smoothness: that "[s]mooth mixtures are made up of disparate elements which maintain their integrity while being blended within a continuous field of other free elements,"[54] while "[s]moothing does not eradicate differences but incorporates free intensities through fluid tactics of mixing and blending."[55] We return to the filmic Blob as the model of a new exemplar, the Vitruvian man updated.

Notwithstanding its horror film evocations, and perhaps in validation of Lynn's advocacy, smoothness has been overwhelmingly adapted as a motif for all types of product design, from apple peelers to automobiles. As philosopher Mark Kingwell has observed, despite being perhaps "a gauge of progress in human affairs"—from the smooth face as a sign of the mastery of sharp tools to the terminological signification whereby performing something "smoothly" is considered to be highly complementary—the blobby smoothness of almost everything seems symptomatic of a return to "the textures of the nursery," "a sort of infantalization of the post-modern imagination."[56] Kingwell goes on to postulate that one of the goals of smoothness is the erasure of an artifact's messy production. As smoothness is often synonymous with ease, as an aesthetic it promises ease of comprehension, ease of consumption, an overall ease of engagement, unburdened by any painful traces of fabrication, of gravity's insistence, of nature's battery, of society's obstreperous individuals.

The inevitable and probably regrettable adaptations necessitated by the human occupation of these attempts at smooth constructions—the occasionally necessary horizontal floor plates, egress cores, standardized ductwork and electrical fixtures (arguably necessitated by unenlightened industries)—seem somewhat tragicomical in these contexts. They are the eruptions of postcarnival "travesty," essentially a return to "normality" as viewed through a posteuphoric hangover.

53 However, this smooth external character doesn't mean an absence of decoration. Lynn believes that one of the advantages of a blob aesthetics is its capability to generate "decorative" knobs and the like in its fabrication. (See *TED Talk: Greg Lynn on Calculus in Architecture*, http://www.ted.com/talks/greg_lynn_on_organic_design.html [Feb. 2005, posted Jan. 2009].) This notion of the microcosmic or perhaps fractile-like decorative element seems derived from art direction in film, and the concepts of "wiggets," "greebles," and "nurnies," whereby details would be added to physical and computer models, especially of spacecraft, in order to imply an immensity of scale in an otherwise scaleless environment.

54 One thinks of Rover in *The Prisoner* television series: a quivering spheroid, apparently birthed from some aqueous medium and that attacks and retrieves potential escapees of the Village.

**Rover, from "The Prisoner"** © ITV Studios Global Entertainment:

55 Lynn, 110–111.

56 Mark Kingwell, "Against Smoothness," *Harper's Magazine* (July 2000), 15. This essay was originally delivered as a convocation address at the Nova Scotia College of Art and Design. In fact, nowhere is the smoothness of the blob more welcome than in the design of children's toys. For its children's line, for example, Nambé had designer Sean O'Hara design bloblike, handmade, seamless, stainless-steel baby rattles that look much like miniature versions of Anish Kapoor's *Cloud Gate* in Chicago.

Architecture passed through its various "humanist" phases, beginning in the mid-15th century, to eventually enter its optimistic industrial phase in the 19th century, followed by the 20th century with its metaphorical machine phase leading to a pessimistic postindustrial phase, and so onward into the first eighth of the 21st century, with its digital-ecstatic phase. We are currently enveloped in a form of carnival-of-the-digital. The rejection of 20th-century modernisms, with their simultaneous beliefs in the distancing of mechanization through metaphor and their adaptation of a genuine mechanization controlled largely through capital forces rather than designed objectives or humanist interests, has led to the manifestation of a "monstrous" and biomorphic post-humanism. (Perhaps one might more appropriately name this a tera-humanism.)

The concept of "post-humanism" seems to have split into a number of variants, the most notable of which include ecological post-humanism (with its belief in the primacy of pan-species accommodation),[57] a cyber-dominated postbiological empiricism,[58] a scientifically enhanced form of humanism (generally, described as a trans-humanism or h+),[59] and the somewhat geeky nonhumanism that is heavily inflected with doses of science fiction and a fascination with alien life forms and occasionally spiced with theories of conspiracy.

What is common throughout these versions of post-humanism is that one discovers that the subordination of humanist objectives can be facilitated by fundamental mathematic operations: the indefinite aspect of mathematics—its virtually endless generative capacities—promotes the production of interminable variants. Selection becomes connoisseurship. Nothing can be definite.

Meanwhile and alas, in contemporary society, representations of the "ideal body" seem to have become the exclusive property of advertising and the various visual media that saturate popular culture. The visual arts seem to counteract this usurpation, either by avoiding the representational body altogether or by manipulating it in a number of modes, through hypertrophy, amalgamation, fragmentation, and the like. By rendering the body in a grotesque manner, the cultural grotesqueness that is served by the ideal body is made evident.[60] In most of the visual arts, these violent manipulations of the body seem to be utilized in order to reveal society's subtle manipulations of the mind.

Strangely, architecture's post-humanist experiments seem to be unaware of the significance of these inverse operations.

57  Granted: there are plants and animals living within every human construction. It is a good idea to accommodate, by amplification or amelioration —depending on their functions within the localized environments (I can't imagine the value of fleas, lice, or mosquitoes, but I await the research)— the cohabitants of humans within a structure. However, in the realm of architectural design, when humans remain the principal occupants and addressees, a certain degree of humanism does not seem to be uncalled for. There should be some graciousness expressed for being a good host.

58  More broadly, this is the case whereby the creations of humans will eventually become more adept at managing the human world than humans themselves.

59  The term *transhumanist* was essentially inaugurated by FM-2030 and disseminated in his *Are You a Transhuman? Monitoring and Stimulating Your Personal Rate of Growth in a Rapidly Changing World* of 1989, though covering work he had been developing since the early 1960s. The concept has been elaborated by futurist/philosophers such as Max More and Nick Bostrom. The term is an abbreviation of "transitional humans," although in many ways it is perhaps more a type of supra-humanism.

60  See, for example, Michael O'Pray's discussion of the frequently disturbing elements of humor, violence, nostalgia, and horror in Švankmajer's partially animated films in his "Surrealism, Fantasy and the Grotesque: The Cinema of Jan Švankmajer," in *Fantasy and the Cinema*, ed. James Donald (London British Film Institute, 1989).

# Caroline O'Donnell

*is the Richard Meier Assistant Professor at Cornell University Department
of Architecture and principal of CODA, an experimental design practice
working at a range of scales from the body to the city. Both her practice
and teaching are rooted in issues of site and the potentially mutant relationship between the architectural organism and its niche.*

# The Deformations of Francesco de Marchi

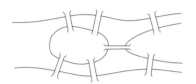 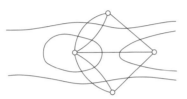 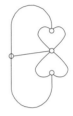 

The origin of topology is normally attributed to Leonhard Euler and his 1736 paper, "The Bridges of Königsberg." In attempting to solve mathematically the popular puzzle of finding a route that crossed each of the city's seven bridges exactly once, Euler diagrammed the city as a set of malleable relations.

This move marked a split from geometry proper, since Euler was not concerned with measurements, shapes, and distances, but instead with "qualitative properties invariant under continuous transformations."[1] Dealing with relations rather than parts, continuity rather than form, the field has since produced such mathematical curiosities as the Klein bottle, the Möbius strip, and the coffee-cup-to-donut transformation.

The term *topology*, however, is not commonly found in literature until the 1920s. Its original appellations, *geometria situs* and *analysis situs* (literally *analysis of position*), suggest a closer relationship with the idea of site (perhaps due to its own urban origins) than the field's content would suggest. Although immediately dissociated with any such earthly reality, the incongruous notion of place still sneaks into the modern term *topo*logy.

While contemplating Euler's abstract and malleable graphic of his city as the origins of mathematical topology, a single urban precedent emerges: one that can be imagined as having paved the way for Euler's own manipulations, that uniquely considered the city as deformable and malleable while maintaining continuity. Francesco de Marchi's deformations, illustrated in his *Della Architettura Militare*, written between 1542 and 1565,[2] provoke fantasies of the *alternative* urban origins of topology: the transformations of the object *by the site itself.*

While his contemporaries pushed aside the dirty realities of context, designing pure geometries on tabula-rasa sites, Francesco de Marchi responded to problem sites in ways that complexified the geometry and embraced topology long before its mathematical explanation existed. In its most distilled form, De Marchi's work demonstrates primitive operations of mutation, transformation, and reaction that are reemerging in architectural discourse today.

Although the mathematical laws on which Renaissance beliefs were based had been expressed earlier by Pythagoras and Plato, they gained new momentum in the late 15th century and entered directly into the discipline of architecture through the resurgence of the work of the classical architect Vitruvius. In his *Ten Books on Architecture*, he often aligned nature and architecture, writing, for example, that "in the human body there is a kind of symmetrical harmony between the forearm, foot, finger, and other small parts; and so it is with perfect buildings."[3] Through this, and the many architectural treatises that followed, the notion that architecture should reflect the "objective" mathematical harmonies of the universe became a basic principle of the Renaissance (see image on p. 24).

More concerned with the principles than the reality of architecture, the treatise was the means of communication of architectural *ideals*. The treatise allowed the architect to communicate the way in which a work—from the scale of the column to the scale of the city—*should* manifest itself under perfect conditions. Underscoring this rift that was widening between the world of the ideal and the real, Renaissance mathematician Niccolò Tartaglia, in his preface to the Latin translation of Euclid's *Elements*, stressed that geometry dealt with figures *in the mind* rather than those imperfect forms that we see in nature with the physical eye.

The *Elements* to which Euclid had dedicated his book were the point, the line, and the area. The combination of these elements produced geometrical forms, and the purest of all of these was the circle. Whether attributed to the divine will of God or the indubitable laws of science, the form of the circle came to represent the geometric order of the world and the cosmos. As Alberti elucidates, "It is manifest that nature delights principally in round figures, since we find that most things which are generated, made, or directed by nature are round."[4]

Round cities are justified by Plato using both a pragmatic and an abstract rationale: "The temples are to be placed all around the agora, and the whole city built on the heights in a circle, for the sake of defense and for the sake of purity."[5] Vitruvius's description propogates this belief, writing that "towns should be laid out not as an exact square, nor with salient angles, but in circular form, to give a view of the enemy from many points."[6] Despite many such textual references to the circular city, the earliest *graphic* example in an architectural treatise is Filarete's rudimentary drawing of *Sforzinda*.[7]

The diagram is an eight-pointed star, formed out of two squares, bounded by a circle. Although there are references to Vitruvius,[8] the mathematical order of the drawing, combined with the fact that the graphic itself had appeared previously in astrological texts representing both the disposition of the elements and the image of the world,[9] suggests that Filarete's motivations were as much symbolic as practical.

Following this diagram, many architects, including Leonardo da Vinci and Francesco di Giorgio Martini, experimented with shape variations, including squares, triangles, circles, and rhomboids, in search of a geometry that could best enclose a city. Whether appearing in their checkerboard or radial versions, the circular city, based unfailingly on the principles of symmetry and proportion, dominated, satisfying, as Filarete's diagram had, "all the longings of the Renaissance for an all-round harmony."[10]

**Diagram of the Ideal City of Sforzinda.** *Filarete's*
*Treatise on Architecture, Volume 2: The Facsimile*
(Yale University Press, 1965), Book II, folio 14ʀ (L)
and 43ʀ (R).

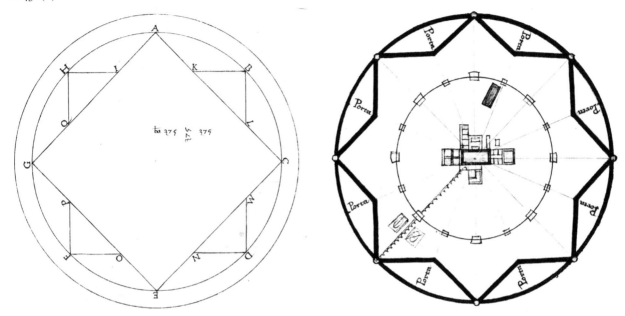

In the mid-16th century, a shift in focus occurred in the design of cities as a consequence of improved military technology. More sophisticated and specialized mathematical skills were required of the military engineer, who came to replace the *uomo universale*.[11]

In this time of extreme pragmatism, Renaissance ideas of geometry were greatly diminished by pressing military issues. Horst De la Croix claims that "the military architect was an exceedingly practical man and his appreciation of the circle was based exclusively on its functional advantages, untinged by any philosophical cogitation on its symbolic qualities."[12] Yet, inevitably, belief in the significance of the circle remained ubiquitous, and clues from the period exist to illustrate that these concerns *did* seep into military design. For example, in his 1557 treatise, Giacomo Lanteri, who has been criticized for an overemphasis on the militarization of the city, describes the circle as "the perfect figure because it reflects the shape and nature of the universe."[13]

It follows then that a nonregular circle would be eschewed by military architects on the grounds that irregularities in the defenses would create weak points (a hypothesis supported by the very few appearances made by the irregular plan in the military treatise). Yet beyond the pragmatics, a certain disdain for irregular form inevitably underlies this logic, since the deformed circle references an imperfect body and a dischordant relationship with the universe. Geometries deformed by the site and other contingencies were, on paper, at least, failures.[14]

In Filarete's treatise, the diagrams of Sforzinda are accompanied by a third illustration—an image of that same Sforzinda diagram, now hovering over a varied landscape.

**Landscape of Sforzinda**. *Filarete's Treatise on Archi-*
*tecture, Volume 2: The Facsimile* (Yale University Press,
1965), Book II, folio 12r.

Although Filarete describes the site, which has been selected after much
investigation, the diagram remains unchanged when inserted into its context: it
hovers above the flattest part of the site, adjacent to (but unaffected by) a river.

Almost all treatises of this period contain chapters concerning the criteria for
the selection of a site for these ideal cities. The argument was polarized between
the flat site and the hilly site, each having its own advantages and disadvantages.[15]
However, in general, the benefits of the flat site were more persuasive: attacking
forces are always in full sight of defenders, horizontal fire is more effective, and
the fortress can be supplied more easily, and relieved in case of a siege. More
importantly, any disadvantages of the flat could be offset by the inherently greater
strength of the geometric symmetry. This implied, of course, that asymmetry means
weakness—the potential for breaches and cracks.

Albeit lengthy and multifarious, the discussion clearly ignores the contingencies that are inevitable in any site. While there *are* references to the inevitable
deformation of the ideal plan in its *implementation*—for example, Girolamo
Cataneo (Lanteri's mathematics teacher and a geometric planner) advised that his
designs must be modified by and adjusted to the local conditions of the terrain—
the deformations were rarely demonstrated graphically in the hypothetical realm
of the treatise. In this context of ideals, rules, and *shoulds*, Francesco de Marchi
stands alone in his treatment of *what ifs*. Francesco de Marchi's *Della architettura*
*militare* presents a baffling variety of military plans.[16] While De Marchi praises the
dignity of architecture, and particularly recognizes the importance of Vitruvius, he
positions himself as a soldier, aiming to bring war into touch with architecture,[17]
and indeed, his written style is more artillerist than theorist.

While his treatise contains many examples of geometrically ordered cities
on perfect sites, what makes De Marchi's work unique among the abundant literature of military architecture at that time is his deployment of a set of hypothetical
problems arising from contextual *imperfections*.

In the more tentative scenarios, De Marchi hypothesizes an ideal city undisturbed by but adjacent to a contextual disruption—a harbor, in the case of City 27. This twelve-bastioned city is symmetrical down to its radial interior planning. Only the site is exerting a massive asymmetrical force, to which the city, until now, remains impervious.

**City 27**

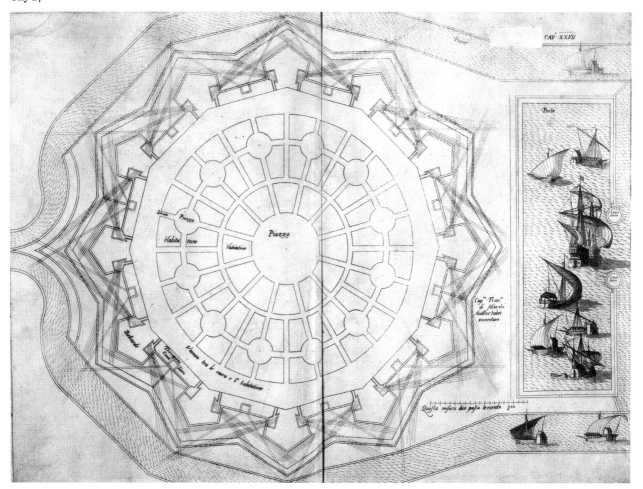

A second step occurs when the city—both the exterior shell and the interior fabric—reacts to the pressure from the context. City 155 shows what reads as a once-perfect circle, conceptually deformed by the force of the sea. De Marchi writes pragmatically and undramatically about this unconventional move: "with great advantage, one can secure a maritime location, where the whole force of fleets can stand there safe from enemies, and there would be no fleet, however strong and large and well-armed it might be, neither galley nor battleships, that would dare to go amidst four towers where they could easily be hit and sunk. These towers could be constructed where there were intervals of rivers, lakes, ponds, canals, as can occur in some sites."[18]

In the plan, what one would expect to be a convex western edge is slightly concave and frontal with the shoreline, its supposed eighth bastion being amputated to form a stumped "launch platform." The piazza is central only to this conceptual circle and not to the actual boundary: in fact, only one block surrounds its western edge, whereas four blocks line its eastern edge. Further, the entire grid of the city has been deformed, widening both the block and street dimension toward the seawall in acknowledgment of this dominant force in the context.

**City 155**

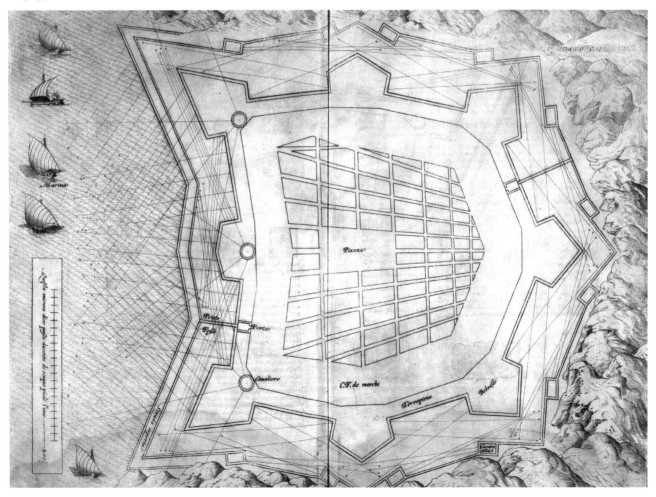

Finally, the contextual element forces itself through the walls and becomes part of the interior of the city, and De Marchi's games begin in earnest.

In City 25, the harbor gate fits perfectly between two seaside bastions, protected just as the other flanks are—by cross fire. The harbor penetrates the walls and occupies a circular area within the radial whole. At the intersection of the center of the outer polygon and the tangent of the inner circle, a new central piazza is located where it should be, both according to the outer circle and with respect to the harbor: stepping off the ship, one is immediately in the center of the city. The circular harbor acts as a cut-out in the city's radial military (center-to-bastion) fabric, but has no effect on the street pattern itself.

**City 25**

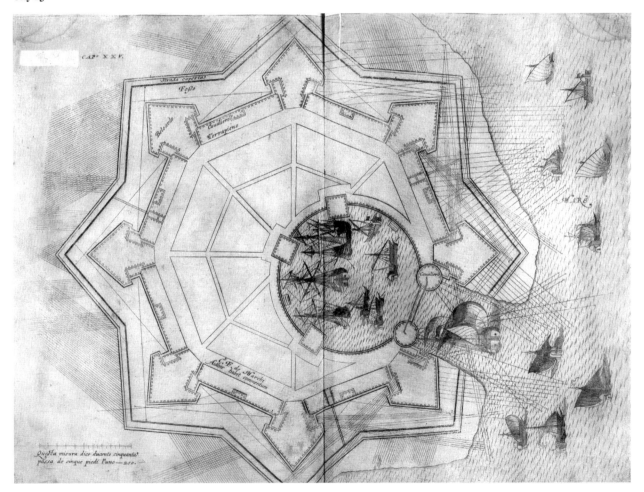

In a similar operation, City 161 is interrupted by the meandering course of a river. Again, the river enters and exits cleanly between bastions, and its centerline aligns with that of the city, so that the location of the central piazza coincides with both the center of the river and the center of the city as a whole. Consequently, the axis of the city and its accompanying secondary piazzas coincide with the axis of the main bridge.

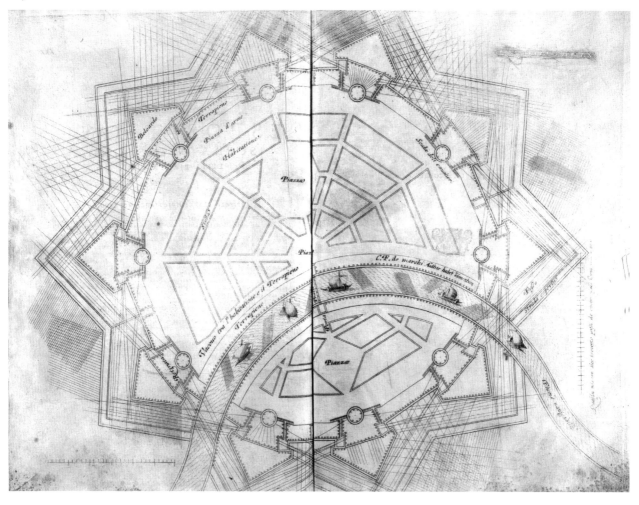

City 48 contains a distinctly larger river, widening more markedly toward the south, with three bridges (two shown) and chains replacing the flanks at each river penetration. This plan demonstrates another radical step beyond the already unconventional moves displayed by its predecessors: whereas the preceding plans overlay the natural form as a passive cut-out from an existing geometrical solution, this new strategy uses the organic form of the river to offset some of the city fabric. Thus, whereas the river-offset streets are meandering, the streets related to the city are wide and straight, as is customary. These major streets do not connect to the bastions and the bastions themselves are not aligned with each other but (presumably) are oriented according to local topography.

True to form, De Marchi justifies the entry of the river into the city on military grounds: "when one part of the land is lost, all of it is not lost, as happened at Parma, when the French once took half the land, but since the river Parma divided nearly the whole land through the middle they could not take the other part, and so they were driven back outside where each side engaged in battle across the river."[19]

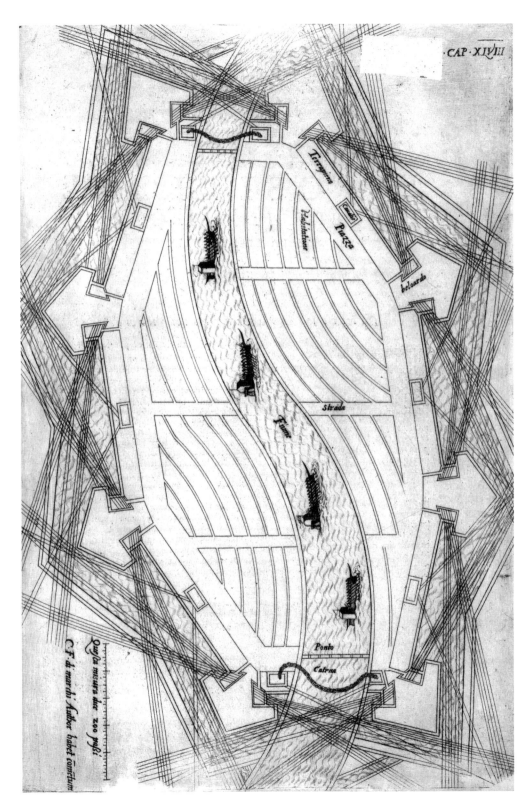

Terrapin

Palazzo

habitatione

beloardo

Strada

Fiume

Ponto

Catena

Questa misura dar 200 pasi

C F di marchi S altor habet conictum

City 59 represents the most extreme struggle between nature and the artifice: here, the meandering river cuts first irregularly through a flank on entry, and on exit, intersects with a bastion. Three bridges cross the river, two on the north-south axis, which is aligned with the east wall and its respective grid-lines, and one aligned with the only east-west axis of the city, which opens to become the central piazza at the intersection of the bridge axes. The city has seven bastions, the three on the right being aligned, and those on the left producing unequal flank angles and distances seemingly related to a factor other than the river. As in City 48, not all of the axial streets connect directly to the bastions, and consequently the circulation between bastions must be managed by the ring road in the discontinuous cases.

Aware of De Marchi's military priorities, one might attribute this meandering plan to emerge from a military logic, possibly as a result of Alberti's statement that "the ancients used to design their streets narrow and winding, imagining that they could be defended better."[20] However, in justifying the curve of the river embedded so completely in the city, De Marchi writes, "I would not want the river to travel in a straight line in the fortification because that would increase the velocity of the water's course, and it seems to me more beautiful to see; that this is the truth one can see in the ancient and famous city of Pisa, for whoever wishes to praise it says that Pisa is along the Arno, which creates a curve: a perspective that is most beautiful to see."[21] Furthermore, he continues to describe the meandering street pattern by offering variation and surprise; walking along the main streets, he writes, the citizen will be "confronted with a new and different vista at every corner he passes."[22]

In truth, it appears that De Marchi is not guided purely by utilitarian considerations, nor, as has been suggested, is he simply performing an exercise in pattern-making.[23] Rather, he communicates the *meaning* of the city *in relation to its context*: by understanding one street, something much larger can be understood—the push and pull that occurs between nature's ideal order and the uncertainty of natural contingency. Despite the dryness of De Marchi's writing, his drawings express, perhaps beyond any possible expression of words, the dynamism and reactivity that emerge from that incongruous relationship.

Today, while the "designed" city is once again being understood as a sign —from the regular geometries produced by architects, including Norman Foster's square city Masdar, and Richard Rogers's circular Compact City in Lu Zia Sui, Shanghai; to symbolic forms produced by developers, such as Nakheel's the Palm, the World, and the Universe in Dubai—these urban forms reference geometric and symbolic figures that are inherently unresponsive to deformative forces. As in De Marchi's last city (City 57), where the sea penetrates the city completely, the tabula rasa condition is reinstated, with all the symmetry and order that contextlessness implies.

And while contemporary architectural practices have translated the mathematics of topology to produce continuous surfaces and deformed geometries, the origin of the deformer has often been abstract and unmotivated. In locating Francesco de Marchi at the beginning of topology's trajectory and in understanding topology as a discipline emerging from a deeper understanding of place, as well as from the urban condition,we may reconsider the role of topology in architecture and urbanism as a motivated deformer, where the context is a force to which our cities, even those of fiction, must react.

City 59

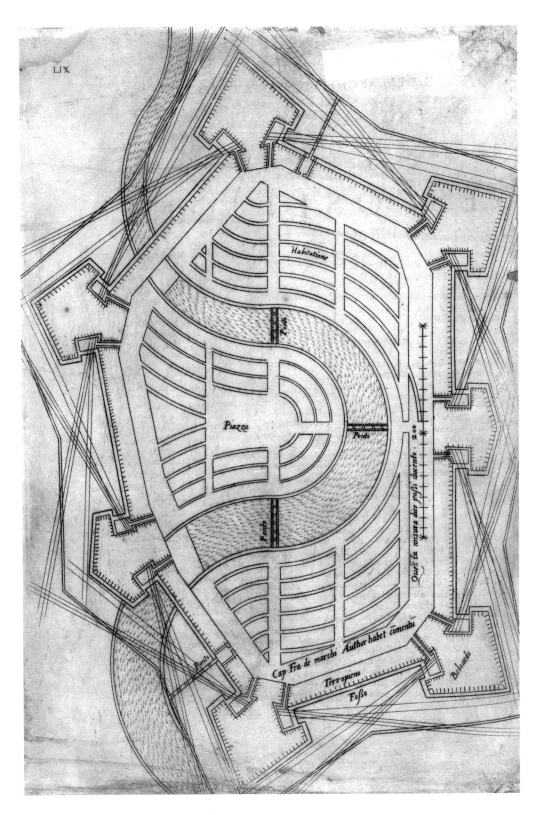

LIX

Habitatione

Piazza

Ponti

Ponti

Ponto

Ponti

Ponto

Questa misura due passi ducento . 200

Cap. Fra. de marchi Author habet comentu

Terrapieno

Foßo

Beluardo

## Endnotes

1  Wayne H. Chen, *The Analysis of Linear Systems* (New York: McGraw-Hill, 1963), 104.

2  Eventually published posthumously by Gaspare dall'Oglio in Brescia in 1599.

3  Vitruvius, *The Ten Books on Architecture,* trans. by Morris Hicky Morgan (Dover, MA: 1960), 14.

4  Leon Battista Alberti, *De re aedificatoria*, Florence in 1485, trans. Joseph Rykwert, Neil Leach, and Robert Tavernor (Cambridge, MA: MIT Press, 1988).

5  Plato, *Laws,* 360 BC, trans. by Benjamin Jowett, http://classics.mit.edu/Plato/laws.6.vi.html. Further, in *De re aedificatoria*, Alberti comments generally on fortifications, "Of all Cities, the most Capacious is the round One; and the most Secure, that which is encompassed with Walls broken here and there into Angles or Bastions jutting out at certain Distances as Tacitus informs us Jerusalem was; Because it is certain, the Enemy cannot come up to the Wall between two Angles jutting out, without exposing themselves to very great Danger; nor can their military Engines attack the Heads of those Angles with any Hope of Success." From S. Lang, "Sforzinda, Filarete, and Filelfo," *Journal of the Warburg and Courtauld Institutes* 35 (1972): 392, trans. Joseph Rykwert, Neil Leach, and Robert Tavernor (Cambridge, MA: MIT Press, 1988).

6  Vitruvius, *The Ten Books on Architecture*, trans. by Morris Hicky Morgan (Dover, MA: 1960), 22.

7  Filarete, also known as Antonio di Pietro Averlino, Trattato di Architettura di Antonio Filareto, Florence 1465. Reprinted as *Filarete's Treatise on Architecture, Volume 2: The Facsimile* (Yale University Press), 1965.

8  And potential misinterpretations: Vitruvius mentions the eight directions of the winds but proposes that the plan of the city work with the directions of the winds, not passively accepts their abstract form. This reading of Vitruvius would have opened up another trajectory in Renaissance city design, and one that would have been more aligned with De Marchi's thinking.

9  Lang, "Sforzinda, Filarete, and Filelfo," *Journal of the Warburg and Courtauld Institutes* 35 (1972): 392.

10  S. Lang, "The Ideal City from Plato to Howard," *Architectural Review* 112, no. 668 (August 1952).

11  Niccolò Tartaglia's treatise on ballistics *Nuovo Scientia* (1537) and his *Quesiti ed invenzione divers* (1538) concerning artillery, mathematics, mechanics, and fortification marks the beginning of the shift from architect-artist to military engineer. Formerly, the architect was also a mathematician, astrologer, inventor, and artist. The new techniques for drawing pentagons, calculating distances, and shaping such things as parapets, ditches, counterscarps, ramparts, and block houses required a complete familiarity with the use of the ruler and compass. Giacomo Lanteri's treatise of 1557, *Due dialoghi ... del modo di desegnare le piante delle fortezze secondo Euclide*, was the first in which design of fortifications was treated as a purely abstract geometrical problem. Lanteri writes, "You must know that arithmetic is necessary to subtract or add measurements, to divide one measurement by another, to know the perimeter of the circuit to be fortified, and to learn how to report the expenses of the works of fortification. To fortify a place is impossible without this knowledge. I am amazed in many ways at the powers of geometry."

12  Horst De la Croix, "Military Architecture and the Radial City Plan in Sixteenth Century Italy," *Art Bulletin* XLII, no. 4 (1960).

13  Martha Pollak, *Turin, 1564–1680: Urban Design, Military Culture, and the Creation of the Absolutist Capital* (Chicago: University of Chicago Press, 1991), 22.

14  In practice, many of the ideal cities of the 15th and 16th centuries, when actually implemented, were forced to deform due to site conditions, existing city form, and civilian needs. Even Palmanova, whose final form was very similar to her paper representations thanks to the siting on a perfectly flat and open plane, was significantly altered in its eventual implementation.

15  In De La Croix's synopsis, "Castriotto believed that mountain sites were stronger. De Marchi was undecided, but also seemed to favor the mountains, while Alghisi was a strong advocate of flat and open sites. Busca devoted nine full chapters to the problem, only to decide that a final choice between the two was most difficult." Horst De la Croix, "Military Architecture and the Radial City Plan in Sixteenth Century Italy," *Art Bulletin* XLII, no. 4 (1960).

16  In his treatise, De Marchi's city plans do not appear in the progressive order that they appear here. Rather, these examples appear sporadically throughout the treatise, intermingled with more conventional platonic forms.

17  J.R. Hale, *Renaissance Fortification, Art or Engineering* (Thames and Hudson, 1977), 33.

18  Francesco De Marchi, *Della architettura militare* (Brescia, Italy: Gaspare dall'Oglio, 1599), chap. 57, trans. by Ashleigh Imus for the author.

19  Francesco De Marchi, *Della architettura militare* (Gaspare dall'Oglio, 1599), chap. 48, trans. by Ashleigh Imus for the author.

20  Leon Battista Alberti, *De re aedificatoria*, chap. 54, trans. Joseph Rykwert, Neil Leach, and Robert Tavernor (Cambridge, MA: MIT Press, 1988).

21  Francesco De Marchi, *Della architettura militare* (Brescia, Italy: Gaspare dall'Oglio, 1599), chap. 48, trans. by Ashleigh Imus for the author.

22  Horst De la Croix, "Military Architecture and the Radial City Plan in Sixteenth Century Italy," *Art Bulletin* XLII, no. 4 (1960), 288.

23  In her article, *The Ideal City: From Plato to Howard*, Susan Lang refers to this plan as an example of the 15th century's tendency "to draw plan as an exercise in pattern-making." It is to this comment that Horst de la Croix responds with his article *Military Architecture and the Radial City Plan in 16th Century Italy*, arguing that the designs were "the products of practical men who were guided primarily by utilitarian considerations." Their feisty argument is printed in *Art Bulletin* 43, no. 4 (Dec. 1961).

*City plans from Francesco de Marchi,* Della architettura militare *(Brescia: Gaspare dall'Oglio, 1599). Courtesy Avery Architectural and Fine Arts Library, Columbia University.*

## James Siena

*is a New York City-based artist. His work is held in numerous prestigious public and private collections across the United States, including the Museum of Fine Arts, Boston; San Francisco Museum of Modern Art; and the Metropolitan Museum of Art, the Museum of Modern Art, and the Whitney Museum of American Art in New York. Siena is represented by the Pace Gallery. He received a BFA from Cornell University in 1979.*

# Error and Generation

James Siena in conversation with Caroline O'Donnell

### Caroline

From the Renaissance until very recently, let's say the 1950s, there was a correct and accepted way of practicing architecture, where proportion, harmony, and part-to-whole relationships, were fundamental. As a result of Colin Rowe's famous essay, the word *mathematics* became synonymous with those qualities of architectural order. Today, however, mathematics in architecture means something different, it means an algorithmic process which creates a range of possibilities: variation, rather than an accepted and correct standard. And it is that trajectory between those two expressions of mathematics—from the Ideal to the Uncertain—that we are looking at in issue 9 of the *Cornell Journal of Architecture*.

It seems to us that there is a resonance between that trajectory and much of your work. Your process has been described as algorithmic, self-organizing, fractal. The titles of your work hint at mathematical influence: *Sequence One, Iterative Grid, Multi-Colored Nesting Unknots, Boustrophedonic Recursive Combs* .... Your process begins with an ideal figure, and repeats, yet it is different in each iteration because it incorporates your own human error as part of the process to arrive at an unpredictable conclusion.

### James

I like to think that my work sites itself all along the trajectory you describe. It's interesting that you talk about the Renaissance as a time of order. I love the anonymous architecture of the medieval period, when builders were the architects. Their view of the world had to do with durability, not with innovation. That somehow comes back to my work. I want a kind of structural durability that maybe calls upon some of that innocence of the pre-Renaissance builder: the idea that there's a consistency and completeness in what I do. With that in mind, the ideas and positions behind the work, despite the presence of "error," are conveyed.

### Caroline

You are right. It was a guild system. The architect as such did not exist prior to Alberti. It was really in the Renaissance that the architect became a liberal-arts-trained intellectual, separated from the craftspeople, executing an intellectual project more than a building project. So the world that you are talking about was a guild-based world where heuristics—rules of thumbs—were everything.

**Sequence One**, 2009. Woodcut on paper. 16 7/8" × 13 1/2" (42.9 cm × 34.3 cm), 36 panels, each, unbound.

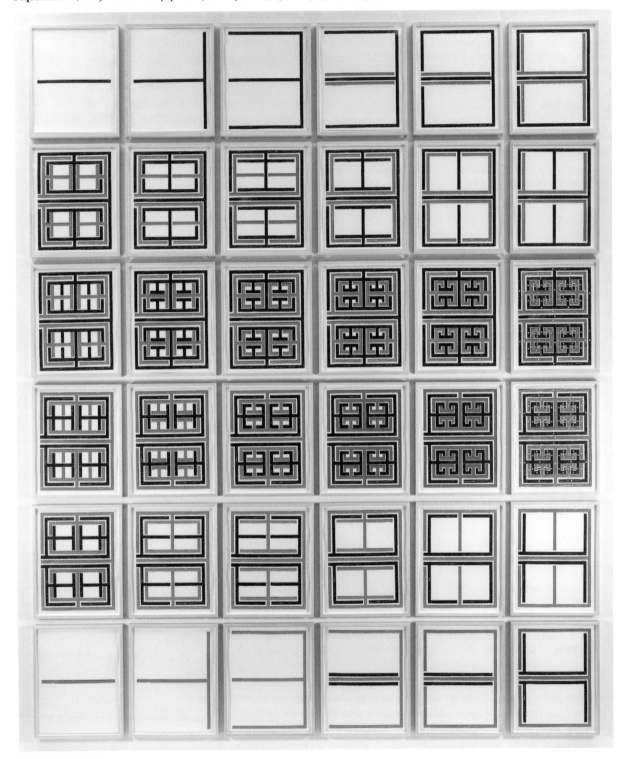

**James**

And change was not encouraged so much as tolerated or, if it occurred, each variation/innovation was agreed upon within the guild. In *A Distant Mirror*,[1] Barbara W. Tuchman talks about the guild system and about this notion of continuity, which interests me enormously. But I am also interested in innovation. Creating something that is both new and respectful of tradition.

**Caroline**

Watching you sketching the hooks earlier, for your in-progress work [working title *Connected Hooks with Arrows (Red)*, 2011–12], one would say you were basically executing a rule-based procedure. You said: there are the elements, and I will join the pieces in the most circuitous way. So one could consider it to be an algorithm. But I have the feeling that no computer programmer could possibly write an algorithm that replicated that. There were unarticulated choices being made, there was proximity of line that was guiding your hand, there was so much more than the instructions themselves.

**James**

And the way lines take-off and come in for a landing. Yes, it is the tendons, muscles, eyes, memories of other people's curves that I've looked at, as well as road systems, trail systems, vehicular trajectories. That human tradition is really important.

**Caroline**

But let's suppose I told you I could write that script. Would that go against the principles of your process?

**James**

No, I would love to see that. But then I would say: let me fuck with your script. We'll throw in hooks that bend, and now run your script. And that, not your script, would be my work.

**Caroline**

See if you can make smoke come out of the machine?

**James**

Yes. Machine Panic. And I've done it. Sometimes—actually, most times—I will intentionally screw it up by changing the lengths or the angles of things.

**Caroline**

Yet it's not an instructional-based art, like Sol LeWitt's, for example; it is not something that you can pass on to another artist to produce. It is *your* hand, *your* memories, *your* tradition that makes the errors that are crucial to the work.

**James**

In most cases, it is. In the Triangle paintings, at first glance they look very mechanical. But they are painted by hand, following lines that are drawn against a ruler. Here, it is not so much about the hand as the mind. I was carrying out this iterative process. I divided the picture plane in two with a diagonal. That's the only move

**Untitled (Iterative Grid)**. Enamel on aluminum, 29" × 22 3/4" (73.7 cm × 57.8 cm)

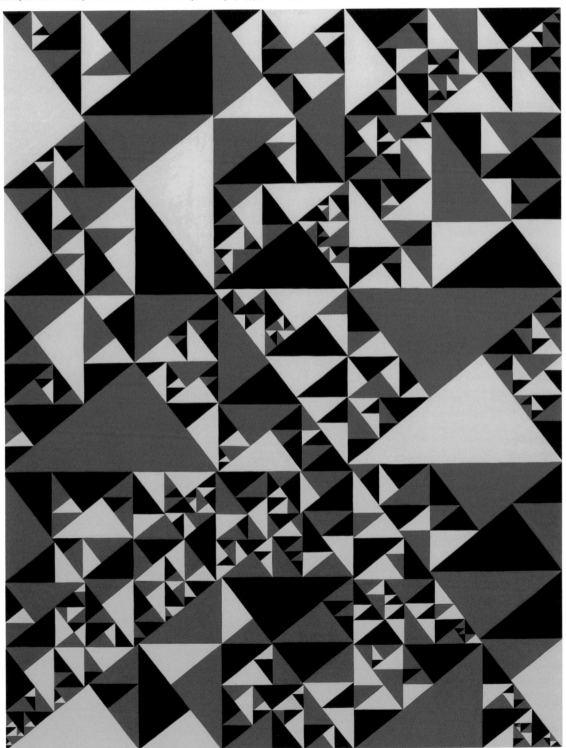

of its kind in this image. All the other moves are the same. I turn it so that this line is parallel to me, and I draw perpendiculars from the two hypotenuses to the right angle of the triangle. And repeat until they start to multiply in a maniacal way. Then I decide we are going to do it in three colors, and the colors cannot touch laterally. Since I am doing it by hand, I may miss one or two iterations. And each error or omission has a cascade effect.

### Caroline
So if you make an error, and that's the mark of a certain humanity, you do not go back and rectify the error, you let the error propagate. And that would be the difficulty in scripting it.

### James
We could say that *life* is a series of errors. Life on this planet. Whatever started the first amino acids propagating, and that became a self-organizing system that was able to somehow copy itself, and some of them got hit by lightning, or boiled by gas vents, or frozen in a storm (to give a few examples), and some did not. And those accidents are intrinsically creative.

### Caroline
The work fascinates me not just because of what it is but because of how it comes to be.

### James
I think what you are talking about is what a friend of mine (Steve DiBenedetto, a terrific artist) called slippage. While there's an integrity to a concept or an image, it has slipped, fallen from grace; yet holds the promise of something new, in spite of its apparent failure.

### Caroline
I enjoy that reading of both conditions struggling with each other.

### James
But the point is not only to unlock the procedure. The point is also to marvel at the complexity of existence. Maybe they look extraordinary in some regard because they are set against reductive modernist notions, but everything is teeming with complexity.

### Caroline
*Battery* is the clearest balance of the procedural and the complex for me.

### James
I circumambulated the surface with ellipses and as I got toward the middle there was less space, so they naturally got smaller. And because of the variations in shape, they started to push themselves into not necessarily the center. I could have laid this out very carefully, made a stencil and created rows but I chose not to. I am ambivalent about this because it is too pretty.

### Caroline
The edge of your painting is controlled by the regularity of the rectangle, but as soon

**Battery, 1997**. Enamel on aluminum. 29 1/8" × 22 3/4" (74 cm × 57.8 cm)

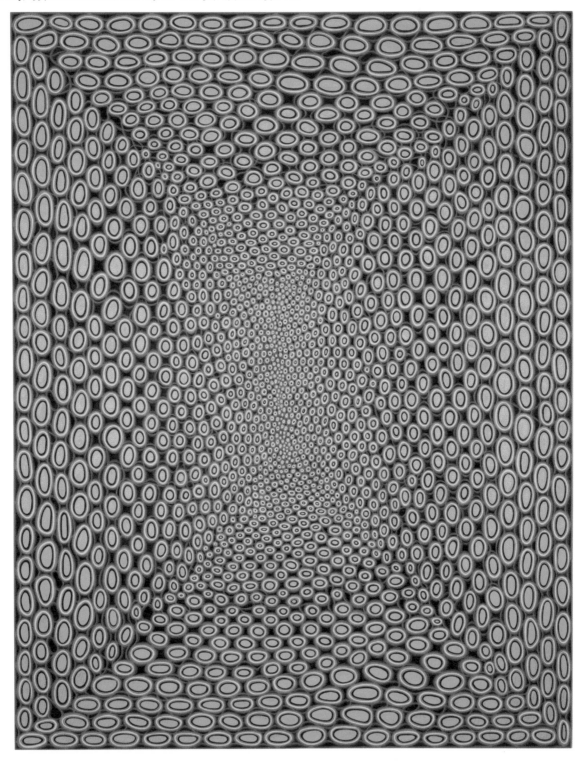

as the errors start to accumulate, it recedes into an extremely turbulent center.

### James

Yes, extreme turbulence but consistency and completeness as well. The ellipses do not touch, the saddle shapes between them have the same alignments: it all makes an internal sense. It's as if there is some kind of growth-mediated art mitigated by error. I'm not sure about that word …

### Caroline

What about the word *mutation* instead of error?

### James

Wonderful word. I also like the word *infection*. I've made works that have variations on the title *Infected Lattice*. Here there is an X motif, and then wherever there is a vertex; I accumulate marks. Marks grow on the vertices, explicitly referencing infection. In the case of the toothpick sculptures, the grid derives from the placement of the now-absent grapes. And maybe that's a poetic reference to the body or to life. I've also made (in the same year as the triangles) overtly sexual paintings and works on paper.

### Caroline

In architecture the role of mathematics and order has often been represented by Vitruvian Man or by the body. It's interesting that your work contains both overtly geometrical, and overtly sexual imagery. Is there an overlap between the two for you?

### James

Well, we were talking about error and generation. That's not too far from sex, is it? Lust has generated mistakes that occasionally develop into something meaningful, making it all worthwhile. But I do find the body more and more compelling as a way into structure and procedure; and that's not too far from sex, either, come to think of it. But there's a strong overlap in the area of the system; we need to be reminded of that when we think of our humanity, or, better yet, our "organity." And the limit of our form, our physical boundary between us and the rest of the world, is, in these works, metaphorized into the body of a painting that functions like a visual machine (or organism: remember the sixties band Soft Machine?).

We're going shortly to an island in the south of France called l'Ile du Levant, to spend a few months working on paintings and drawings. The image with the central line and combs (*Floppy Combs Variation*, 2010) that surround it was inspired by the street plan of that island which is a pedestrian village. It's built on a hill so there's a road called La Perspective, which is aligned with the setting sun, and radiating off of that are paths where most houses are sited.

### Caroline

This brings up my own interest in the role of accident in city planning. My own article in the *Journal* is about a 16th-century military architect named Francesco de Marchi, who designs cities based on the contingencies of site. This is radical at a time when the pure geometry of fortified cities was considered necessary for

**Infected Lattice**, 2004. Lithograph in 2 colors. 17 3/8" × 14 1/2."
Edition 20. Published by Universal Limited Art Editions.
© James Siena/Universal Limited Art Editions, 2004

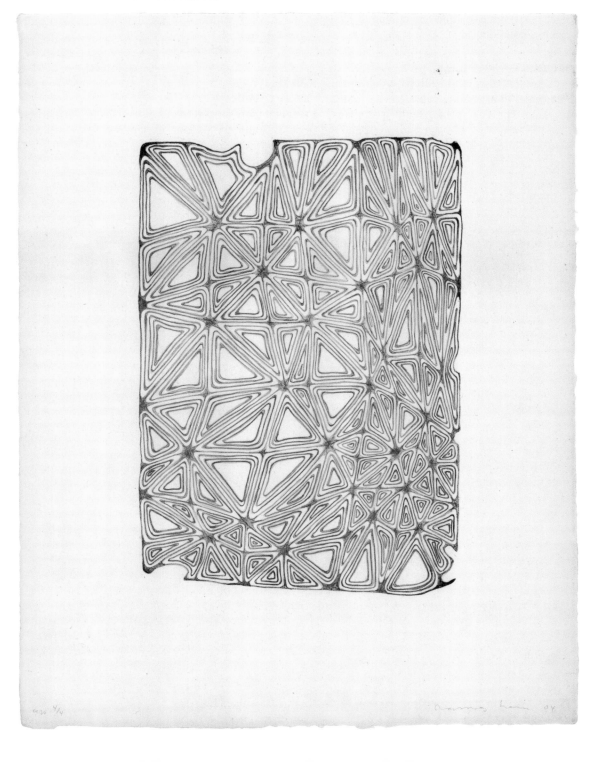

reasons of defense and of geometry. I am interested in an architecture that is reactive
to contingencies in the same way—not for reasons of sustainability, which I also
believe have to or should have to be about reaction, but for reasons of meaning.
A reactive system produces an understanding of the thing itself and the other, and the
struggle produced in between.

### James

We have as a species reacted to a hill by either dealing with the contour, or getting
out the dynamite. I think seeing Colin Rowe's approach in the seventies was
influential on me. The idea of the gestalt street plan … I taught a workshop at the
Studio School in New York last summer, and I had the students go for a walk and
map the walk when they came back. And they got lost because we were near the
West Village, where the orthogonal grid falls apart. So the nonlogical grid was gone,
or perhaps logical, based on landscape which is no longer relevant. But what I said
was, when maps were being made of cities 500 years ago, nobody could see them
from above. They had to conceptualize. They had to go up in the air mentally.
And amazingly, they did it—and even more amazingly, people could read the maps.
Our species learns codes easily! From language to mapping, and beyond.

**Five Unfinished Toothpick Sculptures**, 2005–11.
Courtesy of the Pace Gallery. Photo: Kerry Ryan McFate

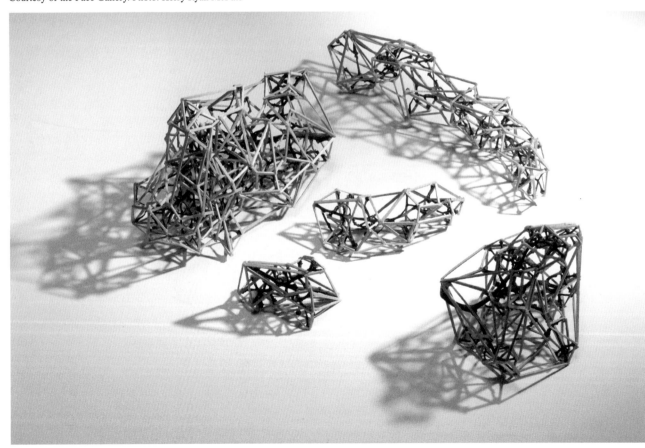

**Caroline**

The figure-ground condition and the arrows in much of your work often reads as a kind of map. I am fascinated by this new work: notating the complex form of the vines using wooden sticks, which is also a mapping, but in three dimensions. How did this work come about?

**James**

When first I made these toothpick sculptures, I painted them black, to unify the inside and outside. Then I realized the shadow was doing that anyway, and there was visual interest in the contrast between the grape stems and the toothpicks. I was also drawn to the singularity of the shape, however complex it appeared to others. Lately, though, I've been clustering the stems in illogical ways before attaching the toothpicks, and the results are initially less harmonious looking, but with time and contemplation they hold an intricacy whose structure comes directly from the random arrangement of stems.

**Caroline**

An architect might read this in reverse: that the interior organic form is derived from the geometrical cage. This tessellation of surfaces is something that computer programs do as a matter of course in order to build things.

**James**

Yes, but as you can see, the stems vary according to species; thick and short, thin and long. And when you do scramble the stems, the program you mention is deeply important. On a craft note, you must leave them for a few years to dry, before working with them, because they shrink. I've found this out the hard way.

**Caroline**

So you are aging the grapeless stem. The parallel to wine is fabulous. At some point it feels like they are trying to get out. Which is ironic, since they generated their own cage.

**James**

They are incredibly strong.

**Caroline**

It could almost be a bridge. But it is not perfectly triangulated. If you don't triangulate, you are risking failure.

**James**

Yes, I am. But without the ever-present risk of failure, what are we?

**Endnote**

1   Barbara W. Tuchman, *A Distant Mirror: The Calamitous 14th Century* (New York: Random House, 1978).

## Jenny E. Sabin

*works at the forefront of a new direction for 21st-century architectural practice—one that investigates the intersections of architecture and science, and applies insights and theories from biology and mathematics to the design of material structures. Sabin is an assistant professor at Cornell University Department of Architecture and a principal of Jenny Sabin Studio, an experimental architectural design studio based in Philadelphia. She was recently named a USA Knight Fellow in Architecture.*

# Material Analogs and the Impurity of Form

The purity of mathematics affords spatial abstractions that unravel and extend the bounds of creative thought in the design process. The impure extends such abstractions toward the material realm and finally into architecture. A design process saturated in computation enables the exploration of the complexities of connectedness, of topological wanders, and the purity of mathematical space. Here, geometry is not solely a practice of defining shapes through mathematics, but is one of projecting and inhabiting form into the ether of mathematical space. This in turn, has impacted modes of representation and the role of geometric abstraction in the design process.

Architects specializing in generative and parametric design strategies—more formally known as design computation—have adopted a bottom-up approach to the negotiation of constraints within the design process. The evolution of digital tools in architecture has prompted new techniques of fabrication alongside new understandings in the organization of material through its properties and potential for assemblage. Internal geometries inherent to natural forms, whose complexity could not be computed with the human mind alone, may now be explored synthetically through mathematics and generative systems. To script and to hack is to sketch opportunistically, where software is a virtual ground to abstract, control, and unfurl. In this sense, software itself is a material, one inhabited by matter and mind, where drawing is formal calculation.

This renewed interest in complexity has offered alternative methods for investigating the interrelationships of parts to their wholes, and emergent self-organized pattern systems at multiple scales. New geometries emerge alongside pressures and inflections elicited by external constraints. The topological wander ceases—one bridge too soon—as the production of architecture begs for the impure, the messy, and the tangible *there* there. The algorithmic design process is tamed and made material through robust feedback loops found outside of the generative systems of investigation and within the realm of architecture. The computer script is extended into the realm of architectural manifestation. A transformation ensues and the purity of mathematical form is made impure through designed contamination. Architecture is not algorithm alone.

**Minimal Surface Studies**. Simin Wang (M. Arch. '13) Matrix drawing of gyroid variations with 3D prints. Subtle changes in the code result in radical transformations in form where designed impurities come forth through fabrication constraints and the development of surface geometry and its thickness. For M. Arch. 1 Core Design Studio 3; Instructor: Jenny E. Sabin

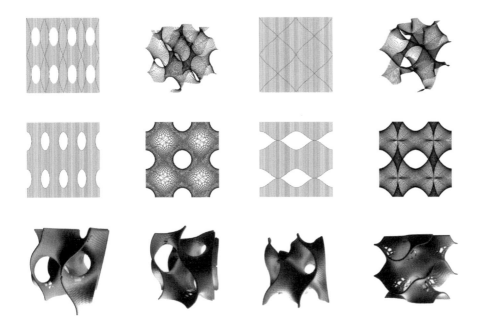

Here, contamination is seen as a process of architectural investigation, a careful and playful choreography between the intent of the designer and the purity of a mathematical and generative system. At each stage, the designers must reconsider their design strategy as new constraints come into the fold—as can be seen in the preliminary generative studies for Simin Wang's studio project for a third-semester graduate core design studio at Cornell. This sets up a rigorous design foundation for understanding how the production of architecture is not simply about form generation, but is a synthesis of a complex array of parameters and effects. In the production of relationships and correspondences, "tools" such as computer scripts are designed and developed to orchestrate the movement between multiple modes of working. Parallel processing, feedback loops, and research are encouraged to provide an environment in which dynamic relationships reveal to the imagination new possibilities of organization at multiple scales. The following is a description of one topological wander taken through a series of designed constraints or feedback loops, this time at the scale of a greenhouse pavilion for the American Philosophical Society Museum, sited in the Jefferson Garden, Philadelphia.

Taking inspiration from the artifacts and themes present in the American Philosophical Society Museum's exhibition, "Of Elephants and Roses: Encounters with French Natural History, 1790–1830, The Greenhouse & Cabinet of Future Fossils" attempts to gather, digest, and disseminate information about nature while also incorporating cutting-edge design and fabrication techniques to ultimately produce a greenhouse of the future.

In the case of 19th-century French natural history, the cabinet or lab may be described as a bounded condition that affords an introspective and synthetic relationship with the field, but at a distance. The unbounded—the scientist out in the natural terrain—offers a sensorial and full-body immersion within the field.[1] For curiosity to take place, a transformation ensues in both situations. In the *Greenhouse & Cabinet of Future Fossils*, the concepts of the field and the cabinet are synthesized and brought together through formal, geometrical, and spatial configurations. The cabinet is newly materialized and parametrically controlled through the modularity of digitally fabricated cold-frame boxes that populate an unraveling structural tapestry. Overall, the *Greenhouse & Cabinet of Future Fossils* attempts to display, gather, and experience nature between two perceptual terrains occupied by the field and the cabinet.

The second mode of transformation operates at the stage of pure mathematical investigation, an unraveling of a three-to-eight torus knot through time. These knot morphologies were chosen for two reasons. The first relates the geometric behavior of an unraveling knot to the desired spatial and formal shift in the Greenhouse from field to cabinet—conveying a spatial and formal transformation as visitors move from the exterior to the interior. The second highlights an abstract and synthetic formal relationship between the configuration of the unraveling knot and the internal structures and relationships revealed in Cuvier's incredible organisms, housed in the Gallery of Paleontology and Comparative Anatomy at the Jardin des Plantes in Paris.

The primary geometrical system of the Greenhouse structure is generated by a select group of profile curves extracted from the unraveling mathematical knots. Mathematical scripts are used as a sketch tool to explore experimental geometries that share synthetic relationships with models found in nature. Through mathematics and generative algorithms and iteration through scripting, it is possible to simulate and inhabit geometry as nature does, absent of representation and translation, in a constant formation, where geometry and matter are one. The Greenhouse configuration as a set of 20 vertical cross-ribs also recalls the bones of giant vertebrates put on display as a public spectacle in the 19th century.

The Greenhouse takes up similar themes related to movement through the formal and mathematical transformations described previously and as an interface with nature at multiple scales and synthetic terrains. From the interior "cabinet," the structure opens up to the world around it through an arched expanse that curves up and over the inner area, creating a space that is simultaneously inside and outside—enclosed but not confined.

The interior gallery under the vine canopy houses the *Cabinet of Future Fossils*, a modular system holding digitally generated and newly fabricated ceramic and 3D printed artifacts inspired by nature, complexity, and generative design processes.

Like the fossils used by French scientists in post-Revolutionary France to classify extinct mammals, these three-dimensional "future fossils" imply an era of the future, a new nature, that will, in turn, look back on these synthetically created "natural" objects of the age of computation and digital fabrication. These forms are also a play on 19th-century "cabinets" that were filled with a vast variety of specimens and fossils, that were at once scientifically relevant and a spectacle for the general public to view.

Finally and most importantly, these forms and the Greenhouse overall, are representative of a shift in digital tooling and crafting in architectural practice,

**Knot Morphogenesis**. Jenny Sabin Studio. Generative study for the Greenhouse, 2011.

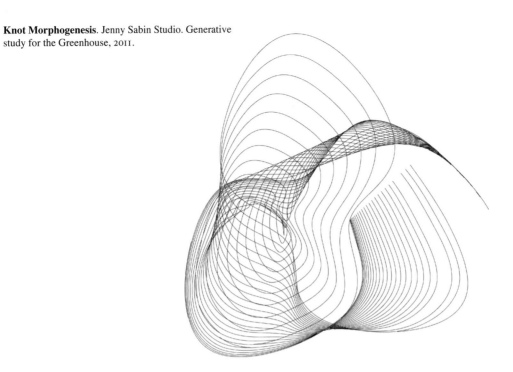

**Greenhouse & Cabinet of Future Fossils**. Jenny Sabin Studio. Rendering and line drawing showing placement of cold frame modules within the cross-rib system, 2011.

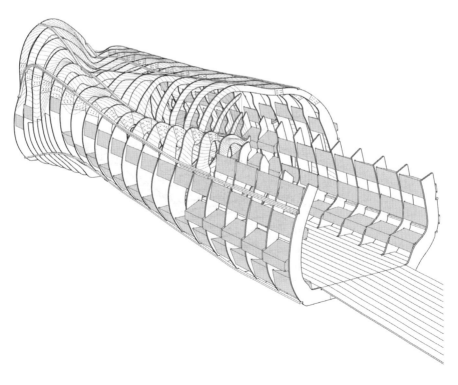

**The Greenhouse & Cabinet of Future Fossils**.
Through its dynamic material configuration, the
Greenhouse attempts to gather, digest, and disseminate
information about nature while also incorporating
cutting-edge design and fabrication techniques to
ultimately produce a greenhouse of the future.
Photos Brent Wahl.

wherein forms are produced as part of a generative design process; an aspect of
computational design that opportunistically abstracts processes and forms found in
nature for architectural investigation. This is certainly not a new idea. Generative
processes extracted from natural models have preoccupied designers and engineers
throughout the Modern era. We simply have better tools to compute abstract
relationships to generate and render complex form.

What is new is our relationship with making and fabrication. The architect
is now in full control of the design-to-manufacture process through the use of
digital tools and mathematically sophisticated models and scripts. In the case of
the Greenhouse, a generative study of knots becomes the geometric and material
ground that is refined and later developed into 20 cross-rib cut files for a computer
numerically controlled (CNC) machine.

Architects are now in the business of making and crafting again. In fact,
this is the biggest paradigm shift—not our ability to digitally generate complex
form. Computational design has impacted modes of representation and the role of
geometric abstraction in the design process. Consequently, plan and section are no
longer primary features of architectural representation; they are three-dimensional
slices of relationships of compiled wholes.

The most important work in computational design today, and perhaps the
most vital to architecture in the future, may be seen in projects that have grappled
with the material and built ramifications of complex form. The creative expansion
of mind and matter will continue to mature as the purity of digital complexity and
mathematical space is seamlessly linked with a playful and rigorous calibration of
tangible constraints found in the making of architecture. The formal expressions

of the *Greenhouse and Cabinet of Future Fossils* may become obsolete, but how such expressions are made impure through digital fabrication and tooling will continue to revolutionize and inspire.

The Greenhouse & Cabinet of Future Fossils *was Commissioned by the American Philosophical Society Museum, funded by Heritage Philadelphia Program, a program of the Pew Center for Arts & Heritage.*

**Endnote**

1 See essay by Dorinda Outram, "New Spaces in Natural History," in *Cultures of Natural History*, Nicholas Jardine, James A. Secord, and Emma C. Spary (ed.) (Cambridge, UK: Cambridge Univer-sity Press, 1996), 251.

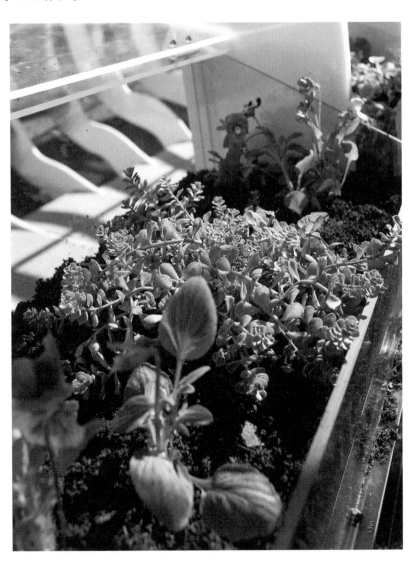

## Mark Morris

*teaches architectural design and theory at Cornell University Department of Architecture. He is author of* Models: Architecture and Miniature *and* Automatic Architecture Designs from the Fourth Dimension. *Mark studied architecture at The Ohio State University and took his doctorate at the University of London's Consortium program, supported by the Royal Institute of British Architects Trust. His research focuses on architectural models, scale, and questions of representation.*

# 1 : Whatever
## The Collapse of Scalar Thinking

> *The Caterpillar: What size do you want to be?*
> *Alice: Oh, I'm not particular as to size, only one doesn't like changing so often, you know.*
>
> Lewis Carroll, *Alice in Wonderland*

We have a scale problem in architecture. It is confusing our discourse, how we represent and talk about our work. Critics are presented with drawings at varying scales or no particular scale at reviews. The same could be said of digitally fabricated models. A good deal of time is wasted at design juries acclimating everyone to the new scale liberalism, where one project might include plans at 1/8" = 1'–0", sections at 3/16" = 1'–0", and models at anyone's guess. One could ask, and students do, why drawings or models are obliged to be at conventional scales. Looking back over our own departmental archive, scale was typically a given in syllabi and review directions, consistently so across decades until now. A student was asked at a recent review what scale her drawings were and she responded, "3/16, I think. Is that a scale? Why does it matter?"

The fact that no one else on the planet besides us, the Burmese, and the Liberians uses imperial measurement anymore undermines the notion that conventional scales are universal. Students have to go metric the minute they find work in any office with international aspirations, so why bother with thinking in fractions of inches? But the problem is not about systems of measurement, but the fading of adherence to any conventional scale that impacts work done in either feet or meters. Conventions may differ from place to place, but they do establish norms or standard criteria for the sake of communication. Using conventional scales develops habits of seeing and imagining to the extent that without finding the scale noted, most architects guess the scale of a drawing or model and quickly move on to the content. It is only when the scale of the drawing is unconventional that the viewer is tripped up.

Other representational habits have waned. Site plans were often drafted using an engineer's scale with decimalized fractions of an inch, 1:10, 1:20, and so on. This tradition came out of surveying. Students rarely turn their three-sided scale rulers, if they even purchase them anymore, to the engineer's side, and then only because they mistake it for metric. Physical models, thought of as extrusions of drawings

**Traveler 156 at Night**. © Walter Martin and Paloma Munoz. Courtesy of the artist and PPOW, 2005.

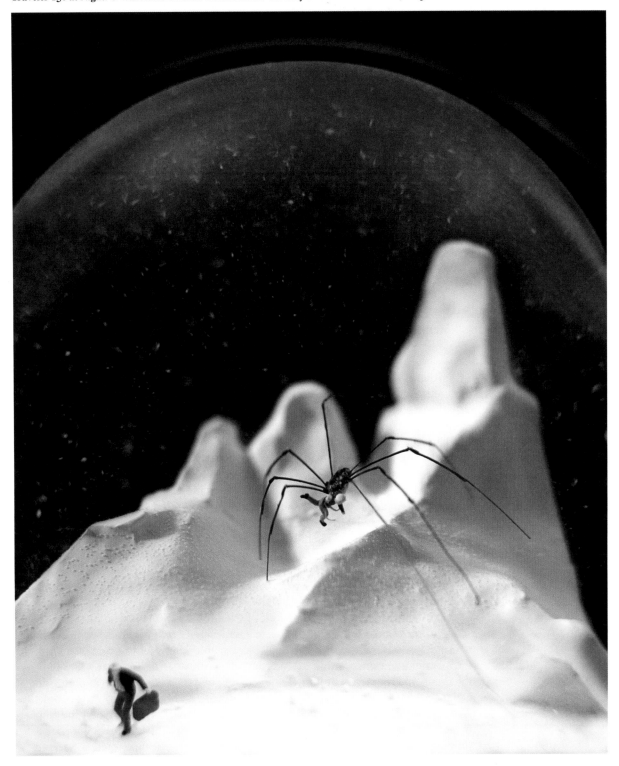

in some respects, either matched or were a useful declination of the drawings' scale; half the scale again, say. "Exploded axons" are popular but are typically built up using a digital model literally pulled apart. Tangible models are wed to digital ones and are increasingly fabricated, milled, or feature fabricated components.

Indeed, it is the computer that has relegated conventional scale to a nicety, if and when it is used. No one prepares their work at a scale, not anymore, and this is a profound shift in how we train architects and practice architecture. With computation came a revolution in how scale is treated in drawings and models. It is conceptually dispensed with, and this was the case from the earliest computer-aided design applications to Grasshopper, Rhino, and Maya. With software, one inputs full-scale dimensions from the start of a project. It would be foolhardy to do otherwise or attempt to think in scale while designing a building in Maya.

One reason conventional scales were adopted in architecture and architects used them so assiduously for so long has to do with the idea of process or stages of development that assume that preliminary things are supposed to be smaller, simpler, and less real than finished or fully manifested things such as buildings. One thinks of a painter's small initial sketch refined and enlarged in various studies, and finally, rendered on canvas. Or, in a biological metaphor, a baby growing, learning, and becoming fully adult. Aristotle's theory of the acorn held that small things have potentiality and an operating cause striving for self-actualization. There is an intuitive sense that the small is preliminary or unfinished. Accordingly, two disparate qualities—size and origination—were yoked together in the case of architectural representation.

Rudolf Arnheim, in *The Dynamics of Architectural Form*, references a similar allometric argument (borrowed from Peter Stevens) and connects it to models and visual perception. He questions any process of analysis that ignores scale. He urges us to view the cityscape as a landscape where formal comparisons and judgments can be made and scale is central to this index of abstraction. One of the few to treat scale as a topic of interest at all in the late sixties and early seventies, Arnheim invents the term *thought model*. Not a material object, Arnheim imagines architects think in model-form, to scale: "No doubt, the architect must imagine with some degree of precision what the actual building will look like when approached from the street or seen from the inside. But much of the actual shaping must be done on thought models of the whole building, mental images that are supported sooner or later by small-scale models built at the office. […] What can be seen in imagination tends, of course, to be less detailed and more generalized, but nevertheless the handling of a mental image bears a striking resemblance to the manipulation of an actual model with one's hands."[1]

Arnheim acknowledges the work of Claude Lévi-Strauss who broadens the scope of scale's conceptual attributes in *The Savage Mind*, where scale is attached to aesthetics. "Being smaller, the object as a whole seems less formidable. […] the quantitative transposition extends and diversifies our power over a homologue of the thing, and by means of it the latter can be grasped, assessed and apprehended at a glance."[2] He connects ease of apprehension with a notion of power over something. Through scale, a sort of conceptual shortcut can be had, "knowledge of the whole precedes knowledge of the parts. And even if this is an illusion, the point of the procedure is to create or sustain the illusion, which gratifies the intelligence and gives rise to a sense of pleasure which can already be called aesthetic on these grounds alone."[3] It is a fundamentally different way of coming to know something, spring-loaded comprehension, the mental buzz of which cashes out as a pleasurable aesthetic experience.

**Structure of Shadow**, Bohyon Yoon, 2009.
Courtesy of the artist.

There is a genuine sense of surprise encountered when a project notionally designed from its inception to its refinement at full scale is output to a scale, any scale, and this is owed to never encountering scale in the first place as an economy of drafting, modeling, or even conceptually as a thought model. The qualitative simplification offered by the quantitative diminishment in scaled representation is foregone for the sake of computation and working more precisely in real terms as if in the real world. But academia is not the real world, training architects requires a willing suspension of disbelief and a capacity for abstraction. Spatially, diminishment implies distance. The distant is visually simplified or abstracted, distilled, and recast in an abbreviated way. Critical distance, having "perspective on something," requires abstraction as a basis for broader comparisons, manipulations, and judgments.

Scale is a useful tool toward graphic and analytic abstraction in the manner of Colin Rowe, or formal and conceptual abstraction in the manner of Rowe's students, for example, Peter Eisenman's use of scaling. He suggests that architecture traditionally has been related to the human scale. A house, a theater, and a skyscraper are the same human scale, in that they each reflect multiples of the size of a human being; this implicitly gives the scale of a human body originary value.

In scaling there is no single privileged scale referent. Rather, each scale change invokes characteristics specific and intrinsic to itself. Scaling "produces a place that is no place, that had no time, that has no scale, that had no origin, and that's the one truth—that there is no truth."[4] Scaling as a technique may have meant more when injected into a milieu when everyone was still habitually working within conventional scales. The destabilization of scaling engendered was all about the friction of scales relying on convention as grist to the mill.

One thing both Beaux-Arts and Bauhaus modes of architectural pedagogy shared was an assumption about scale. For the Beaux-Arts influenced schools, this had as much to do with the composition of drawings on a board as it did with professional emulation. The Bauhaus embraced the idea of prototype and sought easy communication and partnership with industry where architectural rendering approached shop drawing; ergo, the emphasis on the measured axonometric. With nearly universal metrification, a schism erupted between anthropometric and agriculturally derived English Imperial units versus the mathematically pure French metric. Le Corbusier took this as a challenge and sought resolution between the two with his Modulor system developed in 1946, by reintroducing anthropometric measure to the metric, with the Golden Section and Fibonacci sequence thrown in as lures. He spent the rest of his career applying and promoting the system; the Carpenter Center was intended as a Modulor example for Americans to study and embrace.

**Modulor Man Tattoo**, Kelly Lone, 2007.
Courtesy of the artist.

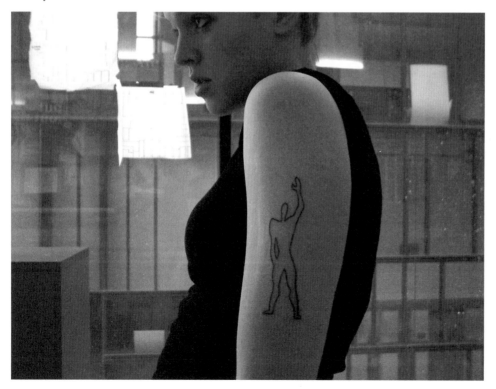

Working at full scale from start to finish gives one the sense that they have already started the building rather than an ideogram of a building. The assembly of a project can originate with accurately dimensioned structural components, systems, and skins that can be evaluated and tested throughout the design process. No scale translations of drawings are required to consult with engineers or building trades. Standard parts—doors, stairs, fixtures—can be imported and applied early on. Original details are not considered fragments, but merely parts to a whole. A sense for the genuine size of things taken from personal and bodily experience can enrich a given project intrinsically.

There is nothing magical about 3/16" = 1'−0, which is a conventional scale. 3/16" 1'−0 does not inherently represent or reveal anything better than another scale (nor is the relation of inch-derived scale units to imperially sized building material beneficial, as lumber and steel dimensions are nominal). The only optimization that could be claimed in that regard is visual, where certain scales read well at a typical sitting distance from a piece of paper. What is significant about any given conventional scale is that it is a set calibration, offset from the continuum of scale and related proportionally to other distinct stoppages along that line. Out of all the possibilities of scale, conventional scales are interrelated increments from the full-sized backward to what is, practically speaking, too small to represent. While conventional, 3/16" = 1'−0 is not a commonly used scale. The student explained that 3/16" = 1'−0 was not a conscious choice. It was the nearest default conventional scale suggested by the computer when the paper size was entered as the student went to render her work. The assumption was to maximize the size of the drawing to the output media—36-inch-wide plotter paper—and the student elected to "scale to fit."

Scaling to fit impacts modeling as well. Having designed a model in Rhino or Maya, one naturally wants to take advantage of digital fabrication. Outputting to a 3D printer eats up a lot of time and money. Given that investment, it is only natural to size rather than scale the model to the limitations of the printing box to whatever those dimensions are. One wants to walk away with the biggest possible object (at least so long as 3D printers remain so relatively small), and here scale completely goes away. The habit with modeling this way is not to scale to fit where the nearest conventional scale is employed, but where these models are sized to fit even if that makes their technical scale something like 3.42/16 = 1'. It is increasingly the norm that a printed model presented at a review bears no scalar relationship to the drawings of the project. The drawings are maximized in their own way, the model in its own way. Here one was has some sympathy for the critics who, even if they crack the 3/16 code of the plots, will struggle to place the scale of the model where conventional scale never had a chance.

It is shocking to see the number of glossy renderings heaped in the dumpster at the end of term. Yet it is not the case that students take no pride in their work; rather, the "work" is no longer bound to its (scaled) representation. Whereas the drawing delineated by hand was the definitive work of the architect and its archiving essential, the rendering is an iteration of a continuous, mutable, virtual model/drawing; an outward sign of an inward process that is no longer bound to scale. There is a marked disconnect between sign and signified, but it is not a symptom of students' apathy toward architecture, just a new way of working. Something has been lost in this shift. Beyond any matter of convention, there was something

**Traveler 174 at Night**. © Walter Martin and Paloma Munoz. Courtesy of the artist and PPOW, 2005.

pedagogically useful in working at set points at a range of scales used as specific calibrations of conceptualization from rough massing to precise details. A building is an enormous and complicated thing. To approach designing one with any confidence, it was useful to work from big-scale moves to smaller ones, zooming in, starting with the most implied distance and coming figuratively closer in stages. This method allayed some creative anxiety, accepting that the development of a project was gestational, that projects literally grew as representations in parallel with the evolving and progressively more sophisticated articulation of spaces, sequence, and structure. It also permitted criticism to arrive at opportune intervals where a professor might better help guide the project from abstraction or sketch phase (lessons of type and morphology) to middle stages focused on adjacency and resolution of program to final rounds of innovative detailing which were, admittedly, fragmentary.

Lévi-Strauss aligned what we will call scalar thinking with a claim that something scaled down typically prompts an aesthetic response. This has to do with a condensation of detail and perceived levels of craftsmanship. "All miniatures seem to have intrinsic aesthetic quality—and from what should they draw this constant virtue if not from the dimensions themselves? [...] Now, the question arises whether the small-scale model or miniature, which is also the 'masterpiece' of the journeyman may not in fact be the universal type of the work of art."[5] Architects may be too close to these things to countenance them as art themselves, but others often do judge them as such, exhibit them as artwork, and trade them within the art world. But the aesthetic experience is not limited to perceiving the work, but also in making it. Gaston Bachelard writes of this aspect, "The cleverer I am at miniaturizing the world, the better I possess it. But in doing this, it must be understood that the values become condensed and enriched in miniature. Platonic dialectics of large and small do not suffice for us to become cognizant of the dynamic virtues of miniature thinking."[6]

Architects can take aesthetic pleasure in their scale representations as well as their buildings. This pleasure can reach an apex when one acknowledges, as Emmanuel Kant claimed in *The Critique of Judgment*, that relative scale rather than size defines the sublime. Kant allowed that the sublime is found at the extremities of scale, the realms of both telescope and microscope. And it is that pleasure that draws many to the discipline. Architects have been caught up in a cyclical pleasure principle tied to making and critiquing scale representations. We still cling to this. The full-scale Maya model is still viewed on a small computer screen, plots of scaled drawings (even if the scales are unconventional) are still pinned up at reviews, and analogically or digitally fabricated models are still mostly miniatures. The aesthetic is maintained, but the strategic deployment of conventional scales in educational settings is not. Aesthetic pleasure is still had in perceiving the work.

Conventional scale is becoming vestigial in many respects. It is an output option rather than a condition of any input. To abide by conventionally scaled representation is a professional courtesy that, for some time yet, will aid in communication and still count as official legal documentation for the purposes of planning and design review. There is no real way to rescue scale for professional purposes beyond these vestigial aspects; Frank Gehry's office may record his initial models to scale, but these are resolved computationally as if full-scale. Architects trained to work in conventional scales will still do so, even doodling accurately at 1/8" = 1'–0", but their new hires will have other gifts.

It is only the practice of using scale as a teaching tool that, I would argue, is worth rescuing. Its value is in bringing projects to fruition at stoppages that optimize the creative process, giving confidence where needed, promoting abstraction in a very basic way, affording "critical distance" for the purposes of self-critique and student-professor tutelage, and even providing aesthetic pleasure. The convention does not matter—Imperial, Metric, Modulor, whatever—provided the options give us consistent effective increments. Educational needs are distinct from professional ones, scalar thinking has been a component of architectural education for some two and a half centuries and it may still prove an indispensible skill that we claim has robust pedagogical value in its own right.

**Endnotes**

1   Rudolf Arnheim, *The Dynamics of Architectural Form* (Berkeley, CA: University of California Press, 1977), 17.
2   Claude Lévi-Strauss, *The Savage Mind* (London: Weidenfeld and Nicolson, 1966). 23.
3   Ibid., 23–24.
4   Peter Eisenman, *Moving Arrows, Eros, and Other Errors: An Architecture of Absence*, Box 3 (London: The Architectural Association, 1986), 4.
5   Lévi-Strauss, 23.
6   Gaston Bachelard, *The Poetics of Space* [*La poétique de l'espace*, 1958], Maria Jolas, trans. (Boston, MA: Beacon Press, 1994), 150.

**Credits**

Kelly Lone is an architect working in the Minneapolis-St. Paul area. Her other life as a freelance photographer takes her to music venues across the country. Her featured self-portrait was taken as a student on a rainy day coming back to studio at Ohio State's Knowlton School of Architecture.

Bohyon Yoon is a multimedia artist working in South Korea, Japan, and the United States. He studied at the Rhode Island School of Design and the Tama Art University in Tokyo, and was a Fellow at the Research Center for Art and the Kyoto University of Art and Design. Yoon's work examines images of the human body and the boundaries of communication.

Walter Martin (Norfolk, VA) and Paloma Muñoz (Madrid, Spain) are a collaborative team working together since they met in New York in 1993. Their work has been widely exhibited. They are best known for Travelers, a series of snow globes depicting a world of unfortunate, dark, and sometimes humorous situations in a frozen winter land. A monograph of their photographs was published by Aperture in 2008. Their work is frequently exhibited at PPOW in New York.

## Jerry Wells & Arthur Ovaska

**Arthur Ovaska** *studied architecture at Cornell University, where he received the professional B.Arch. degree in 1974, and further pursued M.Arch. graduate studies with O. M. Ungers. He collaborated with O. M. Ungers in his Ithaca and Köln offices from 1974 to 1978, before founding the internationally known office of Kollhoff & Ovaska in Berlin in 1978. Ovaska has taught in Berlin, Taiwan, Puerto Rico, and Syracuse, and currently holds a tenured position at Cornell, where he has served as director of undergraduate and graduate programs as well as associate chair and department head from 2004 to 2007.*

**Jerry Wells** *served as chair of Cornell's architecture department for two terms from 1980 to 1989. He is a registered architect in New York, and with the National Council of Architectural Registration Boards. He has served on the Fulbright Committee, the National Screening Committee for Architecture, and was a member of the board of directors for the National Architectural Accrediting Board. He has served on the editorial board of the* Journal of Architectural Education, *and was a member of the Architects in Education committee of the AIA.*

# Dinner with Friends

In conversation with Daniel Marino, Nicholas Cassab-Gheta, and Jae Hee Lee

#### Daniel

The two of you have watched this school grow and change across the various administrations and, Jerry, you held the Chair from 1980 to 1989. You both have definitely seen the ups and downs and sideways of the department, and you've also seen the discipline and practice alongside academia grow and change. This being said, you both teach very important lessons of the discipline that clearly can't be changed by the zeitgeist, so we'd like to frame the conversation around how math, numbers, and related conversations have existed within the department's ideology over the last decades. We will start pre-60s, and with each course, we will progress the conversation. Before the first course arrives, we wanted to ask you both what first comes to mind when we say *mathematics*?

#### Jerry

When I became Chair, I tried to figure out what makes a good architect. I devised tests that we gave to prospective students that were similar to the kinds of things that Robert Slutzky and John Hejduk used to do at the University of Texas. For example, you start out with an 8 1/2 by 11 sheet of paper and you have certain instructions: you draw a continuous line at right angles and superimpose rectangles over it. The only thing we found was that those who had 700 board scores in math on their SATs always made A's in architecture. I could not figure out why, and now I think it is because they had conceptual minds and that made them good prospects for architecture.

**Arthur**

It is true that almost every architecture student has higher math scores than they have verbal scores on the SATs.

**Nicholas**

So it's not so much that you have to *do* math with architecture or even in architecture school—

**Daniel**

They stopped the math requirement for the department a few years ago.

**Jerry**

Over the years they have diminished it: I fought that battle a long time, because I *do* think that a conceptual mind is an important thing for an architect.

**Arthur**

There's a big difference between geometry, trigonometry, and calculus. To me it's geometry that is architecture.

**Metron System,** Lee Hodgden. Courtesy of Arthur Ovaska.

**Daniel**

Arthur, you mentioned geometry's relationship with architecture, and Jerry, you have referred to proportion in the same light. In 1947, Colin Rowe wrote *Mathematics of the Ideal Villa*, which was quickly followed by Wittkower's *Architectural Principles in the Age of Humanism*. How did this emphasis on the role of ordering systems and proportion affect your own educations, since you were in school during this period?

**Jerry**

Colin Rowe, John Hejduk, Bob Slutzky, Werner Seligman: they were all my professors. For them, proportioning systems were a tuning device, not a conceptual idea. Hejduk was especially into that idea: if we did not have 54 golden sections in each drawing you were in trouble.

**Arthur**

I was not yet born in 1947.

*(Laughter)*

**Daniel**

Aware of that, but you studied architecture when this was still a hot topic to your professors.

**Arthur**

I started Cornell in 1969, and I was first taught by a great professor who had been influenced by Colin but did not directly study under him, named Klaus Herdeg. I also had Michael Dennis as a first-year professor, a friend of Jerry's who had also studied under Colin and under Lee Hodgden at Oregon. Lee had also developed his own type of mathematical systems.

**Jerry**

Worked on them until he died and never published the book: his version of proportioning systems …

**Arthur**

I have one of his paintings of the *Metron System*, as he called it. But I think he always made it out to be more important than it really was. Lee was also heavily influenced in some way by Bucky Fuller's mathematical thinking, which is a totally different world from systems of aesthetic proportion.

**Jerry**

We were well steeped in proportioning systems all the way through school. It was Colin who always said it was a tuning device.

**Daniel**

So the drawings and designs would come first and then one would "tune" them for the eye?

**Jerry**

Yes. I analyze that in my seminars, because I really like measured architecture. Today, there is this fascination with the computer and curvilinear forms. I tend to not like things that cannot be measured. Things now lack frontality. In my seminar, over the years, we have looked at many, many architects. Almost all architects, including Zaha, use mathematics in terms of proportioning systems.

**Jae**

But there must be a point where these projects begin to all look alike after this common filter that they all have been through?

**Jerry**

Not really! It's infinitely variable.

**Arthur**

I think it's an interesting question. I am going to come at it from my experience of working with Mathias Ungers. Ungers did not consider the golden section to be "rational" …

**Jerry**

He always used the square.

**Arthur**

He completely dedicated himself to rationality in architecture, but absolutely refused to deal with the golden section. He would deal with the square and with 1.414, the diagonal of the square, which generates a similar series: if you put one inside the other you make a spiral, and so on. That's the proportioning system that the European DIN paper size works with, for example. But the golden section: no, it was probably a little bit too spooky for him. Any kind of discussion I ever had with him asking, "Couldn't we try the golden section?" *No!*

*(Laughter)*

**Arthur**

It was hard to even talk with him about other shapes besides squares, although we once did an octagonal project; he would accept the octagon. He was always using platonic geometries.

*Second Course: Nine-Dot Pea Soup*

**Daniel**

In 1957, there was a debate at the RIBA on the motion "systems of proportion make good design easier and bad design more difficult," a motion that Bruno Zevi refused to support, stating that "no one really believes any longer in the proportional system," and he was agreed with by Peter Smithson who argued that architects would need to look elsewhere in order to generate cultural significance. Did this mark the beginning of the end for proportionality?"

**Roosevelt Island Housing Competition**, O.M. Ungers.
Courtesy of Ungers Archiv für Architekturwissenschaft UAA.

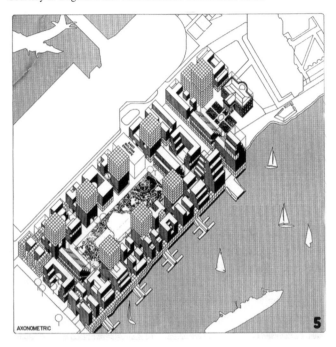

**Arthur**

It probably marked the beginning of the end for Peter Smithson.

*(Laughter)*

**Jerry**

Rem said about proportioning systems a few years back that composition is no longer relevant. I say basically as long as human beings have a brain and an eye, composition will be relevant.

**Arthur**

I wouldn't say much about Bruno Zevi because I always liked Zevi's book *Architecture as Space*. It was the first book that I remember reading as a first-year student that clearly defined architectural space. Schindler also clearly expressed the idea that architecture is space, and that is basically what I still believe.

**Jerry**

I believe that too. That is something we ought to be talking about in schools, because it is not an issue anymore. That's one of the things that made the Cornell education famous—the ability to manipulate space in various ways.

You know what led to Colin Rowe writing *Mathematics of the Ideal Villa*? He was at the Warburg Institute where Wittkower was his professor. He wrote an article suggesting that Villa Garches was Malcontenta stripped of its content.

And Wittkower says: You cannot do that; you cannot compare modern architecture to Renaissance architecture. But basically Colin was right, and he left school because of that argument. He continued to write that article based on his research. You can put the drawings over each other and it is exactly the same proportioning. Another one of my beliefs about modern architecture is that it was in fact traditional architecture stripped of its content. It didn't have architraves and cornice lines and column capitals, but the compositional aspects were proportionally almost the same. I do an exercise in my seminar where we do a transformation of content, Modern architecture and Renaissance architecture, back and forth, and it works, especially in Le Corbusier's buildings; traditional Renaissance architecture stripped of its content and made abstract.

**Plans and Diagrams of Andrea Palladio's Malcontenta and Le Corbusier's Villa Stein,** Colin Rowe, *The Mathematics of the Ideal Villa* *and Other Essays.* © 1976 Massachusetts Institute of Technology, by permission of The MIT Press.

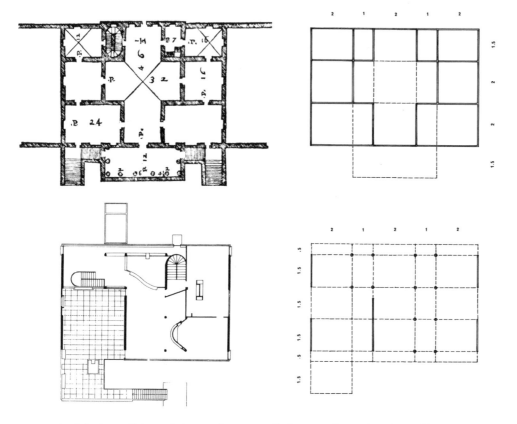

And that condition of abstraction goes all the way through Mies. I like to compare Mies and Mondrian because their work kept progressing toward abstraction. Mondrian ended up with a kind of composition that was a few lines, a few rectangles, and some colors. As for Mies, if you look at the Seagram Building, it's all decoration on the outside. It is the same in every one of his buildings except the Farnsworth House, where the steel was structural. He continued down that line of abstraction to the point where people can walk past his buildings and never even recognize them, because everyone in the world picked up on that way of making skyscrapers. I had a bunch of students with me in Toronto once, who walked past the Dominion Center, which is Mies's biggest building in this continent, and no one even saw it. What has happened is that the general public is not accepting that degree of abstraction. They want *content* back in their architecture, and that is a big thing. That's what Venturi was writing about.

### Arthur

You can see the kind of influence Mies probably had on people like the Smithsons; just take a look at the Smithsons' Hunstanton School. The work that Mies did in the office of Behrens was all about proportion. I like to look at Mies's first houses; they're very traditional, very classical, even Schinkel-esque in a way, or almost Tessenow-like. It's really unbelievable how quickly that transition happened.

### Jerry

Again, I think it is interesting to recall that Picasso and the invention of Cubism were really powerful in terms of spatial definition, and people like Bernhard Hoesli and Colin Rowe were really into that the idea of layered space. Picasso never made a painting that did not have either human or animal content. You can always see the content, so there's a level of meaning there that transcends the abstract condition. Mondrian and Mies never did that.

*Third Course: Nine-Square Scallop with Roe*

### Jerry

What's nine-square about that scallop? Oh … it's got a grid on it!

### Daniel

So, now we're in the late 70s, beginning of the 80s.

### Arthur

Wow, we got there fast.

### Daniel

In *Collage City*, Colin Rowe discusses buildings such as the Palazzo Borghese, and Sant'Agnese in Piazza Navona, neither of which were ideal buildings; they were compositions altered by their urban context. How is it possible for someone like Colin Rowe, who had been so adamant about internalized proportions, to shift his focus so radically from the ideal to the contextual?

### Arthur

Colin had been head of his graduate program in urban design. I think by 1976 Colin was probably much more dedicated to the idea of urban space, and if you think of 1976, there were a lot of strange things going on, with the beginnings of Postmodernism and the whole Venturi phenomenon of reducing everything to the facade ….

### Jerry

Colin was always a mad dog Modernist until those students from Notre Dame came, and Colin was always criticized because he would never do three-dimensional drawings. My first years here, I taught with Colin both third-year and urban design, and Colin dealt with urban design as a piece of Gestalt psychology, looking at the patterns a city makes and connecting up those patterns. There was very little reality in his way of dealing with cities. If you look at some of that work, like the second issue of the *Cornell Journal of Architecture*—it's basically a two-dimensional condition.

The guys from Notre Dame came and had had a very classical education. Colin was gaga over their three-dimensional drawings, and just flipped! Suddenly he was the person who was dealing with Postmodern architecture, well after postmodernism had started.

### Daniel

So you think that the interest didn't actually shift from proportion to contextual.... Do you think there is a way to read one within the other?

### Jerry

What Colin was saying was that the context creates the form, not the opposite way around.

### Arthur

That a building is determined first of all by its context and then arranged, and then in Jerry's terms "tuned" within the context. To me those are two different things.

But, thinking about 1976, again. That was also the year, if I'm not mistaken, that the Museum of Modern Art had the big exhibition of drawings from l'Ecole des Beaux Arts. And suddenly people saw those 18th- and 19th-century drawings exhibited in a modern art context and were quite blown away.

By that time, Aldo Rossi's *Architecture of the City* was out, or was translated into English. People were already aware of Rossi's ideas, like how important the Piazza Navona was as a kind of collective memory piece, or how important Diocletian's Palace was as an idea for something being transformed over time. A lot of things were happening at about that time.

It's strangely interesting that the *tendenza* of the "rats"—"rational architecture"—has somehow disappeared in a lot of modern history and criticism, at least in this country, since it was so strong at the time. People tend to want to leave it out.

*Fourth Course: Möbius Strip Steak*

### Daniel

Now we are onto the meat of our conversation, the 1980s. Jerry, you were chair at the time, actually spearheading the first issue of the *Journal*, and in your introduction, you quoted Le Corbusier on his opinion of how to teach architecture: "If I had to teach you architecture? Rather an awkward question … I would begin by forbidding the 'orders,' by putting a stop to this dry rot of the orders. This incredible defiance of the intelligence. I would insist on a real respect for Architecture…." The Vitruvian orders were based on an aesthetic that had mathematical sensibilities based on proportions and ratios. So in 1981, if the orders and rules of proportion were not being taught, what took its place?

**Jerry**
Well, yes, the stylistic content had changed.

**Daniel**
So what was being discussed instead?

**Jerry**
Abstraction.

**Nicholas**
Abstraction without proportionality?

**Jerry**
No, proportionality was always there, we never dropped it. That was my whole point about how Modern architecture was simply classical buildings stripped of their content. You have to understand how the word *content* works and what it means: it's the stylistic aspects of that point in time in which man is living. Not necessarily ornament. It took a few hundred years to develop the ionic column and it is still on houses in the suburbs today. It is an incredible characteristic that keeps getting subscribed to over and over again. Modern architecture dealt with the notion of stripping that stuff away, and it was a totally abstract condition.

**Jae**
What form did proportionality take in this period?

**Jerry**
There were many strategies that were played with the Fibonacci sequence people were spending a lot of time with, Le Corbusier developed the *Modulor* during the World Wars. He was really incredibly into it, he carried around a tape measure and measured things his whole life. But I don't think we need to make proportionality into this special thing; it really is just the last touch on a project.

**Arthur**
Or it's like getting dressed in the morning. Do you think people can read proportions? We can go back to Dürer and the proportions of the human face. Where is the nose located, what is the length of the forehead and so on, and what is a person's sense of beauty? People seem to somehow agree on it in some way, which is quite intriguing. Dürer was probably the first person to start investigating the proportions of the ideal baby, for instance. Proportion does not have to be just about buildings.

**Daniel**
I think the reason why we are asking you both to dissect proportion and its involvement in teaching the discipline is because it is a relevant term to mathematics, and we don't believe that they should be held separately.

**Jerry**

I can show you many buildings that make incredible use of proportion. Scarpa's Banca Popolare, for example, you cannot move a single line in that building without messing it up in terms of its proportions. And the relative condition of how it works is based upon the idea of the field and figure.

But, let's take the idea of mathematics; it's not always a rectilinear proportioning system. An architect like Antonio Gaudí made really incredible buildings that were all based on mathematics. We all know the catenary models he used and wove into his facades. He was a mathematician, but there was an overlay of content that transcended the mathematics. That's where Le Corbusier got the idea for his roofscape for the Unité.

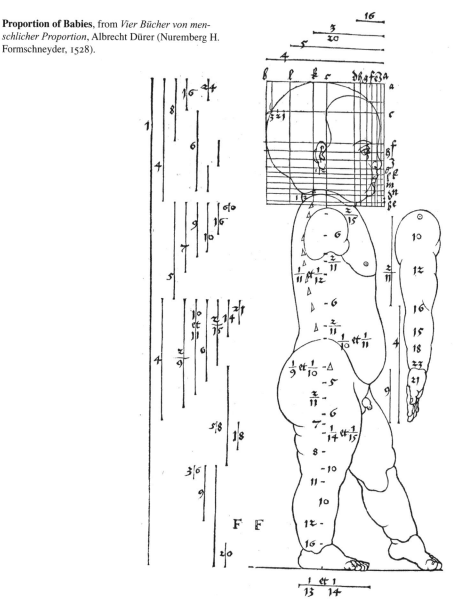

**Proportion of Babies**, from *Vier Bücher von menschlicher Proportion*, Albrecht Dürer (Nuremberg H. Formschneyder, 1528).

**Arthur**

I would put him in the Art Nouveau period, and there's a lot of Art Nouveau stuff that is quite amazing that has also been marginalized in history. Not only Gaudí, but people like Olbrich and Sullivan. You look at what they were doing at that time—it was quite incredible, and done without computers.

And there is also another side to mathematics; in producing architecture, the calculator became the most important tool. In teaching, learning, designing, your eyes and your drawing tools are most important, but when you are producing, you are having to deal with money, square footages, zoning, and developers. The numbers become ultimately important. To me, that's the ugly part of architecture.

But I want to say something different about that time period. I was in Berlin working my tail off at that time, but sometimes Jerry invited me back as a visiting critic, and I was also teaching at Syracuse. What amazed me about that point in time is that you would go to reviews of student work, and in most studios, students would pin up a Xerox along with their project that would be their...

**Jerry**

precedent.

**Arthur**

precedent.

**Jerry**

Funny how we said that at the same time.

**Arthur**

And that was almost always the case. About that time I decided not to use that word anymore, and now use *antecedent* instead: that which has come before. There was always the recognition that things have come before, and that one can learn from them, but at that time there was also a fair amount of copying going on, and it wasn't always about trying to derive concepts from things and reinterpreting them, sometimes it was a little too literal, I think.

**Jerry**

A lot of that comes from the Texas Rangers' method of teaching. You always stood on other people's shoulders but you were also supposed to deal with the *ideas* of precedents and take them through transformations and reapply them to your work.

**Daniel**

Would you say this was an insensitive version of appropriation?

**Jerry**

Architectural ideas happen everywhere in the world and you've got to have a mind that can see them.

*Fifth course: Apple* π

### Daniel

So now we are on to a bittersweet dessert. The 90s and the 00s brought advancement
in the changed ideals of postmodernism and the rapid growth of design intent based
less on theoretical mathematics and more on structural materialistic mathematics.
How did you navigate this strange territory as educators?

### Jerry

Well, I started the first CAD studios, with Don Greenberg. Way back.

### Arthur

As a kind of experimental Option Studio.

### Jae

I remember the tension and disagreement there was when I moved into my second
year here and the incoming freshmen were already trying to use CAD.

### Daniel

We entered the program during the last moments of Mohsen Mostavafi's period
here, and I remember still drafting, or wanting to draft well into my second year:
this is '08. There was this very strange and awkward phase where people started
wanting to present drafted drawings, but they instead kept tracing things they
printed off the computer, because we could not control our computer drawings
as well yet in terms of line-weight, etcetera.

### Arthur

But I think that we have always kept the pedagogical connection between the hand
and the eye, and we have always insisted at Cornell, I think still up until this day, that
you have to be able to see and to make in order have visual and mental control over
your work, before being introduced to the computer. But what I think we are seeing
at some other schools is a certain kind of fetishizing of the computer. There is already
some kind of inbreeding of that fetishism, and people are being educated who don't
know anything else. You can't really talk about the computer.... It's all invasive
now. I remember the first image coming through over the Internet, a picture of the
Forbidden Palace in Beijing. The thing sort of slowly materialized; taking probably
a half an hour until it was done. Everything on the Internet had been text until that
point, while people were predicting that we would be sharing images digitally, nobody
really predicted that people were going to have this tool in their pockets soon.

### Jerry

What has happened is that architectural space ceased to exist; various things have
ceased to exist in terms of the way we teach and the way architecture is presented.
You get the magazines that do two or three images and never show you the plans
of the building, so you can never understand the conceptual workings of a project.
Mohsen used to talk about "design by image." That used to be an embarrassing thing
for architects to do: you had some kind of render that came in after the building was
done, usually as drawings for the client, and you never referred to them again. You

would ask these people to, after the fact, do these pretty pictures, and now architects seem to think that pretty pictures are the essence of the job.

**Daniel**

Perhaps this has been brought on by the economic times, because so many firms are only making paper architecture, they could care less about plan and section, and just make a good render because, as we know, the sexiest image wins the competition or gets you the clients who are surfing the internet.

**Jerry**

You can't research a building on the internet.

**Nicholas**

Yes, because the only thing you see are these seductive images. What does it mean for the culture of architecture?

**Jerry**

It is a bit of a disaster, and I think it will rectify itself, because it can't keep doing that.

**Nicholas**

But at the same time, using computers and these new tools means that the way you design is not in plan and section, so that these plans and sections simply cannot represent—

**Jerry**

But the way you design *is* in plan and section.

**Nicholas**

Not if you are designing in a digital model. That's the way people are doing it.

**Arthur**

There are always these draftsmen or visualizers, or people who can do great images but never really build anything. There always have been.

**Daniel**

Let's talk about the hot terms *parametric* or *algorithmic* architecture. There is a lot of mathematical terminology in architecture today.

**Jerry**

You can make really bad buildings using parametrics, if the parameters are bad. Architects use the English language in the most incredibly ridiculous ways.

**Daniel**

When you guys were educated, and began teaching, it seems like there was a model or single correct way to do things within a single realm. Today there is clearly no right way to do things, at least regarding what is being accepted pedagogically. There is a pluralism that exists in the academic world. Does this make it more difficult to critique, and do we need a more cohesive and collective trajectory?

**Jerry**

There is something that you have to understand about the schools of architecture. They're all different. And you have to research really well. For instance, a few years ago if you came from Princeton, you graduated a Michael Graves disciple; if you went here, you came out a Corb freak. Every school has an identifiable characteristic.

**Daniel**

But now, when we graduate I don't think we graduate as Corb freaks.

**Jerry**

No, no, the school has changed.

**Jae**

Now, more schools have become more like-minded, especially through the use of the computer.

**Jerry**

I think that it is an interesting change, but I don't think it is really healthy for the formulation of ideas. I think we are in danger of letting the computer drive our thinking, as opposed to using the computer to create our work.

**Daniel**

Would you say that the conversation has become more aesthetic-based, versus theory-based?

**Jerry**

Not with my teaching. But yes, that aesthetic is changing; becoming more and more about the design of the superobject. But really, the superobject has been around a long time, and all of these things change through time. They go through cycles. Like the rest of life.

**Arthur**

I generally mistrust any word that has *ism* at the end, but when I see *pluralism*, and I think about how differently things can be interpreted in different contexts, I actually have to get into philosophy and religion for a second. I was brought up a Unitarian, which means that the way you learn about religion is to study every religion other than your own, which means that you had to learn about religion through thinking about other things, which is sort of like architecture to me. You basically grow up with the pluralistic concept that there are lots of other people that don't believe the same things that you believe, and you have to learn through thinking to deal with things. I guess at this point, I believe that there is no *one* architecture.

**Jerry**

Never.

**Arthur**

And if somebody is doing computer doilies, that fine with me. It's just not *my* architecture.

**Jerry**

It all has to do with stylistic content: "You looks around you and you makes your choice." If you don't want to do anything different, you do what is in the current vogue. Fundamentally, it's a choice.

**Jae**

But there is some peer pressure.

**Jerry**

There should not be. I tell my students that they have to win the courage of their convictions. And I don't teach them architecture. I teach them how to learn about architecture. And I don't design their projects. I talk to them about it and let them do it. And you have to realize there will be an aspect of architecture that you will hook onto and love. And if you don't do that, don't be an architect. There's a whole variety of things out there you can love. Basically the education of an architect has to do with loving another architect and mimicking their work. In the end, you will change. Arthur used to love Matthias Ungers, but he doesn't do Matthias Ungers buildings anymore.

Architecture is a really wonderful world; you make it what you want to make it. You don't have to commit to anything, and you can create anything. And basically the architectural education should give you the tools to do that; if you don't pick up on that, you are a bit of a fool. You'll go into a corporate office doing toilet details for the rest of your life.

*Dinner by Caroline O'Donnell with Carly Dean, Jackie Krasnokutskaya,*
*Varvara Larionova, and Ishita Sitwala.*

## Maria Hurtado de Mendoza

*is a Spanish architect and founding partner of the Madrid-based practice
estudio.entresitio. She has taught architectural design at the Architecture
School of Madrid (ETSAM) since 1998, and was a visiting critic at Cornell
University Department of Architecture in the Fall of 2011. Challenge the
Order is the title of Hurtado de Mendoza's visual representation seminar
at Cornell, based on the ongoing research of her Ph.D. thesis, "Systems of
Order."*

# Challenge the Order

> *The order of a system is equal to the amount of information necessary for the
> description of this system.*
>
> J. Monod, *Le Hazard et la nécessité* (Chance and Necessity)

In contemporary practice, architects have tended to reproduce and code certain
states of order/disorder that occur in nature or arise from creative intuition,
describing them as complex because they are beyond immediate comprehension.
The seductive graphical representations of this complexity, of what is apparently
random, inevitably intrigue and distract one's attention. This obsession with
randomness has been described as "a paradigmatic anti-scientific attitude"[1]
—a deserved comment indeed, if randomness occurs without meaning or understanding. With the intention of going beyond the superficial, "Challenge the Order"
investigates the underlying systems in search of a methodology to reproduce a
certain configuration, more generally applied to architecture as a discipline, and
in particular, to the construction of architectural space. In this sense, the objective
is not only to think about geometry as the beginning of form, but to think about
geometry as the beginning of space.

Scientist Christopher Langton believes that between order and randomness
there is an intermediate space called complexity. As a result of the interactions
between elements, new properties emerge that cannot be explained by the properties of isolated elements. A complicated system, in contrast, is also composed
of several parts, but the links between them do not add additional information.
We need to know each of them to understand the system. In a complex system,
however, there are hidden variables that prevent us from analyzing the system accurately. Thus, a complex system has more information than what each part is giving
independently, and to describe it requires the understanding not only of the performance of the parts but of their relationship to each other.

The Spanish psychiatrist Nicolás Caparrós refers to this intermediate space
of complexity as "the fertile place that resists the limits of a definition, diffuse in
nature, where the proportion of order to disorder reaches a limit that is called the
border of chaos, the score or hinge moment or even phase transition. It is the place
of the new, the unusual, creation and emergence."[2] His approach is related to the
*creative clutter* notion of Ilya Prigogine, who proposes "non-equilibrium" as a
source of the new.[3] For Caparrós, complexity does not mean the decline of classical

**Feng Lin**'s (M. Arch. '13) interpretation focuses on the transition from the square to a circle in a linear system. Using 3D software allowed her to arrive at the hybrid form. By placing the same number of points in both shapes, an algorithm calculated their intermediate shapes. The midway curve between a square and a circle is called "squircle" (to name is to know).

**Hua Ye** (M. Arch. '12) used both figures as a way of making "randomness." The diagram above shows a mathematical way to analyze the ratio of a hyperbolic pentacle, which was a sacred geometry symbol in ancient times. Using the diagram for the Children's Center for Psychiatric Rehabilitation, Hokkaido, Japan by Sou Fujimoto, the basic geometric object was duplicated, rotated, and overlapped to create a system in which randomness was found by making the parts visible in a selective way.

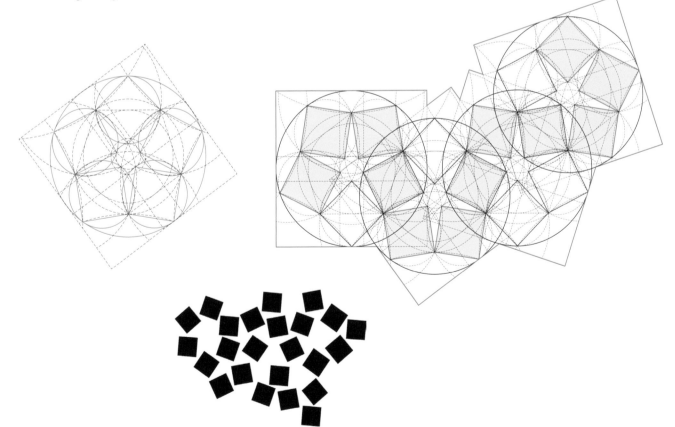

**Simin Wang** (M. Arch. '13) also described these objects showing how a square and a circle look contradictory in 2D, yet can produce a harmonious condition in a 3D object, since all different views of these peculiar objects are either a square or a circle (top, front, and left).

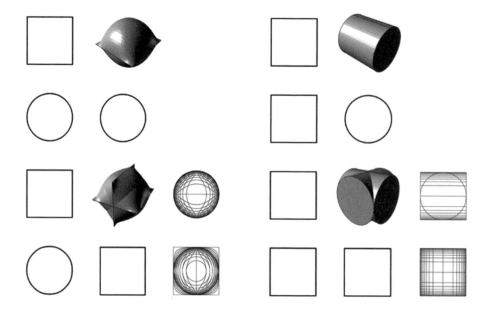

**Alison Nash** (M. Arch. '13) studied quasicrystals and aperiodicity, and how, related to a network of primitive figures, there can be another less evident construction underlying it, with greater potential for a controlled randomness.

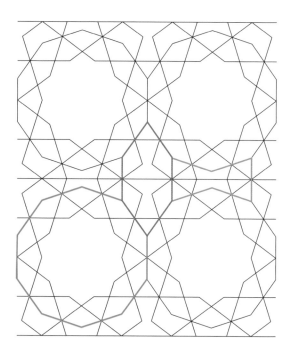

science, but a natural extension of it; some old problems might be relegated or declared unscientific, others, previously nonexistent or trivial, may, with the new point of view, become significant archetypes.

The ways in which the irregular and fragmented is controlled, and turbulence or self-similarity are described are open questions for architecture and its particular way of thinking. While it is certainly risky to establish a classification of different systems of order that interest architecture, this classifier's desire arises as an attempt to understand, or using Koolhaas's words, to "undo the ignorance" about what is interwoven in itself. The terms of mathematics are pervasive in the contemporary verbiage of architects: words such as *parametric, topological, dynamic, emergent, fuzzy*, and *algorithmic* have become relatively commonplace, however, their consideration should not imply the denial of some other words, such as the *ideal*.

The seminar was set up as a series of explorations investigating the space between order and disorder, beginning with a puzzle known for its impossible resolution "squaring the circle." To square a circle has been considered, since ancient times, the question of how to draw a square with the same area of a given circle using only basic drawing tools: the impossibility of its resolution is due to the number $\pi$ (*pi*) being involved in the circle's dimension. The challenge introduced the world of geometric paradox and the possibility of working away from certainty, and opened up the possibility of redefining problems based on contemporary knowledge and tools.

Students were asked to find their own place of encounter between ideas of order and architecture, to reach an original and personal set of ideas, and to consider how their discoveries could be shared as a source of knowledge for the collective. Each chose a single system of order and after coming to an in-depth understanding of that system, proposed a possible translation into architecture.

Architects today are familiar with pure ordering devices such as the grid, or the radial. As architecture embraces more complex systems, new knowledge is required to interact with these (often concealed) systems and to be able to incorporate exceptions, deviations, or transformations. By understanding the ordering systems, the behavior, and the tools implied, architects are freer and solutions are more open and coherent. Geometry is not meant to be the solution, but the frame in which the architectural solution evolves—and to know the rules gives us the required margin to incorporate contingency in a rigorous way. While some may question such a desire for rigor, this work pushes toward a new understanding of rigor in which the *absolute* might be confronted with the *inexact*.

Order, whether it is evident or not, is a key to architecture, and contemporary thinking gives us the freedom to consider both extremes; there is no necessity anymore to choose between one thing and the other: no right or wrong. In fact, these extremes, the orthodox and the innovative ways of understanding order might not be so far apart. Yet still, our ideas of beauty are related to nature, where proportion plays a major role: the golden ratio defines the shape of the human body and face, the Fibonacci series defines the shapes of shells, flowers, fruits, and so on, but we also define as "natural" the indescribable beauty of a harmonious yet chaotic and seemingly random arrangement that arises from rules or patterns embedded within it.

Architecture understood as a way of establishing relationships and organizations represents the holistic meaning of the "whole" as something other than the sum

of the parts, and order can be considered what holds things together. To consider how
new ideas of order imported from the sciences of complexity can be translated and
edited into architecture is something that architects must take time to investigate.
This can only begin with questions, and albeit preliminary, this selection of graphic
inquiries that seek to understand the mathematical system underlying the fixed image
already begins to provoke possible spatial and formal consequences for architecture.

**Endnotes**

1   R. Thom, *Halte au hasard, silence au bruit*,
    Le Débat no. 3 éditions (Paris: Gallimard, 1980).
2   Nicolás Caparrós, Introduction to the
    encyclopedia *Viaje a la complejidad* (unpublished
3   G. Nicolis and I. Prigogine, *Self-Organization
    in Nonequilibrium Systems* (New York: Wiley,
    1977).

## Gisela Baurmann and Daina Taimina

**Gisela Baurmann** *is an award-winning architect who has practiced and taught extensively in Europe and the United States, including at Cornell University's Department of Architecture in Spring 2011. Her work examines cultural techniques as conceptual models of fabrication for application in computational design. Gisela is founding partner of the architecture office Büro NY, based in New York and Berlin. For more information www.BuroNY.com and http://bit.ly/knBIft.*

**Daina Taimina** *was teaching mathematics at the University of Latvia for 20 years before she came to the United States. Currently she is adjunct associate professor of mathematics at Cornell University. In January 2012, she received the prestigious Euler Book Prize from the Mathematical Association of America for an outstanding book about mathematics for a general audience,* Crocheting Adventures with the Hyperbolic Planes. *http://hyperbolic-crochet.blogspot.com/.*

# Crocheting Algorithms

*The loop stitch is a noeud coulant: a knot that, if untied, causes the whole system to unravel. It is an element in making stockings, in knitting and crocheting, and the particular way it is formed is dictated by the tools employed and the use intended. [...] I can only say that it is an extremely refined [art] and yields products whose properties can be achieved in no other way. They carry the elements of their richest ornaments in themselves and in their construction. Elasticity and ductility are the specific advantage of these products; this makes them especially suited to close-fitting dressings that embrace the figure and define it without fold.*

Gottfried Semper, *Style*, 1860.

Crocheting activates a single line—the thread—to generate an elastic surface by moving around and through an empty core. The topology of a crocheted fabric is relatively complex: the thread describes an undulating path along each row, the loops of one row being pulled through the loops of the row subjacent to it.

In crochet, it is possible to create a whole surface of multiple elements from one single thread. Inscribed in the technique is the potential to generate a multitude of volumes, strands, cross-references, and volumetric sequences without ever having to interrupt the fiber's continuous line. Crocheted or knitted fabric specifies local rules of increase and decrease, of temporary pause and subsequent pick up, thus enabling the fabric to splice open and to reunite again later on. It can generate three-dimensional volumes through separating and subsequently braiding, crossing, and back-referencing its own materiality.

In geometry, the most basic and commonly studied category of surfaces are those with constant curvature. In the early 19th century, C. F. Gauss suggested further categorizing such surfaces by the sign of their curvature—positive, negative, and zero. In the case of a constant positive curvature, the surface geometry is spherical, and in case of a constant negative curvature, it is hyperbolic.

**Crocheted Hyperbolic Plane**, Daina Taimina.
Wool, about 50 cm × 50 cm × 50 cm, 2011.
© Daina Taimina. From the collection of Cooper-Hewitt
National Design Museum.

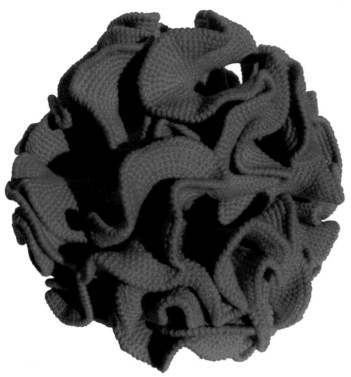

The Euclidean plane (with zero curvature) can be tiled by regular hexagons. At each vertex, there are three hexagons coming together and forming a $3 \times 120° = 360°$ angle. This tiling can be continued infinitely: around each hexagon are six other hexagons. If we start with a pentagon and surround it by five hexagons with the same side length, then at each vertex of this tiling there will be $2 \times 120° + 108° = 348° < 360°$, and the tiling will form a closed surface approximating the sphere. This tiling describes precisely the way a soccer ball is stitched together. If instead of the pentagon, a seven-sided polygon (heptagon) is chosen, then at each vertex the sum of the angles will be $>360°$ and tiling can be continued indefinitely: this will approximate the hyperbolic plane.[1]

Another way to construct the model of the hyperbolic plane is to attach identical annular strips (portions of strips between concentric circles, with the same width $\Delta$ and the same radius as the outer circle), attaching the inner circle of one of the strips to the outer circle of the other. The actual surface with the negative curvature could be obtained by letting $\Delta \to 0$.

In crochet, these techniques can be mimicked by uniformly adding an extra stitch after a chosen and fixed number of stitches in a row. This will result in a crocheted hyperbolic plane.[2]

**Diagram to Crochet the Hyperbolic Plane**, Erica Savig,
2007. Courtesy Gisela Baurmann.

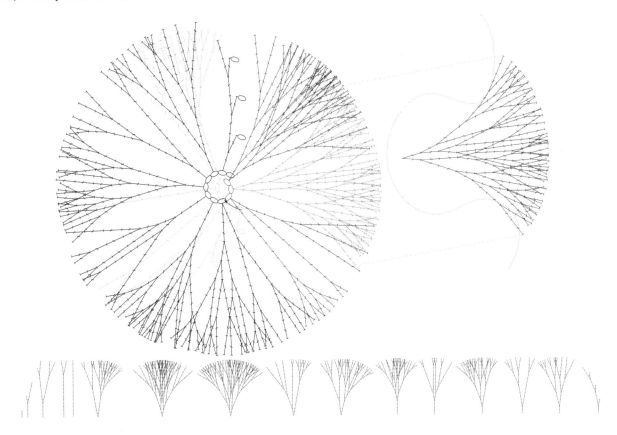

What we now call Euclidean geometry was developed in Euclid's *Elements* around
300 B.C. Among many other hypotheses, *Elements* contained the so-called Parallel
Postulate (also called the Fifth Postulate):

> *if a straight line intersecting two straight lines makes the interior angles on the
> same side less than two right angles, then the two lines (if extended indefinitely)
> will meet on that side on which are the angles less than two right angles.*

The breakthrough in the study of various forms of the parallel postulate came
in the early 19th century when, apparently independently, Janos Bolyai and Nikolaj
Lobachevsky developed a new geometry, which later Felix Klein named "hyperbolic
geometry." In 1854, Georg Riemann showed that hyperbolic geometry holds on
surfaces with constant negative curvature.[3]

Riemann's idea was to start with the concept of curvature and to argue that
geometry was fundamentally about two types of problems: the intrinsic properties of
a surface, and the ways in which a surface is mapped into another surface. Riemann
did even more—he showed that the idea of Gaussian curvature can be generalized
into higher dimensions. He also mentioned that there were three two-dimensional
geometries possible if classified by constant curvature of the surface.

By the end of the 19th century, non-Euclidean geometry had become a widely discussed subject in mathematical circles and had great influence on artists, writers, and philosophers.[4]

Since Euclidean geometry had been taught for many hundreds of years, a large number of people truly believed that Euclidean geometry was an exclusive and absolute truth. To accept the existence of non-Euclidean geometries was revolutionary.

In architecture we may apply the syntax of hyperbolic geometry to generate organizations of multiple linkages. When crocheting the hyperbolic plane, the stitches allow for local specificity as well as feedback between local units and the global fabric. This specificity and feedback can be applied to multiple tectonic elements that generate an architectural project: the organization of program units, structural components of varying scale, facade elements, interior dividers, vertical, horizontal and oblique connectors, and many more.

The radical possibilities of "crochet thinking" in architecture and urbanism lie in its ability to seamlessly shift between increase and decrease of units in the overall fabric, while thinking through the generation of each local constituent progressively. This allows the designer to pay attention to the specificity of each particle/component individually, yet produce a complex overall structure. Whether we apply these rules to parameters of architectural, interior, or urban design, or to physical components of them, we inevitably generate a vast array of possible configurations. A collection of physical expressions created in response to a set of parameters affords us to choose "successful" candidates within this array, according to the requirements that we define.

In the area of digital output, surface materials can be developed that respond locally to stress analysis, requests for changing transparencies or thicknesses, and so on, by condensing or dispersing the filaments/strands for reinforcement throughout the fabrication piece. Multiple possibilities for the arrangement/gestalt of the linear elements generate program-specific base structures. They can be dipped in or covered with *pastose* materials for surface generation to produce an abundance of structural, material, and sensory qualities. Through the increase and decrease of stitches in the base configuration, three-dimensional and multidirectional surface structures can be generated.

Current experiments developed in academic settings demonstrate the first in a series of steps that introduce crochet as a conceptual model for architectural fabrication.

In studio projects and material fabrication seminars, students explore crochet as a conceptual method of design and examine its topological traits as well as its ductility. Using diagrams, 3D modeling, and scripting, space formations are created that reference performance articulation and behaviors of crochet stitching. Students employ the properties of the technique, its local rules, continuity of the thread and algorithmic qualities to discover program continuities that suggest spatial assembly. A series of exercises explore rule-based design methodologies through model-making and analytical drawings and provide an introduction to non-Euclidian geometry. These exercises deepen the understanding of a script syntax and its formal output within the confines of a single line trajectory.

**3D Print**, Ke Xu (M. Arch. '11).

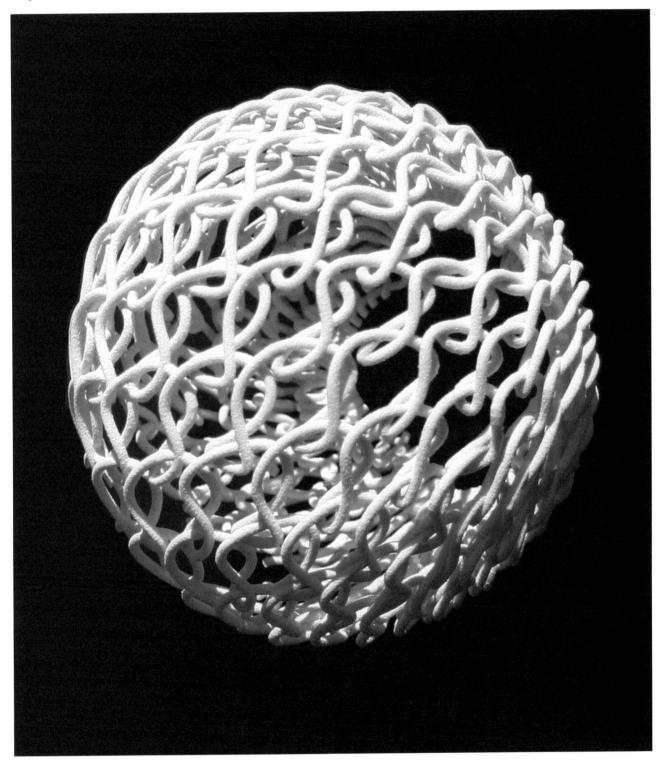

Digital notations of crochet loops generate architectural program diagrams in two dimensions. They are connected following the architectural program's daily routines. A substitution system and the concept of transposition are deployed to exchange agents in one system with those in the other. Ecology, size, connectivity, and organizational layout of a proposed program activity determine its coupling with a specific stitch notation. Subsequently, the local to global relationship of stitch to fabric are read quite literally: program activities are located, connected, and sized according to the stitch's spatial and jointing qualities. Qualitative program definitions emerge.

The computational stitch construction gets introduced to move from the two-dimensional program diagrams to a three-dimensional structural output.

Variation of input parameters, such as number of stitches and rows, stitch increase, thread diameter, openings, and so on, tests the structural, spatial, and material effects.

Transferring the stitch into computation requires carefully tracing the trajectory of the crochet hook and linking one stitch with its preceding and following ones, as well as with its neighbors in the rows above and below. When crocheting a hyperbolic plane, the main trajectory of the thread is a spiral, while the local units, the stitches, connect one row with the next.

In a series of experiments, specific characteristics of crochet fabric are regenerated as fabrication prototypes through computational tools. The analogue material's main characteristics—its transparency, structural capacity, ductility, and thickness, as well as its overall shape—are pursued in individual exercises, starting with transparency and structural capacity, as demonstrated here.

While analogue crochet models exhibit emergent qualities, the topology of a computational model is initially generated in a "frozen state," in order to establish the local connections between units as well as their individual properties. Gravitation, friction, stresses, and pressure will be introduced in a future generation of experiments in order to study the material's ductility in combination with its tectonic properties and material effects.

### Acknowledgments

Detlef Mertins encouraged me to conduct the first crochet studio at the School of Design, University of Pennsylvania. Stan Allen and Dagmar Richter granted the opportunity to explore the concept while teaching at Princeton University and Cornell University, respectively. Seok Yoon, James Kerestes, Jungwook Lee, and Jonathan Asher provided conceptual and technical support. Many thanks to Daina Taimina and Jonas Coersmeier, who helped organize my thoughts in many productive discussions. I want to thank all students, who participated in exploring crochet as a generative tool in architecture at Cornell University's Department of Architecture: Frances Gain, Shujian Jian, Huidan Kang, Donghyun Jake Kim, Han Joon Kim, Yuen Ying Serena Lee, Feng Lin, Lorena Quintana, Dick Kar Ida Tam, Ke Xu, Wendy Yang, Fanbo Zeng, Huang Zheng and at the University of Pennsylvania's School of Design: Dan Affleck, Emily Bernstein, Leslie Billhymer, Young Suk Choi, Joshua Freese, Kenta Fukunishi, Vincent Leung, Danisha Lewis, Andrew Ma, Lauren MacCuaig, Kara Medow, John Ryan, Erica Swesey Savig, and Alan Tai.

### Endnotes

1  Daina Taimina, *Crocheting Adventures with Hyperbolic Planes* (Wellesley, MA: A.K. Peters Ltd. 2009), 135.

2  David Henderson and Daina Taimina, "Crocheting the Hyperbolic Plane," *The Mathematical Intelligencer* 23, no. 1 (2001): 17–28.

3  More history in Daina Taimina, *Crocheting Adventures with Hyperbolic Planes* (Wellesley, MA: A.K. Peters Ltd., 2009).

4  Linda Henderson, *The Fourth Dimension and Non-Euclidean Geometry in Modern Art* (Princeton University Press, 1983).

**Surface Panelizations**, Huidan Kang (M. Arch. '11),
Ida D. K. Tam (M. Arch. '12), and Frances Gain (M. Arch. '11).
Computationally constructed stitches populate the surfaces.
They are connected and interlaced to generate a continuous
fabric.

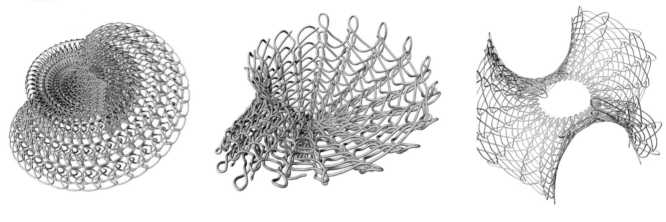

**Crochet Program Diagrams**, Young Suk Choi and
Joshua Freese, 2007. Courtesy Gisela Baurmann. Digital
notations of crochet loops generate architectural program
diagrams in two dimensions. They are connected
following the architectural program's daily routines.

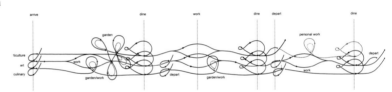

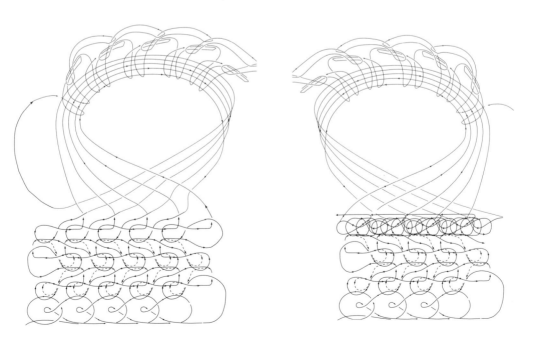

**Surface Panelization**. Jake Donghyun Kim (M.Arch
'12) and Serena Yuen Ying Lee (M.Arch '12). Variation
of input parameters, such as number of stitches and
rows, stitch increase, thread diameter, openings to test
structural, spatial and material effect.

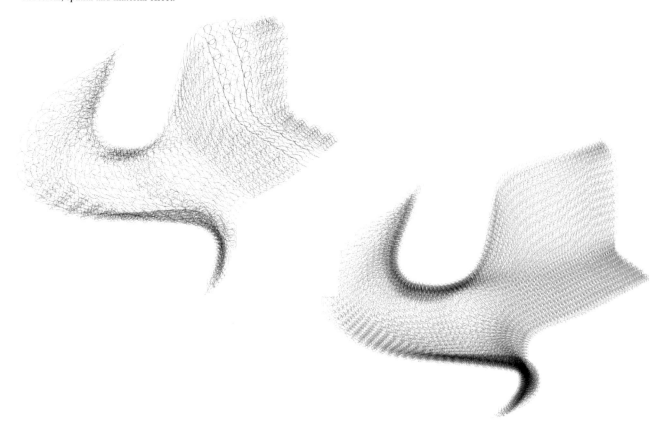

# Mario Carpo

*teaches architectural history and theory at the School of Architecture of Paris-La Villette, at the Yale School of Architecture, and at the Georgia Institute of Technology (Atlanta, GA). Carpo's research and publications focus on the relationship among architectural theory, cultural history, and the history of media and information technology. Among his publications,* Architecture in the Age of Printing *(The MIT Press, 2001) has been translated into several languages. His latest monograph,* The Alphabet and the Algorithm, *was published by The MIT Press in 2011.*

# Parametricism, Digital Scholasticism, and the Decline of Visuality [1]

**Porcelain Teapot with Oriental Ornamentation,**
Manufacturer Ginori Doccia, 1750–1755. Photo:
A. Dagli Orti © DeA Picture Library/Art Resource, NY.

Human-made objects are no longer what they used to be. Digital parametricism has changed the way we make objects, what we make with them and what we make of them. For the last few centuries, and until recently, we had two ways of making objects: hand-making, and mechanical machine-making. Objects that are made by hand tend to be visually different from one another, even when they are serially reproduced, because that is the way freehand making, and free, unconstrained human bodies, work. Think of a signature: no two signatures made by the same hand are identical, even though all signatures made by the same person are expected to be similar (otherwise they could not be recognized as autographs). Then came mechanical machines. Mechanical machines use casts, molds, stamps, or matrixes, and all imprints of the same matrix are the same. But mechanical matrixes are expensive to make, and once made, their cost must be amortized by using them as many times as possible. This is the world of mass-production, economies of scale, and standardization; at its core, this is the technical logic of industrial modernity.

Digital making does not work that way. Digital notations are in a permanent state of drift, and they can change all the time randomly, automatically, or by the intervention of some external, unpredictable agency. Indeed, digital scripts are increasingly designed for variability, or open-endedness, right from the start. And digital fabrication in most cases does not use mechanical matrixes, hence in a non-standard series variations can be mass-produced, in theory, at no extra cost. In short, in a digital design and fabrication chain, product standardization is technically and culturally irrelevant; and in a digital design environment, modern authorship is replaced by some new format of hybrid or participatory agency—a joint venture of sorts among any combination of human and technical actors and networks.[2]

Whether we like it or not, this "hybridization of agency" is an essential aspect of digital parametricism, because it is embedded in its very technical nature. In mathematics, a parametric function is a function where the value of some parameters can vary. Likewise, parametric notations in digital design and fabrication contain terms that are left indeterminate—only the limits of their variations are set. These open values can be determined, or finalized, by the same person who wrote the original script, or by others. Some values may also evolve all alone, or almost they may emerge, adapt, and self-organize. The possibilities are infinite: but most of them are deliberately left outside the control of the authors of the first, original script. A parametric function is an open-ended algorithm; a generative, incomplete notation. At the beginning of the digital turn, Gilles Deleuze and Bernard Cache invented a special term to define this new kind of technical object—they called it an objectile.[3] In philosophical terms, an objectile is a generic object: it is a general script that defines an open-ended class of individual or specific objects, which will all be different, as individuals, but also all similar, as they all have something in common. What they have in common is the code or script that was used to make them, and which is, in a sense, inscribed in them.

The morphogenetic metaphor in this theory is as evident as is its Aristotelian and Scholastic provenance. In parametric making, the script is the genus, and the sets of individual objects are species; the script is the definition, and the series of events it creates is the extension. Scholasticism has already been related to one architectural style. Gottfried Semper was famously the first to define the Gothic as "petrified Scholasticism,"[4] which the great classicist did not mean as a compliment; with different nuances, the notion was taken over by Wilhelm Worringer,[5] and many others, and is today a commonplace. In 1951, Erwin Panofsky outlined several types of isomorphisms between Gothic architecture and Scholasticism:[6] first and foremost, Panofsky argued, both the Gothic and the Scholastic minds cherished the intricacy of articulation (in logic, an arborescence of definitions and divisions), and both Gothic and Scholastic articulations are a game of variations within the same class (e.g., all capitals at the same level in the nave of the same cathedral are often similar, but seldom identical). But the analogies between the Gothic, Scholasticism, and today's parametricism are vast and wide-ranging, and are not limited to form, or style. Scholasticism was the most successful "comprehensive unified theory" (in Patrick Schumacher's words)[7] in the history of the West; additionally, participatory, collective, and often anonymous making, that mantra of today's Web 2.0, was the rule on most medieval building sites, even though medieval builders could not see it that way, because the modern idea of individual authorship did not yet exist at the time. As Lars Spuybroek has eloquently pointed out, today's parametricism is indeed in many ways a revival of the Gothic Revival—or a John Ruskin 2.0.[8]

Yet another pioneer of the digital turn, the already mentioned Bernard Cache, has recently concluded a thorough investigation of Vitruvius's design method, and proven with compelling arguments that the method of Vitruvius was also quintessentially parametric.[9] Yet Vitruvius was no Gothic. The game here is a bit different, because in classical architecture most capitals in the same row in the same Greek temple, for example, are often quite identical to one another; but all Doric capitals manufactured following the instructions that Vitruvius outlines in his Book IV,[10] for example, can only be, once again, similar (but not identical) to one another. They all belong to the same class—they are all defined as "Doric Capitals," and they can be visually recognized as such. But Vitruvius's algorithmic design process does not control the final finished shape of each individual Doric Capital; each maker will need to add something at will—and at the same time in compliance with Vitruvius's rules.

Indeed, based on this evidence, one would be tempted to conclude that all premechanical theories of manufacturing are bound to be parametric; just as most postmechanical, digital theories of manufacturing are. Evidently, hand-produced variations are slower to make and fewer in number than those we can mass-produce today using digital tools. But, with the exception of speed and performance, and a few other details, both hand-making and digital making generate designed variations because, when making by script, both follow rule-based, generative notations (alphabetic or algorithmic, based on text or on computation, logocentric or logiconcentric). This is the opposite of mechanical making, which mostly reproduces identical copies of archetypal visual models using mechanical matrixes, stamps, casts, or molds.

This parallel between hand-making and digital making, and between the alphabet and the algorithm, may be a truism—too evident to be meaningful; but if it is true, its consequences, including aesthetic consequences, are staggering. For it appears that we are now moving out of a visual universe of exactly repeatable visual imprints and into a new world of endlessly changing, invisible algorithms: either designed for change (customization, or evolution) from the start, or not, but then often tweaked and changed all the same. In this new world, objects and their outward and visible forms are only the occasional and ephemeral epiphany of a

**Alessi Tea and Coffee Pots, Plans**. © Greg Lynn/FORM.

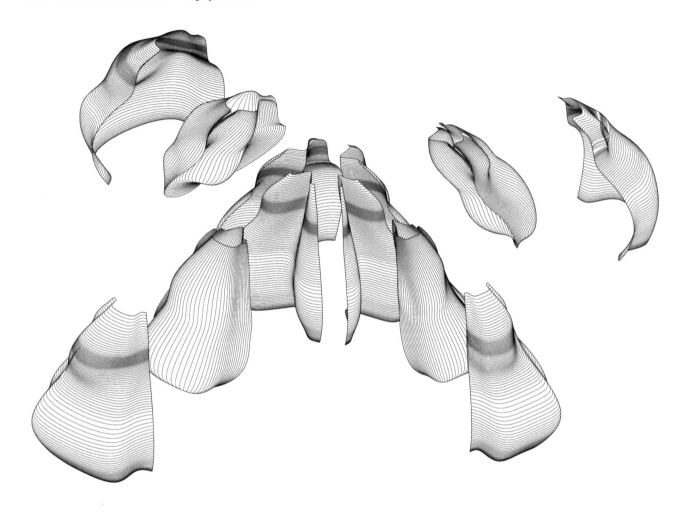

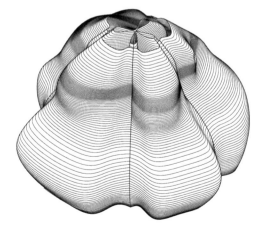

script embedded in them, of which every manifestation can be different, randomly or automatically or by design—or by the design of some random human agent. In the mechanical age, our apprehension of human-made objects used to be based on the identification of identical copies: in a world of mechanical prints, either one visual form is identical to another, and then it has the same meaning, or it is different, and then it has another meaning, or no meaning at all. In a parametric environment, on the contrary, identification is not based on identicality, but on similarity and resemblance—just like in nature, where the reproduction of similarities is the rule (as in the classical topos of the resemblance between father and son), and identical copies are the exception (as in the case of two monozygotic twins).

In the old mechanical world, indexical signs, and some categories of iconic signs, were particularly powerful, because they were predicated on immediate visual identification—on our capacity to relate the copy to the original or archetype that it reproduced. In the new parametric world, only some form of social consensus can bestow conventional meaning on endlessly variable visual signs. Charles Sanders Peirce famously called this class of signs "symbols," and once again, not coincidentally, symbolic meaning was powerful in premechanical times, for example in the Middle Ages, when only society at large could attach stable meaning to unstable signs. In his famous study of Medieval imitation, Richard Krautheimer tried to account for the medieval capacity to identify objects of all sorts and shapes as equally valid copies of the same model—for example, the Shrine of the Sepulchre in Jerusalem, of which each medieval city had one or more look-alikes; except that none of these look-alikes "looked alike," as most copies were different from one another and all were different from the original, which by the way no one at the time had seen. Krautheimer concluded, with some perplexity, that, by our standards, that is, by modern standards, medieval visuality appeared to be "almost emphatically non-visual."[11]

The same also applies, and will increasingly apply, to today's postmodern visuality, born of the new digital and parametric environment. In a visual environment where visual forms can change so fast and so often, appearances will count for less and less, and our capacity to interpret them will count for more and more. The meaning of parametrically generated, variable forms will be increasingly contingent on our capacity to see them in context, and to relate them to others, by comparison and selection, generalization and abstraction, recognizing variations, inferring patterns, and sorting events into classes; choosing some, discarding others, and making some sense out of them—trying to make cosmos out of chaos.

This may sound disturbing, but it is not far-fetched. After all, parametricism is only a mild and much domesticated version of the universal paradigm of variability, which is inherent in all things digital. Unlike media objects, like texts, images, sounds, or software, which can morph and change endlessly and effortlessly, physical objects must cope with physical constraints. Parametricism is a way (and, incidentally, not the only one)[12] to enforce some form of curatorship and supervision onto the otherwise open-ended drifting of digital notations: parametric systems only allow variations within given limits; versioning must stop at some point in time, so that fabrication may ensue; and these limits in scope and time are set by authors. But media objects have already transcended these contingent limitations. And we are already striving to come to terms with the formal and functional consequences of unbridled and systemic "aggregatory" versioning. We are learning, by trial and error, that digital images (that is, the totality of today's reproduced images) are no longer indexical traces of the originals they represent; that all electronic documents can be edited anytime and often anonymously by almost anyone; and that digital texts and documents, technical and literary alike, are increasingly destined from the start to an endless meandering of unpredictable accruals, deletions, and revisions. We know that any Wikipedia entry can read differently today from what it read yesterday, but we also know that if the next change is a blunder, someone, somehow, will soon set it right. Likewise, we know that the software we are using today may work a bit differently tomorrow, after the next, inevitable, automatic "update"—which we never signed on for, but which there seems to be no way to unsubscribe from. But we also know that changes will be incremental and most of the time, not catastrophic. And the same applies to all that is run or managed through networked digital systems—that is, to the quasi-totality of our technical environment. This environment being ever more based on permanent versioning by participatory scripting, or even by automatic self-adjustment, we are getting used to that inevitable, diffuse, quintessential ricketiness which is inherent in all things that can change all the time because they are scripted by many and by no one in particular—a new, evolutionary, participatory, messy, confusing digital style of many hands. We can try to make it look like something we are familiar with, and which we have the feeling we can control using the same good old authorial tools we knew. Historically speaking, this is seldom a winning strategy.

### Endnotes

1   An earlier version of this text was presented at the symposium "The Eclipse of Beauty: Parametric Beauty," Harvard GSD, March 9, 2011.

2   See Carpo, *The Alphabet and the Algorithm* (Cambridge, MA: The MIT Press, 2011), in particular chapter 4, "Split Agency," 123–128, and Carpo, "The Craftsman and the Curator," *Perspecta* 44, *Domain*, T. Gharagozlou and D. Sadighian (eds.) (2011): 86–91.

3   Gilles Deleuze, *Le pli: Leibniz et le baroque* (Paris: Editions de Minuit, 1988); *The Fold: Leibniz and the Baroque*, Tom Conley (trans.) (Minneapolis: University of Minnesota Press, 1993).

4   Gottfried Semper, *Der Stil in den technischen und tektonischen Künsten oder praktische Ästhetik* (Frankfurt a.M.: Verlag für Kunst und Wissenschaft, 1860), XIX ("Eben so war der Gothische Bau die lapidarische Uebertragung der scholastichen Philosophie des 12. und 13. Jahrhunderts.") and 509 footnote 1 (the Gothic as "steinerne Scholastik").

5   Wilhelm Worringer, *Formprobleme der Gotik* (Munich: R. Pieper, 1912); translated as: *Form Problems of the Gothic* (New York: G.E. Stechert, 1920; London, G.P. Putnam's Sons, 1927), *Form in Gothic*, Sir H. Read (authorized trans.) (New York: Schocken, [1957] 1964; London: Tiranti, 1957).

6   Erwin Panofsky, *Gothic Architecture and Scholasticism* (Latrobe, PA: Saint Vincent Archabbey, 1951).

7   Patrik Schumacher, "Parametricism and the Autopoiesis of Architecture," *Log* 21 (2011): 63–79; see. in particular. 63. See also Schumacher, *The Autopoiesis of Architecture: A New Framework for Architecture*, vol. I (London: Wiley, 2011).

8   See Lars Spuybroek, *The Sympathy of Things: Ruskin and the Ecology of Design* (Rotterdam: NAi, 2011).

9   Bernard Cache's doctoral dissertation on Vitruvius's design method, "Fortuito supra acanthi radicem," was defended in January 2009, and is unpublished to this day. See also: "Vitruvius Machinator Terminator," in Cache, *Projectiles* (London: Architectural Association, 2011), 119–139.

10  Vitruvius, *De Architectura*. IV: 3, 4.

11  Richard Krautheimer and Trude Krautheimer-Hess, *Lorenzo Ghiberti* (Princeton, NJ: Princeton University Press, 1956), 294 ("To Petrarch [...] it mattered little whether or not a site was commemorated by a monument, or merely haunted by memories. His approach was entirely literary, almost emphatically nonvisual.") See also the famous (and controversial) notion of a "non-visual" form of imitation in the Middle Ages in Krautheimer, "Introduction to an 'Iconography of Mediaeval Architecture,'" *Journal of the Warburg and Courtauld Institutes* 5 (1942): 1–33, in particular, 17–20. Reprinted in *Studies in Early Christian, Medieval, and Renaissance Art* (New York: New York University Press, 1969), 115–151; see, in particular, 117–127 and nn. 82–86.

12  See Carpo, "Digital Style," *Log* 23 (2011): 41–52.

**Michael Young**

*is an architect and an educator practicing in New York City, where he
is a founding partner of the practice Young & Ayata. Michael currently
teaches design studios and seminars at the Cooper Union, Yale University,
Columbia University, and Princeton University.*

# Digital Remediation

*The fact that a continuum can be divided in all possible ways, however, is
exactly what makes it continuous according to Leibniz. He defines the abstract
property of continuity as the potentiality for infinite division in arbitrary
ways: there is an arbitrary number of different possible infinite partitions of
a continuous whole.*

Richard T. W. Arthur, "Leibniz on Continuity," *PSA: Proceedings of the Biennial Meeting
of the Philosophy of Science Association.*

While geometry is an integral aspect of architectural construction, discourse, and
representation, it is never a pure autonomous idea: it is always mediated. If we
look at just these three areas, the status of geometry shifts wildly. In construction,
geometry involves the measurements that translate drawing to building; in
discourse, geometry is a foundation for deductive logic and procedural argument;
and in representation, geometry can be the object represented (form), or the mode
of representation (projection). Geometry dances beneath, above, and between
architecture and its design methodologies. By focusing on geometry's shifting
roles in architectural mediation, we can begin to clarify some of the key concerns
for architectural representation, and specifically interrogate how digital modeling
software is remediating architecture's relation to and with geometry.

Mediation brings with it multiple associations in this context. Most important
for the discussion that follows are the associations to Walter Benjamin's essay
known in its first two versions as "The Work of Art in the Age of Its Technological
Reproduction." In reflecting on ideas of medium and mediation in Benjamin's essay,
Tobias Wilke writes, "The medium names the comprehensive force field that links
the human sensorium to world and that is constituted in doing so by the interplay
between natural (physiological, physical) and historical (social, technological,
and aesthetic) factors." This quote in itself is not a bad description of architectural
representation, for architecture is not only the art form to master reception by the
masses in a state of distraction as Benjamin famously suggests, but it is also the art
form whose mode of discourse and practice is fundamentally built on mediation,
specifically through the multiple negotiations between abstract geometry, visual
expression, and disciplinary interpretation.

One crucial historical shift in architecture's mediation occurs during the
Renaissance with the development of scaled, measurable, notated project drawings.
These drawings are hybrid objects where the graphic visualization of a building
is fused with the regulatory measures of plane geometry. Although geometry
and architecture share ancient roots, the desire to tie the image of architectural

**Course in Airplane Lofting**, Burgard High School, Buffalo, NY, USA, January 1, 1941.

drawing to the rational notations of geometry was one of the crucial developments of early modern architecture. These desires begin the remediation of the medieval stonemason's oral, procedural, full-scale, material construction toward the late Renaissance architect's numerically notated, visually mimetic, proportionately measurable design drawing. Both practices employ the plane geometry descended from Euclid's *Elements*, but the mediation is radically different. First, planar geometric measure allows a precise, pragmatic notation to stand between representation and construction; numeric calculations on the small drawing translate toward material construction in the large building. The significance is that the design control of a building can move away, physically, theoretically, and socially from the building site. Second, geometry becomes fused with the visual image of a building's representation, allowing aesthetic arguments to consider beauty "perceived" as being structured by abstract geometric logic "conceived," meaning that architectural aesthetics could be taught as a code of proportional rules and judged in drawing prior to construction. Third, with the woodblock and the printing press, the mechanically reproduced treatise combined text, representation, and geometry into the same printed page, facilitating an explosion of architectural theory tied to textual discourse, which in turn allows a dissemination of architectural ideas beyond the oral secrecy of the guilds. These treatises required representations to be flat, reduced, and measurable in order that they could be combined with text and numeric notations, and then printed as a plate of coded visual information.

This transformation in the practice and theory of architecture is undeniably of massive importance. But is this transformation the effect of a change in geometry? Or is this transformation the effect of a change in the mediation of the geometries that already exist?

Although orthogonal drawings were known in antiquity, combined orthographic projections begin in earnest with Antonio Sangallo and Albrecht Dürer at the start of the 16th century, are not common in architecture until a century later, and not until Gaspard Monge at the very end of the 18th century do we have a fully resolved system of orthographic projection. If one thinks about these developments as changes in mediation, then the long gestation period for orthographic projection begins to make sense. Each phase strives to achieve what will later be done effortlessly through a change in technology. In many ways, the orthogonal elevation drawings used by early Renaissance architects were not conceived of as projections at all, but more akin to template drawings for the flat measured mappings of elements on an elevation. In this light, the awkwardness of these drawings becomes understandable as they strive to fuse architectural image with the measurements of plane geometry, something more easily achieved through the geometry of orthographic projection. (See Spiral, *Underweysung der Messung,* Albrecht Dürer, on page 22).

In order to understand the changes instigated by digital representation in architecture, one must be clear about the changing relations between geometry and mediation. The digital modeling software used by architects is structured around plane geometry and projective geometry, measured through coordinate geometry and differential geometry, and represented parametrically. These geometric concepts range from thousands to hundreds of years old. Modeling software does not bring any "new" geometry, but it does radically change the mediation. This change in mediation opens connections to practices, techniques, aesthetics, and concepts that are tangential to much of traditional architecture. It remains to be seen if this reme-diation will have an equivalent impact as found in previous epochs.

It is often revealing to look at the efforts that an art form goes through prior to a shift in technology. Benjamin's "Artwork" essay provides another salient concept: "The history of every art form has critical periods in which the particular form strains after effects which can be easily achieved only with a changed technical standard—that is to say, in a new art form." If we look at the representations that architects were developing in the decades preceding the advent of the digital model in the 1990s, we find several significant trends. One aspect related to the themes of our present discussion regarding geometry and mediation is suggested by an analysis of the curvature found in the drawings of Enric Miralles and Carme Pinos for the Olympic Archery Range in Barcelona of 1989–92. There are three principle curve lines found in the plan. The first curve is the plan representation of the retaining wall dividing earth from space. The second curve is the primary wall enclosure dividing interior from exterior. The third curve is the landscape line dividing hardscape from softscape. In the analysis shown here, the first act is to measure these curves. The notation is a mapping of translations and rotations regulated through length and angle. These dimensions are all that is required for the full measured description of the first two of the three curves, the retaining wall, and the enclosure wall. But the third curve, the landscape curve, resists the reduction to line and arc and will require a shift in geometric notation. This shift is a move to the notations of tangency, difficult in a manual mediation, fundamental in a digital mediation.

As a generalization, most of the digital modeling software used by architects (Maya, Rhinoceros, 3ds Max, Catia, Generative Components, Revit) can find their origins in a combination of the entertainment industry (film, video games, animation) and the transportation/military industries (ships, airplanes, cars). There are fundamental aspects of digital modeling software more deeply connected to the geometric mediations of automotive, airplane, and shipbuilding traditions than to architecture. Many of the geometric questions in these practices are questions of continuity. The desire is for pieces of surface to join other pieces as smoothly as possible—a necessary condition when surfaces negotiate the flow of water or air. Ship/Plane/Car designers created the need for surfaces that just could not be described with straight lines and arcs, or easily processed through numeric notations. The mathematics for the numeric description of these surfaces came into existence with the application of calculus to geometry. But differential geometry was rather foreign for designers tied closely to artisanal material design practice. It is not until the 1960s that a system of numeric mediation was developed that harnessed the desires of car body designers. This was the digital mediation of curvature that eventually came to be known as non-uniform rational basis splines (NURBS).

In contrast, architecture was successful relatively early on in a numeric resolution through drawing. The design is measured and geometrically resolved in the virtual space of the drawing prior to the construction of the building; construction was to reproduce these drawings precisely, only larger. Because of this, architecture developed different relations to geometry, not only pragmatically but aesthetically as well. It was the hope of Renaissance architects that the beauty of a design could be judged completely from the drawing. Proportion, the relations of part to whole, could be studied in nature, in man, in antiquity, and then taught as "first principles"

**Miralles Lines, Curvature Analysis through Graphic Differential Geometry 1: Curve Identification.**
Plan Curves starting from left: the retaining wall, the enclosure wall, the paving/landscape division. Each curve possesses a different character in the negotiation of rate of change. Underlay courtesy of Carme Pinós.

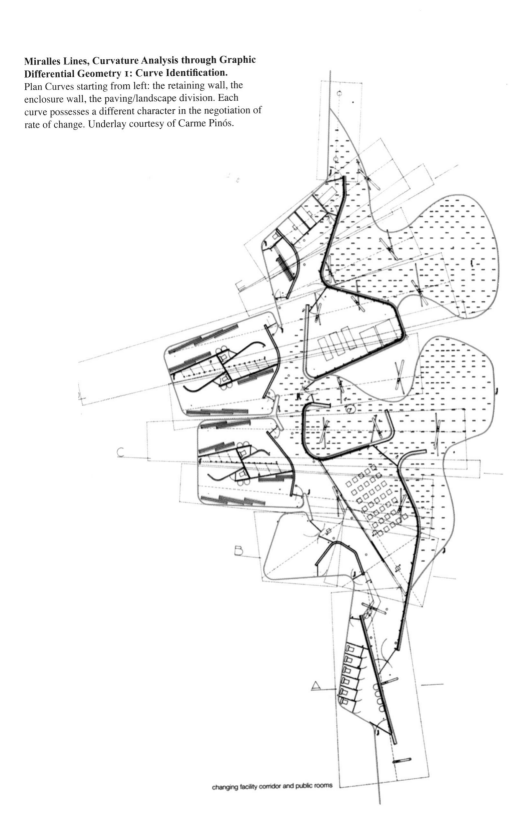

changing facility corridor and public rooms

**Miralles Lines, Curvature Analysis through
Graphic Differential Geometry 2: Linear & Radial
Measurement Notations**. These notations can translate
the retaining wall and enclosure wall into numeric
notations, but fail to numerically describe the complex
curve signifying the paving/landscape division.

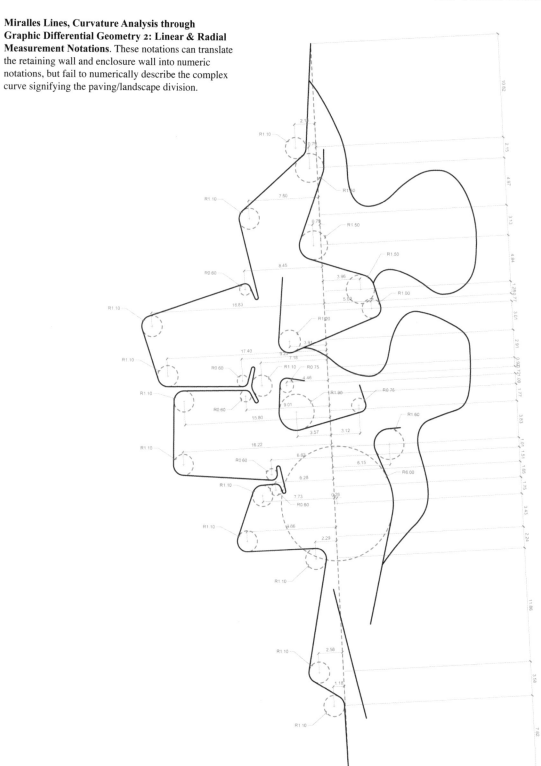

through the mediation of geometrically regulated images. Whether these proportions were understood as natural or conventional, proportion judged visually through a drawing in reference to the abstract ideals provided by geometry proved to be the testing ground for aesthetic beauty. But theories of proportion tied to concepts of ideal beauty were of little value to a ship designer if they produced disjunctions and discontinuities in the surface of the ship's hull. What did matter was the aesthetic that could be seen *and* felt as one surface met another in a smooth continuous manner. This is a visceral sensation, not an idealized linear rationalization. In order to describe and design these surfaces, shipbuilders developed a process that negotiates drawn geometry (lofting), material experimentation (splines and sweeps), and sensory aesthetic judgment (fairing).

During the sixth and seventh centuries, throughout the Mediterranean, there was a shift in building a ship's hull from a "shell-first" toward a "frame-first" construction. This was a conceptual and technological revolution. It meant that the surface of a ship was considered as a sequence of sectional lines transforming along the length of the ship from its midsection toward the front and rear. The ship's hull was thus defined at 90° to its visual elevation through lines that were not edges of the surface but were lines through which the surface was generated. These sectional ribs were constructed as transformations of a master mold or template. Each rib along the length of the boat was a slight modification of the adjacent ribs. This required geometric diagrams that would regulate these transformations along a proportional gradient. This mode of construction also required the sections to be described through profile curves drawn in the plane.

"Lofting" loosely describes a group of techniques that generate a surface description through sectional profiles. The minimum situation is two guide curves, which results in a ruled surface. These straight lines join the two curves at points of common tangency, described by where a flat plane would touch both curves.

(L) **Ship Draught from Matthew Baker's Manuscript**, 1586. From Peter Jeffrey Booker, *A History of Engineering Drawing* (London: Chatto & Windus, 1963).

(R) **20th-Century Ship Drawing** from Richard M. Van Gaasbeek, *A Practical Course in Wooden Boat and Ship Building* (Chicago, IL: Friedrick J. Drake, 1918).

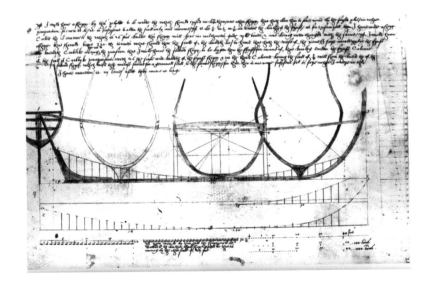

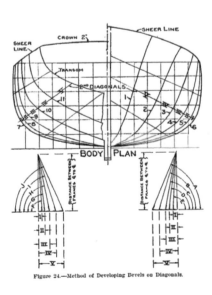

Figure 24.—Method of Developing Bevels on Diagonals.

The joining lines in turn can be sectioned to produce intermediate guide curves, and the process recursively repeats itself. By the 17th century, lofting developed into the use of three sets of interrelated sectional curves describing the surface of the ship's hull in three perpendicular directions: body plan (front), sheer plan (side), and half-breadth plan (top). These techniques are some of the most sophisticated forerunners of Mongean descriptive geometry. Once the hull curves are interrelated through the three views, a complex surface of double curvature can be lofted as a network of contour lines.

Lofting mediates a three-stage translation: drawn geometric diagrams, full-scale fair splines, and mold templates for hull construction. The curves are never completely measured on the small-scale drawing in the sense that architects understand plans; they are constantly negotiated as graphic lines and material lines, at reduced scale and full scale, and only when all the interrelations of these networks prove to be fair are the templates constructed. The curve becomes the primary representational element not as the boundary edge, but as a notation of the edgeless condition interior to a surface of freeform curvature, a contour.

Fairing is a process of testing these lofted lines for continuity. This is done visually by looking down the length of the line checking for kinks, and tactilely by running a hand along a material line or "spline" to check for smoothness. Fairing requires sensory judgment of geometric and material relations, and the ability to manipulate a curve locally to be smooth and continuous. As the ship lines are drawn at full scale on the loft floor (the floor was elevated to be flat and level for inscription of the full-scale lines and the construction of templates; this elevated floor is what gives "lofting" its name), the curves are marked out by long strips of flexible wood or metal called "splines," and held in place by weights sometimes referred to as "ducks."

A spline is a material line, using the properties of bending in the material and moments of force constraining the spline into various configurations. These weights that hold the splines in place allow local variations of the curve, in order to ensure smoothness and continuity of the curves as they vary in complex manners across the hull. Manipulating a related series of curves controls the continuity of the surface. These manipulations are performed point by point, weight by weight, with subtle local variations based continually on tactile and visual sensations of fairness.

A physical template cut from a fair curve could become a guide for future curves. This is how ship templates and eventually French curves came to be developed. These are templates from material constructions that would come back into a drawing to guide the stylization of graphic lines. These templates could also be run along another guide-rail template carving out clay or sand as a complex doubly curved surface; this technique is called a "sweep." Often shipbuilding curve templates would be referred to solely as sweeps. It should be noted that many of these terms touched on above are also used in modeling software. Terms such as *lofting, sweeping, patching, splines*, and *fairing* have become digital algorithms, but all of these techniques were once design mediations moving between the physical and abstract, the material and geometric, the template and the line, the hand and the eye, in order to resolve the continuities of surface.

The major steps taken to develop a description appropriate for computer-driven computation came from the automotive design industry of the 1960s. The question that faced these designers and engineers was how to provide a numeric description of free-form surfaces with an interface intuitive enough for designers to feel that they could handle the subtle variations of curvature that functional and aesthetic performance required. The need for a numeric definition of these curves was driven by the rise of numeric control in fabrication. In order for any digital fabrication system to handle a construction, it had to be described through numbers.

Two key players in this development were Paul de Casteljau and Pierre Bézier, who worked for the French automobile companies Citroen and Renault, respectively. Both engineers developed a method for a parametric representation that could allow a direct user interface in the construction and manipulation of free-form curves and surfaces. The algorithm goes under the name of De Casteljau, while the curves are called Bézier, due to publishing time sequences. Both engineers were attempting to solve very pragmatic problems. In the description of surface curvature at the time, auto body designers would use templates, French curves, and sweeps to mold clay, sand, or other materials in the desired shape. These templates could then be used to transfer lines of the car body to a drawing, then scaled up to have jigs and molds fabricated. This was more or less traditional shipbuilding technique and technology, not radically different from the way free-form surfaces were described during the 15th century. But in the mid-20th century, the automotive and aircraft industry were running into new problems as every other component in the assembly was increasing its precision. The surface pieces were not always able to keep up with diminishing tolerances and, importantly, milling and fabrication machines were beginning to appear that could be Computer Numerical Controlled. Their task required a new mediation of the geometry. Paul de Casteljau began with an old construction for a parabola called a "thread construction." Its simplest example is two rigid sticks with strings connecting equal divisions on both sticks, the sequence flipped so that first is connected to last. This simple construction defines a parabolic curve, but is also an example of a recursive algorithm of repeated linear interpolation.

**Thread Construction of Parabolic Curve.** Simplest example of de Casteljau's algorithm, Michael Young, 2011.

**Degree 2 NURBS Curve**, with lines tangent and normal. This example shows the stitching of the 2° two Bézier curves at the midpoint of the control polygon as a basis spline. A single iteration of De Casteljau's algorithm has been graphically represented. Michael Young, 2011.

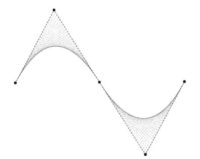

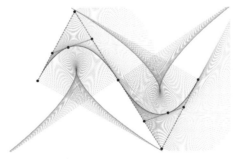

The sticks will become the control polygon, the ends become the control points, and the strings become the vectors tangent to a curve. This construction is at the heart of Bézier curves, which join together to form basis splines, which are rationalized to create NURBS modeling software, the most common way to define curvature and surface in a digital environment.

Non-uniform rational basis splines are a calculus-based parametric mediation of curvature. Tangent vectors are the primary elements of curve measurement, and Gaussian surface analysis allows the measurement of surface curvature through the differentiation of vectors normal to a surface.

**Degree 3 NURBS Curve**, with lines tangent and normal. This example shows a single, degree three Bézier curve. A single iteration of De Casteljau's algorithm has been graphically represented. Michael Young, 2011.

**Degree 3 NURBS Curve Field**, with lines tangent and normal. This example shows the transformation of a curve through several stages, generating a surface, notated as a field of vectors. Michael Young, 2011.

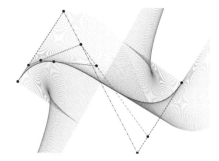

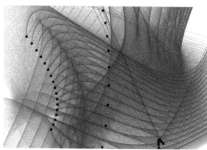

The mathematical representation of curves and surfaces in a digital environment is parametric. Much has been made of parametric representation in contemporary architectural discussions, both practice-based arguments with BIM software and design-based apologies, but it is necessary to remember its roots and why design software is for the most part parametric. A parametric representation allows numeric definition without explicit dependency to the *xyz* coordinate axes that define the global digital space. Instead, a parameter—time, for example—is introduced and the spatial equations are redefined to depend on the domain of this new parameter. This is crucial for digital modeling since the design must be able to be transformed as an object in space. If digital entities were defined through explicit equations, every time you moved an object it would change because it would be dependent on the global *xyz* values. Parametric representation also defines an entity through a bounded domain. This bounding of the parameters means that every curve has a start and an end. The curve's vectors have a directionality informing the sequence with which it is computed. Furthermore, the parameters that the surface or curve equations depend on can be associated to more than one entity. The manipulation of one variable thus begins to affect a large number of associated entities. These parametric associations can build a surface, or can tie together multiple objects as an aggregate of relations.

The mediation for the control of geometric transformations is fundamentally different between the analog and digital. In an analog regulation, the instruments of a straightedge or compass leave a residue of their action. These traces accumulate as a design develops; layers of translucent paper are often used to sort out the sequence. In a digital environment, there is no trace or index of the transformations. To visualize a previous state, the designer has to undo the operation, or make several copies of each state. But as the graphic index is lost, there are new qualities that emerge from the digital mediation of transformation. Transformations regulated parametrically represent a range of possible states available along a vector; each instance is a simulation. Most software can also nest several transformations into a single operation to allow what appears to be deformation. Twists, bends, tapers, and stretches are examples of this. There is not really any new transformation here, but a combination of simpler transformations associated parametrically. It begins to appear that you can deform a surface. This is a major conceptual change for the mediation of geometry. Within a traditional mediation of geometry, a deformation is an immeasurable, intuitive act that typically involves a physical exchange between matter and force. It is important to remember that splines used in shipbuilding are deformable lines. There is a deep connection here in the desire to manipulate a curve or a surface in a free, deformable manner with tactile and muscular sensations of pressure altering the material. The movement of control points alters the net of control polygons, which alters the computation of each associated curve, and thus any associated surface can be locally, internally deformed in what appears to be real time. This is the kind of interface that a car body stylist or film animator desires; control points, tangent threads, and normal vectors would just get in the way of visualizing the object under design. Similarly, the lack of residual index left by the parametric representation of design transformations is preferred by these industries; they are after the associations and affects of a final design image and do not require a procedural logic with which to justify their actions.

It is now time to return to the analysis of the Miralles and Pinos plan. As will be recalled, the complex curvature of the free-form landscape curve could not be rationalized into arcs and straight lines. The discussion of shipbuilding curves and tangent notations provide us with a compelling option for describing this curve. Viewing curvature through the lens of calculus and differential geometry alters the designer's understanding of a curve. A single tangent notation gives a graphic description of the rate of change of curvature, and as a collective of tangents, how fast and in what ways these rates change. The line normal to the curve also becomes a unique graphic device as a vector showing the instantaneous radius of curvature. Lines tangent and normal can become part of a graphic notation relating conceptual and aesthetic aspects of curvature. Curves loose a singular signification due to particular shape, and instead gain the qualitative character of curvature. The control points define an envelope for the curve to develop. It is within this envelope that the curve will be approximated through subdivisions of a control polygon. You do not draw the curve; you sequentially set spatial vectors within which the curve will be simulated. The first two points set a direction of tangency for the start of the curve; the last two points set the ending tangent vector. These tangents establish the control polygons, which like a marionette, allows transformations of curves at a distance. Once the three Archery Range curves are described through the notations of tangency, their control polygons can be constructed. These control polygons can be linearly interpolated between themselves to build a field of curve instances between states. This technique is the digital descendent of shipbuilding lofting.

If curves are measured as the locus of a moving line tangent to the curve, the curve is dissolved into variations of vectors, or notations of force. If surfaces are measured as the regulated transformation of curves, then the surface dissolves into a field of vectors. The lines tangent give a vector notation of movement along the curve, and in a surface, the lines normal give a vector notation between curves as the surface deforms. Geometrically, the digital construction is explicitly notated. But, aesthetically, we no longer see surfaces or lines, but fields of forces, their movements structuring organizations of density, accumulation, and direction. Surfaces become notational extensions into fields of variable intensity.

**Miralles Lines, Curvature Analysis through Graphic Differential Geometry 3: Tangent & Normal Notation**. In order to find a common notation that can describe all three curves, a notation of lines tangent and normal to the curves is introduced. Each tangent vector describes the trajectory at an instant along the curve. Each normal vector is extended to the center of the circle that best approximates the radius of curvature at that instant.

**Miralles Lines, Curvature Analysis through Graphic Differential Geometry 4: Curve Interpolation**. Once the tangents of each curve are known, control polygons can be constructed. New curves may then be interpolated between each of the three given control polygons. This is a graphic equivalent of the techniques for lofting a surface.

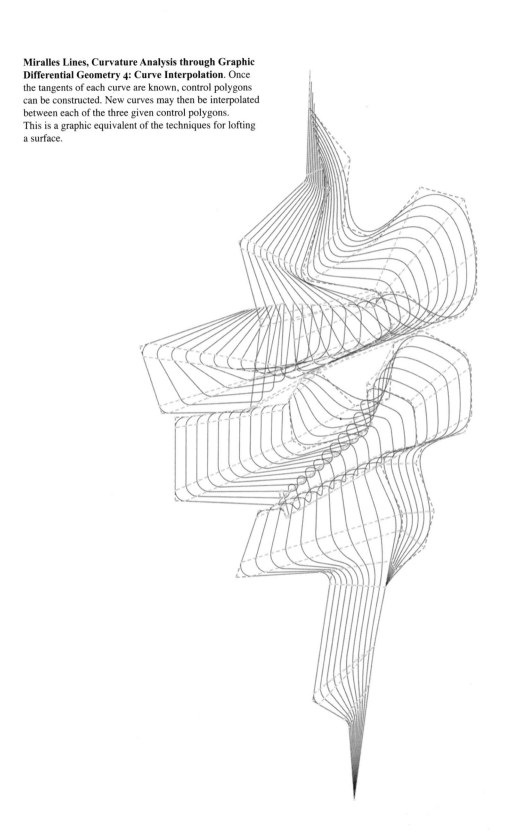

**Miralles Lines, Curvature Analysis Through Graphic Differential Geometry 5: Vector Fields of Tangent and Normal Notations**. Density, Length, and Color are variable along a gradient, these are the only variables.

The gradient variations of these quantities require an aesthetic response from the designer to evaluate and control the emerging qualities.

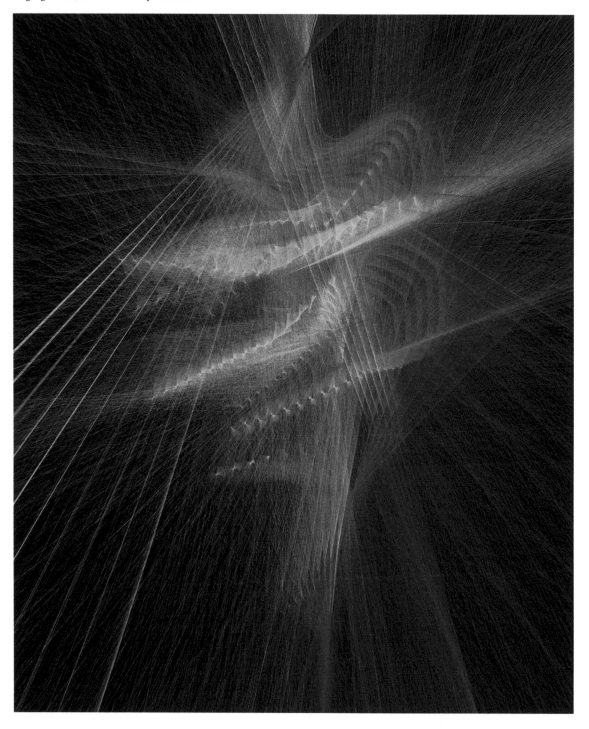

As architecture re-mediates it relations to representation through digital tech-nologies, it becomes imperative to understand the nature of this change. Not only to be able to guide the software toward specific architectural concerns, but to be able to understand the conceptual and aesthetic desires that are latent in the mediation itself: and in this balance begin to experiment with other possibilities that the software may open. The lines tangent and normal to a curve are in many ways the graphic notations of the digital tectonic building a curve. To work through their representation is to pull in a deep historical discourse in which architectural notation seeks to record and reveal the acts of construction through acts of representation and vice versa. But of equal importance here in the final drawing of the analysis of the Archery Range plan are the aesthetic concerns that begin to accumulate around the variable intensi-ties of vector notations. These aesthetic affects are not new; they are in fact very painterly and in many ways best understood in reference to late 19th-century aesthetic discourse. What is novel is the mediation of painterly atmospheric sensations through differential geometry. To pursue the aesthetic as well as the pragmatic in any tech-nology is to begin to use that system for what it truly is: mediation.

**Endnotes**

1 Tobias Wilke, "Tacti(ca)lity Reclaimed: Benjamin's Medium, the Avant-Garde, and the Politics of the Senses," *Grey Room* 39 ((Spring 2010): 40.
2 Walter Benjamin, "The Work of Art in the Age of Its Technological Reproducibility," *Grey Room* 39 (Spring 2010): 33.
3 Filippo Camerota, "Renaissance Descriptive Geometry: The Codification of Drawing Methods," in *Picturing Machines: 1400–1700*, Wolfgang Lefevre (ed.) (Cambridge, MA: MIT Press, 2004), 175–176.
4 Wolfgang Lefevre, "The Emergence of Combined Orthographic Projections," in *Picturing Machines: 1400–1700*, Wolfgang Lefevre (ed.) (Cambridge, MA: MIT Press, 2004), 210–211.
5 James Ackerman, "The Origins of Architectural Drawing in the Middle Ages and Renaissance," in *Origins, Imitation, Conventions* (Cambridge, MA: MIT Press, 2002), 49–53.
6 Mario Carpo, "The Making of the Typographical Architect," *Paper Palaces* (New Haven, CT: Yale University Press, 1998), 159–160.
7 Both the medieval use of plane geometry as practi-cal trade-based constructions and the Renaissance theories of proportion derived from Vitruvius are ultimately examples of the first written discourse on proportion known from classical antiquity; Book V from Euclid's *Elements*.
8 Mario Carpo, *The Alphabet and the Algorithm* (Cambridge, MA: MIT Press, 2011), 21–22.
9 Dan Pedoe, *Geometry and the Visual Arts* (New York: Dover Publishing, 1976), 102–103.
10 Mario Carpo, *Architecture in the Age of Printing* (Cambridge, MA: MIT Press, 2001), 11–14.
11 Bruno Latour, "Drawing Things Together," in *Representation in Scientific Practice*, Michael Lynch and Steve Woolgar (eds.) (Cambridge, MA: MIT Press, 1990), 46.
12 "But the last advantage is the greatest. The two-dimensional character of inscriptions allow them to merge with geometry. As we saw for perspective, space on paper can be made continuous with three-dimensional space. The result is that we can work on paper with rulers and numbers, but still manipulate three-dimensional objects 'out there' (Ivins, 1973). Better still, because of this optical consistency, everything, no matter where it comes from, can be converted into diagrams and numbers, and combina-tion of numbers and tables can be used which are still easier to handle than words or silhouettes (Dagognet, 1973). You cannot measure the sun, but you can measure a photograph of the sun with a ruler. Then the number of centimeters read can easily migrate through different scales, and provide solar masses for completely different object." 46.
13 Wolfgang Lefevre, "The Emergence of Combined Orthographic Projections," in *Picturing Machines: 1400–1700*, Wolfgang Lefevre (ed.) (Cambridge, MA: MIT Press, 2004), 210–211.
14 Walter Benjamin, "The Work of Art in the Age of Its Technological Reproducibility," *Grey Room* 39 (Spring 2010): 27.
15 Robin Evans, *The Projective Cast: Architecture and Its Three Geometries* (Cambridge, MA: MIT Press, 1995), 113–116.
16 Walter Benjamin, "The Work of Art in the Age of Its Technological Reproducibility," *Grey Room* 39 (Spring 2010): 31.
17 In an effort to focus on the mediation of geometry, this paper will address only the latter of these two. A similar effort would be valuable in looking at the meshing, rendering, and lighting engines that come from entertainment design practices.
18 Gerald Farin, *Curves and Surfaces for CAGD* (San Francisco, CA: Morgan Kaufmann, 2002), 1–2.
19 Gerald Farin, *Curves and Surfaces for CAGD* (San Francisco, CA: Morgan Kaufmann, 2002), 1–2.
20 Mario Carpo, *The Alphabet and the Algorithm* (Cambridge, MA: MIT Press, 2011): 70.
21 Caroline van Eck, "Verbal and Visual Abstraction: The Role of Pictorial Techniques of Representation

in Renaissance Architectural Theory," in *The Built Surface, vol. 1*, Christy Anderson (ed.) (Hants, UK: Ashgate Publishing, 2002), 167–169.

22  Indra Kagis McEwen, "On Claude Perrault: Modernizing Vitruvius," in *Paper Palaces* (New Haven, CT: Yale University Press, 1998), 324–326.

23  Eric Rieth, "To Design and to Build Mediaeval Ships (Fifth to Fifteenth Centuries)—The Application of Knowledge Held in Common with Civil Architecture, or in Isolation?" in *History of Science and Medicine Library, Volume 11: Creating Shapes in Civil and Navel Architecture*, Horst Nowacki and Wolfgang Lefevre (eds.) (Leiden, Netherlands: Koninklijke Brill, 2009), 122.

24  Horst Nowacki, "Shape Creation Knowledge in Civil and Navel Architecture," in *History of Science and Medicine Library, Volume 11: Creating Shapes in Civil and Navel Architecture*, Horst Nowacki and Wolfgang Lefevre (eds.) (Leiden, Netherlands: Koninklijke Brill, 2009), 31–33.

25  Gerald Farin, *Curves and Surfaces for CAGD* (San Francisco, CA: Morgan Kaufmann, 2002), 441.

26  Howard Thrasher, *Aircraft Lofting and Template Layout* (San Francisco, CA: Aviation Press, 1942), 125–128.

27  Peter Jeffrey Booker, *A History of Engineering Drawing* (London, UK: Chatto & Windus, 1963), 68–70.

28  William Nelson, *Airplane Lofting* (New York: McGraw-Hill, 1941), 82.

29  Richard M. Van Gaasbeek, *A Practical Course in Wooden Boat and Ship Building* (Chicago, IL: Friedrich J. Drake, 1918), 179–180.

30  Edward L. Attwood, *A Text-Book of Laying Off or the Geometry of Shipbuilding* (London: Longmans, Green & Co, 1918), 16, 19.

31  Richard M. Van Gaasbeek, *A Practical Course in Wooden Boat and Ship Building* (Chicago, IL: Friedrich J. Drake, 1918), 179–180.

32  Gerald Farin, *Curves and Surfaces for CAGD* (San Francisco, CA: Morgan Kaufmann, 2002), 2–11.

33  Helmut Pottman, Andreas Asperl, Michael Hofer, and Axel Kilian, *Architectural Geometry* (Exton, PA: Bentley Institute Press, 2007), 259.

34  Gerald Farin, *Curves and Surfaces for CAGD* (San Francisco, CA: Morgan Kaufmann, 2002), 8–9.

35  Ibid., 43–45.

36  NURBS: Non-Uniform Rational Basis Splines.

37  Non-Uniform: Knots, the joins between Basis or B-Spline curves, can be uniformly or non-uniformly spaced along the length of a curve.

38  Rational: Mathematically defined 3-space polynomial equations for all curves. This allows each control point to be weighted differently than the others, which is achieved through central projection. Conics such as hyperbolas, ellipses, and circles are thus definable.

39  Basis Splines: Several Bézier curves joined together in uniform knots, a piecemeal curve. The curvature is smooth at the knot, as the end of one curve shares tangency and vector length with the start of the next, creating parametric continuity.

40  Bézier Curve: Parametric method of determining a smooth curve within a control polygon through linear interpolation. Control polygon is divided in equal ratios, lines join the divisions, and these are further divided along the same ratio; this sequence is iterated according to degree of curvature to determine a point on the curve. The collection of all points and their corresponding tangents determine the complex curve. Named for Pierre Bézier, who published it first, it uses Paul de Casteljau's algorithm.

41  Curvature Degree: Refers to the highest exponential in the curve's equation. Degree 1 = Straight Line, Degree 2 = Quadratic Curve (Conic), Degree 3 = Cubic Curve, and so on. The degree of curvature cannot be higher than the sides of the control polygon determined by the control points of a curve.

42  David Celento, "Innovate or Perish: New Technologies and Architecture's Future," in *Fabricating Architecture*, Robert Corser (ed.) (New York: Princeton Architectural Press, 2010), 63–65.

43  Patrik Schumacher, "Parametricism and the Autopoiesis of Architecture," *LOG* 21: 63–79.

44  It should be said that the author has deep reservations about many of the claims made in defense of parametric tools as a design style. This paper does not have space for this argument and will have to wait to be pursued.

45  David F. Rogers, *An Introduction to NURBS* (San Francisco, CA: Morgan Kaufmann, 2001), 2–4.

46  Ibid., 156–157.

47  Helmut Pottman, Andreas Asperl, Michael Hofer, and Axel Kilian, *Architectural Geometry* (Exton, PA: Bentley Institute Press, 2007), 453–468.

48  Gilles Deleuze, *Francis Bacon: The Logic of Sensation* (Minneapolis, MI: University of Minnesota Press, 1981), 50.

49  "These are two very different categories. The transformation of form can be abstract or dynamic. But deformation is always bodily, and it is static, it happens at one place; it subordinates movement to force, but it also subordinates the abstract to the Figure."

50  Bernard Cache, *Earth Moves* (Cambridge, MA: MIT Press, 1995), 49–51.

51  David F. Rogers, *An Introduction to NURBS* (San Francisco, CA: Morgan Kaufmann, 2001), 46.

52  Gerald Farin, *NURBS From Projective Geometry to Practical Use* (Natick, MA: AK Peters, 1999), 110–112 and 159–161.

53  Heinrich Wolfflin, *Renaissance and Baroque* (London: Fontana Library, [1888] 1964), 29–37: "The contour is quite annihilated, and the continuous, static lines of the old style are replaced by and indistinct and gradually fading boundary area," 31. "The painterly style gives the illusion of physical relief, and the different objects seem to project or recede in space," 31. Alois Riegl, *Historical Grammar of the Visual Arts* (New York: Zone Books, [1898] 2004), 129. "Once movement was deemed acceptable, transitory and accidental qualities entered art," 129. Wilhelm Worringer, *Abstraction and Empathy* (Chicago: Ivan R. Dee, [1908] 1997), 21. "A crucial consequence of this artistic volition was, on the one hand, the approximation of the representation to a plane, and on the other, strict suppression of the representation of space and exclusive rendering of a single form," 21.

## Shohei Shigematsu

*joined OMA in 1998 and has led the OMA office in New York since 2006, overseeing OMA's operations in the Americas, including the recent completion of Milstein Hall at Cornell University. Shigematsu was also project leader for the winning competition entry for the CCTV headquarters in Beijing and the Shenzhen Stock Exchange Headquarters. He is a visiting faculty member of Columbia University's Graduate School of Architecture, Planning and Preservation; Harvard University Graduate School of Design; and Cornell University's College of Architecture, Art, and Planning.*

# Fo' Sho: A Conversation on Uncertainty

Interviewed by Carly Dean, Alison Nash, and Heriberto Rodríguez Valenzuela during a visit to Milstein, in October 2011, and at OMA's New York office in December 2011.

**Milstein Hall Exterior**. Photo © Brad Feinknopf 2011.

#### Heriberto

We are looking forward to discussing the role of mathematics in the design and construction of Milstein Hall, and the unexpected and serendipitous conditions of the existing building. The word *mathematics* has many different interpretations for architects. To begin, what does mathematics mean to you?

#### Sho

We often talk about mathematical beauty when we conceive of a form. Mathematics, or physics, and engineering are a fundamental part of our design. We often talk about how architecture can be integrated into engineering as much as possible. In many of our buildings, you cannot tell which one—engineering or architecture—is governing. This is an ideal tension we would always like to achieve in our design work.

#### Alison

Historically, mathematics at Cornell has tended to imply a certain order and proportion in architecture that emerged during the Renaissance and reemerged with Le Corbusier, and later, with Colin Rowe. Although issues of proportion and order were being discussed in schools of architecture until very recently, they seem to have been lost on our generation. Do you think that these mathematical premises have a role in OMA's design projects?

#### Sho

The subject of mathematics implies two different applications today. One application of mathematics rationalizes free-form into something buildable and understandable. The other application of mathematics in parametrics goes beyond what you are imagining, to almost lose control. With parametrics, you are expected to get results that you were not expecting. OMA uses mathematics in the former option, treating proportion not as an unpredictable formula, but as a set of givens. Often proportional issues are linked to functional issues. A lot of dimensions are often set by typologies. In a way, it is not mathematical but rather trying to embrace the givens and then trying to find more combinational beauty or proportional beauty out of the givens. In short, OMA cares very much about proportion and form.

#### Heriberto

There seems to be a disconnect between the slow process of building architecture and the fast speed of culture and media. How did the economic recession and social movements influence the construction of Milstein Hall? The design was unveiled in 2006; was there any change after that unveiling?

#### Sho

There were many changes, but they were subtle. The basic idea was always the same. But to respond to your previous comment, I think the building did not necessarily *respond* to those changes but *anticipated* them by creating such an open-ended space. It is difficult to say whether it was part of our ultimate decision or ultimate conviction. We anticipated flexibility for the future in arts and architecture learning.

#### Alison

How did you envision that Milstein can affect learning and teaching?

**Milstein Hall** © Matthew Carbone

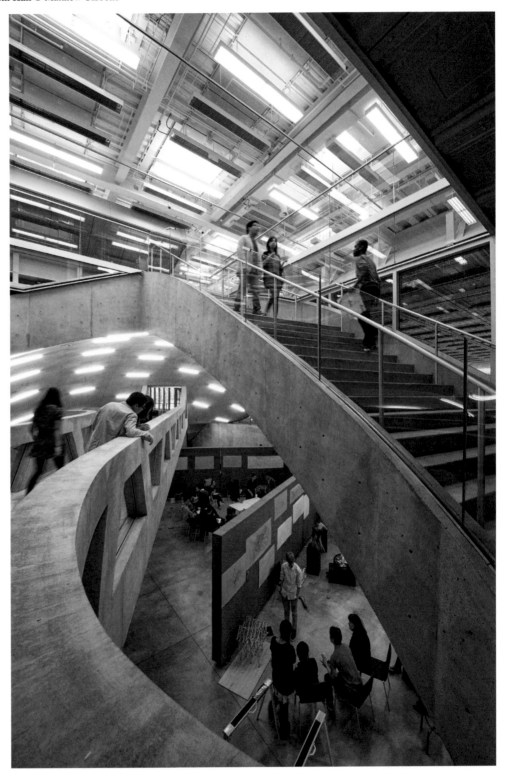

**Sho**

Our ambition was to maximize the flexibility of the upper plate. This actually triggered a lot of intense discussion with the students and faculty about programming to encourage interdisciplinary discussion. In one of the many iterations, the library was located in the University Avenue cantilever. But, in the end the upper plate was dedicated to studios only, with direct access to additional studios in Rand and Sibley Halls. It is happening now in a different way than originally planned. So, it was a master planning process. The building became a platform to discuss pedagogical and operational issues.

**Carly**

On one hand, the engineering in Milstein Hall seems very precise. The Vierendeel that becomes a diagonal truss, for example, is a precise response to both program and structure. On the other hand, the dome, despite its complexity, was built (form-work) and poured in quite a traditional way. How was this balance calibrated between the rough and the precise, and what meaning does it hold for you?

**Sho**

We deliberately used two very different construction materials: steel and concrete. I wouldn't say either process is more traditional than the other. Although steel construction was established later, concrete construction with complex geometries requires many computational studies in Rhino and other programs. Ultimately, I do not know which one is more high-tech.

It is rather diagrammatic to have such contrasting materials without any transitional element. The resulting juxtaposition is beautiful. It provides a variety of spaces and also serves as a pedagogical message to the students who were able to witness these two construction processes and the outcome.

We also sought to explore how the building's architecture and landscape could coexist in an urban scale and an architectural scale. In our master-plan proposal for the AAP, we planned for a strip of interconnected indoor and outdoor public spaces extending along University Avenue. We chose to elaborate the ground condition of the AAP campus in the building's materiality with a continuous concrete plaza that is lifted to form the dome. Likewise, the upper plate of uninterrupted studio space functions as a bridge between the existing facilities in Rand and Sibley Hall.

**Carly**

Our Building Technology class used to meet in Sibley, and as we were learning about construction methods, we were seeing the steel frame being erected and welded, and we were seeing the dome being poured. It was a unique experience. And I think the interstitial space between Milstein and Sibley, the undercroft area, is important. Recently, local Ithacans have been using this space and the dome for skateboarding. I don't know if you have seen the signs "No skateboarding, please respect our new building." How does this kind of unexpected usage complicate or enrich the building and the experience of the dome space?

**Sho**

There was initially opposition to the covered area because there was a fear that it would basically become a dark wind tunnel. But we wanted to provide a more urban environment within the campus. The moment where you can see the bus stop along University Avenue from the Dome crit space feels particularly urban. The combination of the landscape element and a simple box on top succeeds in providing this strange density unique to the campus.

### Carly
Did you ever imagine that people would enjoy skateboarding on the dome? The seating bubbles seem to be intentional obstacles for these kids.

**Skateboarder, Milstein**. Photo by Carly Dean.

### Sho
Yes. We thought they would. The seating bubbles were primarily intended for informal crits but also to at least interrupt the skateboarders. The bike rack acts as a barrier as well. Naturally, they see it not as an obstacle but as a challenge. I'm happy to attract urban activity into the building.

### Alison
Milstein's continuous ceiling is clad with pressed metal panels, reminiscent of 19th-century industrial, yet ornamental, ceilings in the region. It is one of the few signs of ornamentation that we see in Milstein. At the same time, in the studios housed within, some of our advanced studios are producing extremely complex and arguably ornamental forms. Do you think that using algorithms or parameters to create these ornamental architectures is an arbitrary approach to design, or is there potential in that approach?

### Sho
The ceiling panel was a 3D model that was communicated with the contractors. So, a direct connection between manufacturing and computation is happening in that regard, to maximize on the panel's durability and acoustical performance. But I think it is a good point; parametrics has more and more potential to deal with the repetitive and mundane rather than very special things. You are rather expecting the opposite.

**Milstein's Continuous Ceiling**. Courtesy of Cornell
University by William Staffeld

### Alison
Since you have had the opportunity to see how digital tools can be used in construction, what is your opinion on their potentials for creating regenerative architecture? Can parametrics be used not only for production of form but also as a design method?

### Sho
There are many ways to look at the potential of parametrics, and one is that there is a big gap between drawing and manufacturing at this moment, so there are many mistakes—from the different panel size to glass size, etcetera. If those inefficiencies are solved by BIM or by digital fabrication that automatically find the optimum size and connect straight to manufacturers and so on, that is one way to see the potential of parametrics. But parametrics implies that the designer is manipulating the parameters, and I would still like to believe that my own intuition is stronger than computer parametrics. When you are engaged in the architectural process, it is not necessary to say this is the result of 500 studies and, therefore, this is the best thing. You just have to say what you believe in and that is real human communication: I don't think it's healthy to exclude that real encounter so much.

### Heriberto
You do not see parametrics as a productive process in architecture?

### Sho
As a design tool I don't see it yet, because it endangers the profession to a certain degree.

### Alison
The idea that a computer could design something is a danger?

### Sho
It's not the old-school worries you might imagine. But with any art form, because you don't know the *ideal*, you continue to seek for it, and you continue to wonder, you continue to design. If parametrics claim to find the final, ideal solution,

I think it's a bit strange. In my opinion, not knowing the ideal is healthier for any art form.

### Heriberto
What are your thoughts on the future of architecture, as media culture begins to accelerate, making architecture seem comparatively slow?

### Sho
This is why we, as a firm, conceived the entity called AMO that deals with non-architectural commissions with architectural thinking. That is one way to catch up to the speed of cultural production. The other way is basically to widen our territory of performance from being an architect and belief in architectural thinking to have more surface area to communicate to society. And that way you are unavoidably influenced by media.

### Alison
Do you believe that data can be used generatively in the design process, and how is it productive for your practice?

### Sho
As a student, there was a dominant Dutch school that used data as a drive to generate forms, but I don't think that's ideal. Data supports your intention or argument—not vice versa. OMA's research focuses not on relentless data mining, but on forming a hypothesis to utilize the data for a better narrative.

### Alison
Are there any specific architectural projects that exemplify this relationship between data and form?

### Sho
Our midrise for 23 East 22nd Street is one example. Typically, real estate is governed by floor area, but we thought that the developer could also sell volume. The developer had also purchased the air rights from adjacent buildings but he did not want us to go higher than 250 feet, because he had already presold all the units. This design maintains the cubic footage of each unit—so when the floors are bigger, the floor heights are smaller; and when the floors are smaller, the heights are bigger. We generated something that resembles the typical New York step building.

### Alison
So in this project, you have appropriated developers' profit formulas and matrices to figure out the puzzle of program?

### Sho
Yes. Whether working for a developer or doing an architecture department building, there are always interesting givens that can contribute to objective data analysis. It is not a design tool, it is just information. Architects still need to think subjectively and make design decisions.

**L. P. Kwee Studios, Milstein Studio Plate**. Courtesy of Brett Beyer Photography.

**Alison**

How does the idea of subjectivity play out in your work?

**Sho**

Mathematics has a formula, right? By using a very simple formula you can solve and address very complex issues that exist in the world; however, parametric design studios only talk about how well they used the formula. These studios never explain if they liked this formula or if there were any personal reasons for it. With parametrics, you are educated to be only objective. In my point of view, pedestrian decisions [in parametrics] don't generate any new energy. In *real* communication with the client, and within our studio, what really matters is what you're really passionate about, what you really like about certain things, what you're critical about, or what you're really interested in. I'm critical because when I was a student I wished that a school could have taught me more about how to appreciate instincts or passion. You have to be an artist…

This is just a tip for students: don't just present your portfolio in a rational path with a rational expression. Show your studies, show your struggles, show your emotions, and your opinion of the outcome or the process. Students need to develop a point of view, not just present a sequence of rationales. This is something that I try to enforce with the studios that I teach: data analysis only plays a supporting role in design. Intuition, fostered by criticality and by developing your own interest, should lead design decisions. The danger of parametrics is it eliminates the reliance on intuitive design by using data alone to deliver the ultimate design decision.

**Alison**

Do you see a relationship between the academy or university's theorizing about architecture and the practice of architecture in terms of the economy?

**Sho**

As you know, I am from Japan, and Japan has been in a depression for a long time, and I am interested personally in postcrisis. In my lectures on the subject, I've talked about the end or transformation of the market economy that we call the ¥€$ (Yen, Euro, Dollars) regime. Also, I describe the postcrisis effects on architecture and urban design that motivate thought, invention, and theory of architecture as directly related to the current economy. When economic indexes are in decline, there is a rise in humanistic indexes like planning, connecting, thinking, and feeling. For example, health care and religious architecture are the two typologies that always proliferate when the recession happens. Many architectural and urban manifestos were written during the recession because, obviously, when architects don't have work, they either come to the university or they try to do something that compensates their time—typically, historically, that is the case.

Japan had its ups and downs but if you look at it in a 40-year span, it shows constant decline. I do not think that the U.S. will ever go back to the boom of 2007. The Middle East, Africa, China, and South America are already in the process of experiencing that modernization fate. From working in different economic, political, and cultural conditions in different countries, I've learned that it's very important to be open and aware of diversity.

**Carly**

With a number of projects in the Middle East, Africa, China, and South America, an influence of Japanese culture could yield an interesting output. How has your own culture come in to play in your work?

**Sho**

I was born in Japan in '73. After the war [World War II] Japan had a steady growth until almost 30 years later. My parents' generation lived their lives through an economic upturn, whereas I only lived during the downturn of Japan, after the oil crisis. I found it very important to travel outside of Japan. As an architect it is critical to know what modernization means to a city, but at the same time now, with work in China, the Middle East, and booming countries, I am interested in what it means to be in downturn. I led a number of studios at other schools about the potential of postcrisis, because the upturn and downturn is a back-to-back condition. It has a kind of dialectic relationship. As an architect you need to understand life in a declining country or shrinking country like Japan, or parts of Europe, or even parts of America.

**Alison**

A lot of architects, developers, and entrepreneurs are reconsidering rust belt cities in the United States for that reason, because when there is an economic downturn, the flip side is its potential for growth.

**Sho**

During a downturn, potential is always there. I am a also interested in new ways of interpreting modernization in the urban landscape, rather than creating another downtown New York or another downtown Shanghai. I'm a bit tired of the prescribed hypercommercial, capitalist outlook on the city and the fixation on the ultimate outcome. I am trying to not be influenced by specificity and diversity rather than individual culture. In the end, I am influenced less by traditional Japanese culture, but more by my generation and the specific geo-political-economical conditions into which I was born in Japan.

**Carly**

Contemporary mathematics incorporates probability, chaos, and uncertainty to deal with unpredictable outcomes. This emphasis is reflected in the global economy in terms of the densification of cities, the building of informal settlements, and the instability of future climate. Do you see mathematics and economics as parallel, and do you find these ideas relevant to your work?

**Sho**

I like the way that you apply the notion of mathematics to economy or climate, or movement of people on the globe. It is all linked.

**Alison**

Mathematics is at least trying to describe some of those conditions, either using statistics or equations in atmospheric science. How do you deal with uncertainty in your work?

**Sho**

We embrace uncertainty. I think that if you lose the sensibility to enjoy uncertainty, architecture is not fun anymore. Each time you deal with different conditions —climate, economy, complexity, industry—uncertainty is there. Embracing uncertainty is a good ending for a mathematics theme. If math is a structure that can deal with uncertainty or the questions of the universe, then a parallel tool or realm definitely exists in architecture.

**Carly**

In our interviews, it has been interesting to hear points of view of many different architects. Many shy away from mathematics, they seem to never be at peace with it, or embrace their own strengths. Many seem to be tongue in cheek about failing calculus or structures.

**Sho**

Me, too. I associate physics with math. How do you think of mathematics?

**Alison**

I think of mathematics as a language.

**Sho**

I like that idea that mathematics is a language that we all use, especially in architecture. That math is a common language, between architecture or the economy, or politics, or science. I think it is a catalyst. Like a language, architecture has a structure, and rules, and growth, but can create completely unknown results: it can deal with uncertainty. I think that is beautiful. I can personally describe my life like that. We have a common set of rules or language, and by dealing with uncertainty and expectations of the known, we create something unknown.

## Dana Čupková and Kevin Pratt

*are the core of EPIPHYTE Lab, an architectural design and research collaborative based in Ithaca, NY. Their work engages the built environment at the intersection of ecology, computationally driven processes, and systems analysis. Dana Čupková is a visiting assistant professor and Kevin Pratt is an assistant professor at the Cornell University Department of Architecture.*

# Fuzzy Metrics

*Fuzzy: hairy, furry, fluffy, downy, wooly, blurry, unclear, nebulous, hazy, vague, misty, bleary, indistinct, uncertain, ambiguous, unclear, confused.*[1]

## Fuzziness

At first glance it seems that mathematics is all about clarity, while *fuzziness* implies the opposite: a softness of touch, the sensuality of something enjoyably fluffy, or even cute, covered with furry haze.[2] It seems improbable that fuzziness could be a concept used in applied mathematics as a method of specific problem solving, given that mathematics (especially in the design disciplines) is usually associated with precision, numerical determinism, and the possibility for a singular truth. "Design truth"—a scary thought, one might think, as the glow of numerical matrices encases the design world in an impenetrable, and yet fuzzy, veil of data. But while optimization routines and partial feedback loops wrestle with the beauty of objectified mathematical topologies, the ambiguities encompassed by a contemporary architectural practice embedded in a planetary biosphere are growing exponentially.

There are other ways to interpret fuzzy: blurry, uncertain, confusing.[1] Here we are on firmer (or at least more familiar) semantic ground. So, as a kind of disciplinary reflex to the memetic culture of the 21st century,[3] we have already constructed, analogically, a literalization of blurriness. Hairiness or fuzziness as a formal, experiential, or atmospheric aspect of design has emerged as yet another breed of contemporary production, strongly associated with the notion of style, exemplified by such buildings as British Pavilion at the 2010 Shanghai Expo by Heatherwick Studio. Yet our interest in thinking about fuzziness lies elsewhere. It lies in using computational protocols to investigate a multilayered stochastic network of intuitive and observed patterns. We understand such a matrix as a territory of probability, a layering of intervals, and not as a singular underpinning for globally computable solutions. This is a merged territory between the mathematical and the empirical; a patch system of partially computable protocols and observed concurrences between the built and natural world.

## "The map is not the territory"[4]

However, taking such a stochastic approach requires coming to terms with a contemporary shift in the disciplinary territory of architecture. The discipline of architecture constructs itself between the twinned poles of art and science, producing a schizophrenic condition characterized by an attraction to, and repulsion from, both the determinacy of the quanta and the ineffability of the sublime. Of late, the availability and ubiquity of digital methods has driven the profession to adopt tools incubated in departments of engineering and computer science, while at the same time creating a peculiar resistance to explicit modes of analysis. Thus, as the outside pushes in, some notion of disciplinary singularity attempts to reassert itself, and pushes out. One casualty of such resistance has been the systemic assimilation, within the discipline, of ecological thinking in the service of global sustainability, since sustainability necessitates some acknowledgment of the concept of the computable metric as a means to measure the potential impacts of design on the biosphere.

The reluctance to embrace such pressures and accept certain quantitative methods has its roots in a fear of numerical determinism, is husbanded by a habitual obsession with convention, and buttressed by the fear of loss of identity. Yet our fussy disciplinary boundaries need to be more fuzzy and inclusive of new knowledge. In the end, this will depend on understanding that just because phenomena can be quantified (or even qualified) does not mean that their interactions and ultimate effects can be determined with any certainty over time, and further that such uncertainty does not imply illegibility. Ironically, the existence of such a middle ground, between determinacy and disorder, has been accepted and systematically studied in other disciplines—especially in applied mathematics—for decades.

In advanced mathematics the terms "fuzzy system" and "fuzzy set" refer to an approximate mode of reasoning; to a non-binary logic based on the notion of dynamic range, of an interval with elastically modifiable boundaries. Imprecision and gradient are fuzzy. A partial truth has greater value, because it admits to indeterminacy and can thus be used in a probabilistic analysis. The potential for degrees of a multiplicity of simultaneous memberships in disparate groups (intervals) is the basis for this particular expansion on classical set theory. It is, at root, a stochastic vision of reality, in which logical chains branch and intertwine, forming thickets of probable outcomes. Fuzzy logic theory[5] has enabled advancement in the fields of probability theory, data and knowledge mining, pattern recognition, robotics, artificial intelligence, genetic algorithms, non-linear dynamic analysis, forecasting, simulation, and cognitive psychology. Fuzzy sets are a cornerstone of the mathematics of uncertainty. And the world *is* uncertain. Despite this fact, contemporary building practice tends to describe architecture with certainty as an objects situated in a spatial and cultural field, objects contained within closed systems having definable boundaries. Ecology, on the other hand, posits that all entities within the system have thermodynamic relationships to each other and are bound together in complex systems of energy and information exchange: an ecosystem. And as the boundaries of ecosystems are uncertain, they are open and transient.[6] Without such dynamism there could be no change, no evolution; our planet would be static and cold. The systemic boundaries in

ecology are nonexclusive and temporal. Just like in fuzzy sets. But in contrast
the production of a particular design necessarily and inescapably dictates distinct
boundaries to discreet objects. The process of design, with its dependence on an *a
priori* vision of the future, stands in opposition the mindlessly effective processes
of evolution. Thus the question becomes: how can architectural objects be "fuzzed"
into the site? How can they nest in hierarchical sets of niche based relationships
while maintaining the potential for a plurality of memberships in the future? In
other words, how can they be designed to retain the ability to adapt to an uncertain
future? One of the issues is that the disciplinary notion of "architectural site"
systemically resists this temporality, the fuzziness of an evolving niche. Context is
generally reduced to an abstraction of the site conditions, rendered as a culturally
constructed understanding of the ground, as either palimpsest, analogic geometry,
or infinitely occupiable surface. The necessity to respond and adapt to specific
dynamic environments (from the bio-synergetic point of view) requires us to
expand the definition of a context, to treat it as a series of nested complex systems
embedded into larger patterns of dynamic exchange. To, in effect, construct the
cultural through an understanding of ecology, and abandon the fixed idea of *place*
in favor a fuzzy notion of indeterminate and spatially concurrent *places*.

## The Computability of Patched Objecthood

Architecture is by default a component based practice, its efficacy bound by
the economics of repetitive construction. Increase in component variation tends
to be driven by a desire for distinctiveness and ornament, whereas a decrease in
variation (often termed "value engineering") is all too often driven by the need for
economic viability. Due to the evolution of parametric digital tools and techniques
one can (easily) produce an unlimited amount of variation, resulting in an expressive
diversity of parts. Given the preponderance of formal concerns that seem to be a
somatic imperative of contemporary practice, this reliance on digital geometric
mutability tends to produce internally self-referential, non-scalar systems with low
information content[7] (in that the essential *point* of differences between parts remains
mysterious) and a need for a high degree of construction customization. Ironically,
the fundamental disconnect between the abstraction of computational topology
and the concreteness of the built environment, when coupled with a capacity for
generative multiplicity, all too often leads to projects whose inanity is matched only
by a commitment to a heroic, baroque un-constructability.

Yet specific information (such as climate, structural, or material resistance)
does suggest a way to produce concrete information and effects through the use
of analytic data as input for inquiry. Unfortunately, a current tendency to embed
multiple performative and programmatic requirements into singular mutable
elements, which require a high degree of specificity, stands in contradiction to the
need for adaptation over time. Put more simply, we cannot overcome the "inanity
problem" merely by introducing "performance" as a variable that controls one aspect
of the multitude. Such an approach leads to a *hyper-specificity* that has only a low
degree of adaptability and limited time-based effects.

Therefore the methods by which we define adaptive strategies on multiple
nested and interlinked scales are critical. And how these strategies respond to the

notion of energy capital and power usage—as well as a desire for material effects in support of social systems—could demonstrate a different approach in using ecology to anticipate an architecture that is, within a certain lifespan, tightly bound to the specificity of place; yet not hyper-specific in and of itself (in other words, systemically, if not at the component level: fuzzy). This logic anticipates the need for a system of parts having the ability to dynamically transform both during the process of design and construction and throughout its functional lifespan. It inspires us to rethink architectural material and its componentization in more complex way. It suggests a need for biomimetic strategies, using biomimetic process not for the creation of a formal analogy but to develop an understanding of performance, systemic logic, and materiality, where component evolution produces variation through degrees of adaptive mutation in multiple, loosely bound layers, and not within a single, continuous surface. At the most basic level it requires us to recognize that hierarchy, which is a distinguishing feature of all ecosystems[8] will be a necessary organizational principle of architectural *eco-logic*.

## Green Negligee

Some suggestion of how such processes might play themselves out can be gleaned by looking at a project we have named[9] *Green Negligee*. The Negligee is a modular retrofit system selectively attached to prefabricated concrete panel housing blocs in Petrzalka, Slovakia. The *Green Negligee* attempts to address social, urbanistic, and ecological problems created by the area's top-down CIAM-inspired compositional and organizational schema, while at the same time dealing with energy consumption issues stemming from the fact that the un-insulated concrete building blocks perform poorly in Slovakia's temperate climate.

**Aerial view of the Green Negligee**, EPIPHYTE Lab: Tensile network, component systems, energy harvesting devices, plantings, and communal apartment blocks.

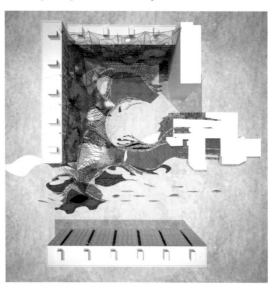

Constructed across the Danube from Bratislava (the de facto capitol of the Slovak Republic) in the sixties and seventies, as a communitarian parallel to the modernist, social democratic model of a "functional" city, Petrzalka is an example of a state-controlled planning process that resulted in rigid programmatic segregation and a compositional urban scheme dominated by the application of a panelized prefabricated concrete system to the task of social engineering. Despite the stigma usually attached to this type of social housing, the real estate itself has become quite valuable due its proximity to the city center and shifts in post-Soviet demographics. The privatization of state owned apartment blocks with centralized utility systems has created ambiguities about the extent of ownership beyond the line of the single apartment. Privatization has also led to questionable ownership of auxiliary spaces and energy systems, neglect, and maintenance problems, as well as imposing on residents the human costs of living in fundamentally unsustainable buildings. The issue of landscape ownership is particularly problematic. Historically the district was used for viticulture; during the era of collective ownership, the strong cultural need to transform the ground within the stark figure of the rectilinear plan was channeled into cultivation, planting, and gardening. In the post-Soviet era, this desire has been suppressed by the loss of coherent ownership of public spaces. Thus, because of the general deterioration of the collective, nature is reasserting itself. Every crack is overgrown and filled with weeds. As a result, the figure-ground is dissolving, adding textural and spatial complexities.

The effect of the weeds is fuzzy. The *Green Negligee* project takes its inspiration from these weeds. The purpose of the *Green Negligee* is to leverage the embedded (yet currently suppressed) social desire for collective cultivation and leisure, and the political and economic ad-hoc social conditions that have developed since the fall of communism, to create a system that can be used to engender a sustainable future for the Petrzalka district. It attempts to accomplish this by blurring the hard boundary between the buildings and the landscape with lightweight, secondary facade elements that host a variety of low-maintenance quasi-naturalistic systems, energy harvesting devices and native biotic species that, in their aggregation, create alternatives to installed building service systems, new social spaces, and opportunities for emergent biodiversity.

These social spaces bind the disjointed and atomized physical spaces of the existing blocs into semi-autonomous zones of habitation that nest into larger, pre-existing ecological systems that define the district as a whole.

Given this desire to integrate the designed and ecologically and socially pre-existent, the first step in the design process was to understand the dynamic environment that exists, currently, on the site. To create, in effect, a layered dynamic map of the site that could function, virtually, as a kind of test bed to evaluate potential methods of intervention. This test bed was constructed by aggregating existing site information in a four-dimensional digital model, while running simulations on the model to deduce the existence of conditions that would eventually influence the nature of intervention. In parallel, we gathered information about existing economic and social systems, paying particular attention to the way that modes of ownership in the post-Soviet era have created rather novel structures for collective decision making and programmatic re-appropriation of existing functional spaces. We also surveyed existing building service and structural systems, assembling a picture of the way that the existing engineered systems both meet (or fail to meet) the basic needs of the inhabitants, and how these systems interact with both larger engineered and natural systems that serve and define the entire region.

A few key insights came out of this process. One: that the collapse of a top-down authority has led to atomistic patterns of ownership, and that pressures from the transition to a market-based economy has led to the formation of ad-hoc decision making structures at the scale of the building, as well as localized uncoordinated reprogramming, meaning that efforts that require much coordination at the macro- or site scale are impractical. Two: that the population is beginning to reorganize at the local scale to oppose the co-option of public space by external market forces, but it they lacks any particular physical mechanism to effect its plans. Three: that existing service systems are both inadequate and almost completely dependent on off-site sources and sinks to generate energy and dispose of wastes, meaning that local ecosystem services remain largely untapped. Four: that the physical layout of the buildings and the landscape, in interaction with climatic and hydrological forces, create multiple overlapping zones for opportunistic intervention, which reveal themselves through dynamic mapping processes. In other words, there exists, between figure and ground, a third zone, defined by the ephemeral forces of sun, wind, and water, and uncaptured by existing modes of bureaucratic control: an unoccupied niche.

**Paramatric Datascape**, EPIPHYTE Lab: Example of dynamic environmental mapping technique used to discover the ephemeral hidden landscapes formed by the interaction of climate and site. These invisible boundary conditions are determined based on radiation mapping and computational fluid dynamics analysis. They define niches where componentized energy and waste processing systems would be more or less functional and could be deployed. The goal is to define zones of overlap, or gradients, where viticulture, wind harvesting, and gray-water filtration are effective.

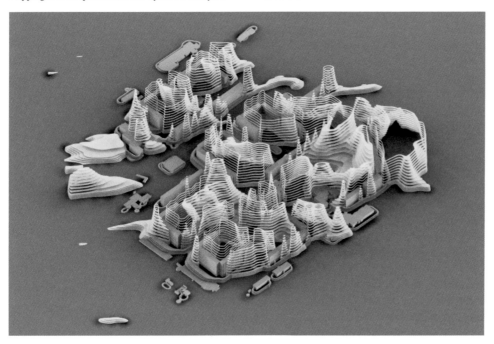

Given that, axiomatically, nature abhors a vacuum, we designed a system to fill that niche. Using the dynamic digital map as a base model, we have proposed a hierarchical system of parts that can be implemented at the sub-building scale, and then be aggregated to interlock both with the larger built environment and the existing landscape. The primary component system forms tensile cable networks that create a secondary surface between ground and facade—a host for the functional systems that produce both spatial effect and systematic integration. These networks enable a new form of landscape distribution, subdivision, and ownership as the vertical tensile system transforms into an obliquely malleable catenary landform. This modular net is itself anchored to the existing buildings which, due to their method of construction, are massively over-structured and are thus able to bear significant additional loads and the existing landscape, which is, for the most part, intermittently occupied and given over to automobile parking.

The form of the net is developed using relaxation algorithms applied to boundary conditions between areas of relative environmental and programmatic differentiation revealed by the digital map of the site. Given that in any defined zone a multiplicity of these boundary conditions exist (between areas of lesser and greater turbulence, available radiation, existing view corridors, etc.), particular surfaces and different subdivision patterns can be selected to create terrains that are more or less suited to different purposes—to form enclosures, private winter-gardens, and semi-enclosed public spaces, to be hosts for localized viticulture and other water-purifying horticulture, and to support localized energy-generating devices.

Systems of secondary components populate the nets. They operate according to a patch logic, defined by intervals associated with particular ranges of performance. This allows aggregated systems to intertwine, producing second-order architectural and spatial effects. Potential component distributions are determined through interaction with the digital map, which delineates *fuzzy* zones of relative effectiveness, and their specific layout derived from matching these potentialities with programmatic and formal intent.

The components are not integrated into the cable network: rather they overlay the network in a loose pattern, meaning that they do not require a geometric specificity that is dependent on the underlying geometry of the net itself. The multiple component types have a myriad of functional overlaps, including the collection of water, the transformation of wind and solar energy into electricity or mechanical energy, and the provision of armatures to support both biotic communities and the growth media they require. Each of the secondary component types has a definite interval of variation, which is again governed by material properties, methods of assembly, and functional constraints. Because the components are relatively small and loosely attached to the net, it is imagined that they could be reconfigured without necessarily disrupting the system as a whole during a functional lifespan.

The components themselves aggregate into larger overlapping systems. They tend to organize themselves sectionally, and spread horizontally to define space. An example of such an aggregation might be: wind-powered devices at higher elevations to take advantage of prevailing winds (which come from the northeast) and power existing building systems and devices like lights and pumps that are part of the network. Shingles, of different types, that congregate on the near vertical surface of the network near the facade to form a secondary system of enclosure to both shade and trap solar radiation. A mixture of trellis and planter components, occurring where the network turns horizontal, which capture and filter both runoff and graywater, host grape vines that allow for localized viticulture, and create a semi-enclosed public space. The component network is married to a landscape that has been reconfigured using berms, swales, and gabions to both reinforce the attributes of the public spaces created and further store and process runoff water descending from the component patchwork. The landscape manipulation also serves to contain new spaces, which are necessary to service the new systems. Such a system could begin life occurring across a single structural bay of a building, and expand over time as both financing and political will become available.

**Loose Fit Modularity**, EPIPHYTE Lab: The adaptive logic of the overall system negotiates between environmental variables and the collective desires of the building co-op.

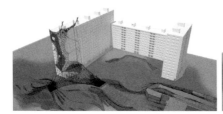
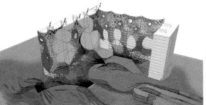

**Formal Study**, EPIPHYTE Lab: Relaxation of lightweight
tensile system network and pattern distribution logic for
vibro-wind components according to wind speed data.

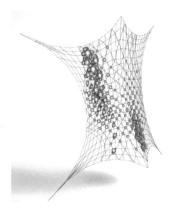

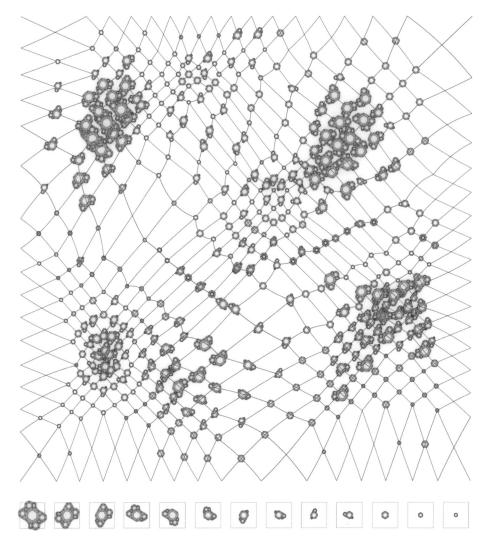

# Fuzzy Conclusions

It is important to understand that the configuration described above does not so much represent a singular design, which would be repeated ad infinitum across the larger site, but rather a particular scenario that might fit a localized set of conditions and intents. The process of making a "best guess" at a configuration suitable to a particular locale might be best described as making a series of choices at each level of the system hierarchy from a set of fuzzy potentialities—delineated by overlapping sets of analytical and observational data—that emerge from the indeterminate analysis. Because the digital representation of any particular scenario is parametric, the systems can, during the design phase, be "tuned down" and tested, that is, a series of scenarios can subjected to the same analytical procedures that were applied to the site before potential the intervention has been inserted. The hierarchical organization and loose fit between systemic levels also allows for a localized specificity that enables the system to scale all the way down to the human dimension, and be reconfigured over time. For example, imagine if a fairly large horizontal area of the cable net has been populated with trellis and planter components creating an overhead garden. If, in the future, a section of the public space under this system is converted to a playground, the patch of network above it can be covered with shingle, either in place of or above the plants, to form a pavilion of sorts that would enable children to play in the rain. Although this example seems rather prosaic, it is worth remembering that, ultimately, the point of the system is not to create the appearance of adaptability, or an image of green architecture to be sold to prospective investors, but rather to create some kind of, however imperfect, armature that supports potential methods of sustainable living that are developed out of the quotidian process of everyday life itself.

Rather than imagining the intricacies of form, the intent is to construct a system logic imbued with both formal and performative tendencies, while retaining enough malleability to escape the particuarity of a single instantiation. It is, perhaps, this tension between intent (system) and available modes of representation (image) that explains why the discipline of architecture has struggled to assimilate the idea that a project can be carefully designed, and yet resist a definitive tectonic formulation. It is, after all, difficult to apply traditional ways of making architectural judgments (relative proportionality, compositional effect, etc.) about the relative merits of a particular design to a proposal that remains, even during the course of its occupied life, fuzzy. It is here that we come to the most difficult piece of interdisciplinary thinking that, as architects, we have to accept, if we are to seize the territory made available made available to us by the intersection of computational potential and systemic, ecological modes of thought. It is simply this: we have to expand our definition of beauty and to acknowledge potentiality, to see value in systems that can become, outside of our direct control, something remarkable. If you ask a mathematician whether or not this:

$$\int_a^b f(x)\, dx$$

(the definitive form of the integral) is beautiful, she will tell you yes. Not because of the way the ink has arranged itself on the page, or even because, as a method, the integral represents a particularly elegant way of solving a particular problem, but because the definitive integral is a fundamental piece of a system (the calculus) that enables anyone to act, freely, as a lever to move the systems that create the world.

**Acknowledgments**

The *Green Negligee* project was in part supported by the Arnold W. Brunner Grant AIA NY Chapter.

Epiphyte Lab's project participants: Principal Investigators Dana Čupková & Kevin Pratt (Design and Production Team) / Michael Esposito, Travis Fitch, Shujian Jian, Siyuan Ye, Daniel Marino, Karbi Chan Yuet, Jeremy Burk (Analysis Team) / Andrew Heumann, Sebastian Hernandez. Special thanks to Francis Moon, Ephrahim Garcia. and William Jewell for their feedback.

**Endnotes**

1   English Thesaurus, Microsoft Word (Microsoft 2010).
2   <http://en.wikipedia.org/wiki/Lolcat>
3   See: *Cultural Software: A Theory of Ideology* by J.M. Balkin (New Haven: Yale University Press, 1998) and *Viruses of the Mind* by Richard Dawkins (Seattle: Integral press, 1991).
4   Alfred Korzybski's original quote (1931) is cited by Gregory Bateson, in *Steps to an Ecology of Mind* (Chicago, IL: University of Chicago Press, 1972) where he explores notions of subjective representations of objective realities: <http://en.wikipedia.org/wiki/Map-territory_relation>
5   Fuzzy mathematics were originally discussed by Zadeh Lotfi, in "Fuzzy Sets," in *Information and Control*, Vol. 8 (New York: Academic Press, 1965), and "Fuzzy Algorithms," in *Information and Control*, no.12, 1968, pp. 94–102.
6   The example of a cattail comes to mind. Is cattail part of a land system or a water system? The answer is either—depending. Depending on water level and degree of rainfall the cattail adapts.
7   "The notion of the amount of information attaches itself very naturally to a classical notion in statistical mechanics: that of entropy. Just as the amount of information in a system is a measure of its degree of organization, so the entropy of a system is a measure of its degree of disorganization." Norbert Weiner, *Cybernetics or Control and Communication in the Animal and the Machine* (Boston, MA: MIT Press, 1948).
8   Explained perhaps most eloquently by H.T. Odum, in the fourth chapter of *Environment Power and Society* (NY: Wiley & Sons, 1971)
9   With posthumous apologies to both F.L. Olmstead and the city of Boston.

# Gang Chen

*is an assistant professor in the Department of Earth and Atmospheric Sciences at Cornell University. He teaches atmospheric dynamics and climate dynamics. He researches global atmospheric circulation and climate change by developing and analyzing simple and comprehensive computer models from the laws of mathematics, physics, and chemistry.*

# Predictability of the Atmosphere

Despite the chaotic nature of the atmosphere and the complexity involved in reconciling the motion of water, air masses, the spinning Earth, and solar radiation, atmospheric forecasts are much more accurate than the prediction of many other chaotic systems, such as elections or the stock market. The predictability of the atmosphere is special in that it relies on both observed (instrument derived) and mathematical (equation derived) inputs to yield results. Both inputs have been crucial over the past few decades, for the dramatically improved daily or weekly weather forecasts.

While it remains impossible to predict an individual weather event beyond a month—owing to the sensitivities of a chaotic system to small errors in the initial conditions—it is possible to predict the changes of a collection of weather events over decades with climate warming. This long-term prediction is possible because these collective changes of weather events are fundamentally dominated by the changes in the energy balance of the Earth's climate system, rather than the fluctuations induced by chaos.

Much of meteorology was developed as applications of mathematics and physics to the motion of the atmosphere. Using Sir Isaac Newton's laws of motion, one may readily conceive that the motion of the atmosphere can be predicted with certainty as the motion of macroscopic objects, such as the stars, planets, or aircrafts. For example, by interpreting and synthesizing the information contained in thousands of weather maps, an experienced meteorologist was able to develop an empirical picture of the initial direction and speed of various weather patterns. The weather was predicted by looking for similar weather patterns from past records, and then, extrapolating forward using basic arithmetic: the known quantities of distance to travel ($d$), and speed of a weather system ($c$), yielding the time to arrive at the destination ($t = d/c$).

In the 1920s, an English meteorologist, Lewis Fry Richardson, pioneered numerical weather prediction by attempting to forecast local weather using direct computation methods. Using a mathematical model and inputting data for the principal features of the atmosphere, Richardson attempted to predict the local weather over the course of the following six hours. For example, one can predict the changes of surface pressure ($ps$) from a discretized representation of the rate of change in a column of air mass: *convergence of column integrated air mass,*

The Earth showing sea-level pressure or Rossby wave depressions (blue) and crests (orange), mapped using the grids of longitude and latitude on December 27, 2010. The blue color (low pressure) indicates the locations of storms, and the fluctuations from blue to red are atmospheric waves. The red solid lines highlight North America. Courtesy of the author.

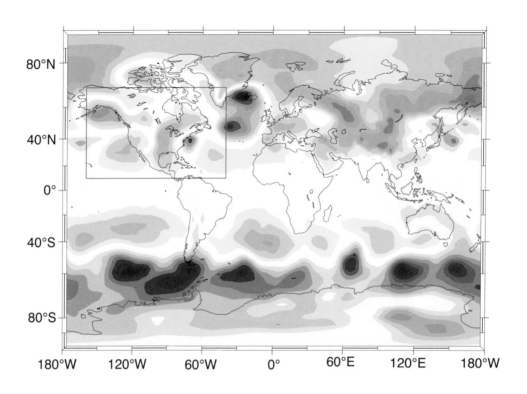

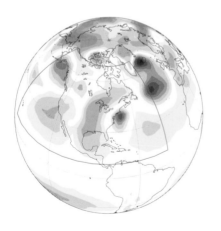
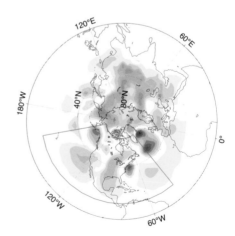

and the convergence of air mass can be determined by the current state of the atmosphere. The model resulted in an erroneous conclusion: by failing to exclude unphysical pressure surges, it predicted a huge rise in pressure—larger than the pressure increase from the center of Hurricane Katrina to its edge—while the actual pressure remained static. Despite these results, Richardson's forecast method later proved to be essentially accurate.[1] This remarkable achievement opened the door to the era of numerical weather forecast by discretizing the differential equations of the atmospheric motion necessary for weather prediction.

Since the 1950s, computer models have been widely used in meteorology and climate science. There are generally two types of computer models: those that focus on short-term (e.g., a week) weather prediction in operational numerical weather forecast and those that concentrate on long-term (e.g., a century) climate prediction in the models of Intergovernmental Panel on Climate Change (IPCC) Assessment Reports. Both types of weather forecast models and climate models apply numerically the basic laws of mathematics, physics, and chemistry to describe the atmosphere and other components of the Earth's climate system.

The atmosphere fluctuates from day to day, and this fluctuation imprints on the pressure at sea level, which in turn reflects the fluctuation of the weight of air masses above. Meteorologists generally map the global distribution of this pressure by longitude and latitude.

The roughly daily fluctuation between the high (red) and low (blue) pressure is analogous to the crest and trough of traveling waves after a stone is thrown into the lake: the low-pressure center indicates the location of a storm. These *Rossby waves* are key components of the atmosphere, their behavior provides the primary source of predictability for weather patterns.

The atmosphere is divided into finite grid boxes by longitude, latitude, and height; the discretized differential equations predict the changes of energy, mass, momentum, water, and chemical species within each grid box and the exchanges among neighboring boxes.

Inside each grid box, radiation and chemical reactions are calculated from the laws of physics and chemistry. For example, the emission, transfer, scattering, and absorption of the solar radiation and terrestrial infrared emission are calculated from the physical laws of electromagnetic waves traveling through the atmosphere. Meanwhile, the absorption of radiation by greenhouse gases such as water vapor or carbon dioxide is determined by their molecular structures and chemical characteristics, which have been established in chemistry.

Additionally, some subgrid scale processes are empirically parameterized (i.e., *subgrid parameterization*) on the basis of the notion that a collection of random events can produce a predictable average effect from their common characteristics. While a circulation larger than the size of a model grid box can be directly calculated by the governing equations, a circulation smaller than the size of a model grid box has to be empirically calculated based on the general characteristics of the specific grid box. An example from electoral prediction can illustrate this point: while it is difficult to predict which party any individual citizen will vote for in a presidential election, it is possible to predict the winning party for a given state, based on its demography.

**Waves in a Large Free Sphere of Water**, Don Pettit. These images of a sphere of water in zero gravity show a singular surface wave behavior when a puff of air is blown across its surface. Multiple wave occurrences happen on the Earth simultaneously, resulting in a more dynamic and chaotic system than this simulation. Courtesy of NASA. (Source: http://spaceflightsystems. grc.nasa.gov/WaterBalloon/)

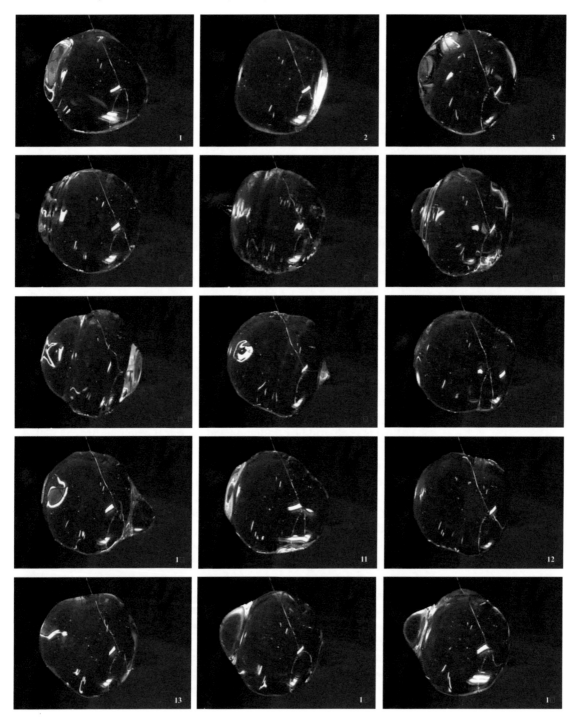

Analogously, clouds, whose size are often less than the size of model grid box can be simply represented in the computer models by the parameters such as its size and height, the number of water droplets in the cloud, and other characteristics. The relationship between the clouds and these cloud parameters are determined by field campaigns from aircrafts, satellite observations, or cloud-resolving numerical models. The relationship between cloud parameters and observations is used in calculating the radiative budget of the atmosphere or the microphysical processes for rainfall or snowfall. As it is impossible to describe mathematically these cloud characteristics precisely—because of their range in size from a water droplet to a cloud of several hundred kilometers—the subgrid scale parameterizations are a major source of uncertainty in these models.

The use of computer modeling for prediction prompted the intriguing realization that a more nuanced understanding of the interrelatedness of atmospheric inputs was necessary for the accuracy of the results. Analysis of computer modeling results showed that a forecast outcome using deterministic physical laws is very sensitive to the initial conditions of a numerical calculation. With slightly different initial conditions or a small error in monitoring the current state of the atmosphere, the forecast results for a future weather pattern may be entirely different due to the chaotic nature of the atmosphere. Consequently, weather prediction capacity shifted from being deterministic to being probabilistic, by allowing a small range of errors in monitoring the initial state of the atmosphere. Deterministic methods relied on the accuracy of the input in the algorithm to produce the prediction: mathematically speaking, given a specific input, the same output will always result. Probabilistic methods attempt to incorporate uncertainty into the algorithm by using logical probabilities instead of crisp true-false values, and through the inclusion of degrees and ranges of interpretation based on previous occurrences.

**Finite grid box divisions** are based on latitude, longitude, and height. Weather forecast models and climate models are the numerical discretization of the basic laws of mathematics, physics, and chemistry for the atmosphere and other components of the Earth's climate system. Courtesy of Alison Nash.

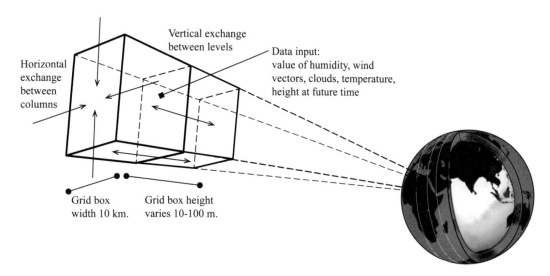

From Newton's law of motion, the acceleration of wind ($a$) can be determined by their relationship to the total forces ($F$) exerted on the air mass ($a = F/m$). If we are certain of the initial conditions and know the exact forces acting on the atmosphere, the changes of air motion can be predicted without any errors. However, errors in initial conditions are inevitable and inherently part of using observational instruments. These errors will compound exponentially in a chaotic system like the atmosphere, leading to the lack of accurate predictions for individual weather systems beyond a couple of weeks.

By using a traditional method of prediction: the extrapolation of traveling Rossby waves forward in time, the atmosphere can be predicted, to some extent. The holiday blizzard on December 27–29, 2010 can be used as an example of this method.

**December 27–29, 2010 sea-level pressure in the North America region highlighted in red previously**. Note a major storm in blue on the East Coast of the United States. The arrows describe the magnitude and direction of surface winds. Courtesy of the author.

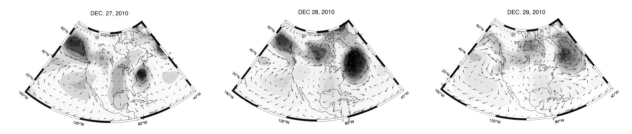

A notable storm (blue) is seen to move northeastward along the East Coast of the United States. A jet stream can be identified along the eastern coastline, guiding the motion of the storm. The arrival of a storm may be predictable by an extrapolation of past motion forward in time, similar to the way the arrival of a train can be calculated by a departure-time train schedule if the distance and speed are known.

However, the accuracy of this prediction is deteriorated by chaos inherent in the atmosphere. As the weather systems build from the potential energy from differential solar heating ranging from the equator to the poles, atmospheric waves occasionally break down nonlinearly due to the saturation in wave amplitude, in a process similar to the breaking waves at the shore, resulting in a chaotic atmosphere.

Further challenging to prediction is the simultaneously linear and nonlinear nature of the atmosphere: this characteristic makes weather prediction possible but potentially uncertain. As in the previous example, the speed of the traveling Rossby waves provides a source of predictability; however, the waves occasionally break down when their amplitude is saturated; therefore, the source of predictability is lost. The conditions for these wave breakings are highly nonlinear and unpredictable and are evidence of the chaos inherent in the atmosphere.

Edward Norton Lorenz (1917–2008) at MIT first pointed out the sensitivity of deterministic numerical weather forecast methods to initial conditions. In a forecast experiment in the 1960s, he found that a tiny change of a non-dimensionalized initial condition from the full .506127 to .506 resulted in a completely different weather scenario. Commenting on this observation, he wrote that, "one meteorologist remarked that if the theory were correct, one flap of a seagull's wings could change the course of weather forever."[2] Known popularly as the "butterfly effect," this result can be illustrated in two computer simulations. The computer models are identical, except for a slight difference in the initial conditions

**Two computer simulations show the sensitivity of the evolution of storms to initial states of the atmosphere.** The figure shows the sea-level pressure (color) and surface winds (arrows) on days 1, 10, and 20 from very similar storm-free quiescent initial states. The two computer models are identical, except for a slight difference in initial conditions; the resulting duration of the storms in the bottom panel is longer. Courtesy of the author.

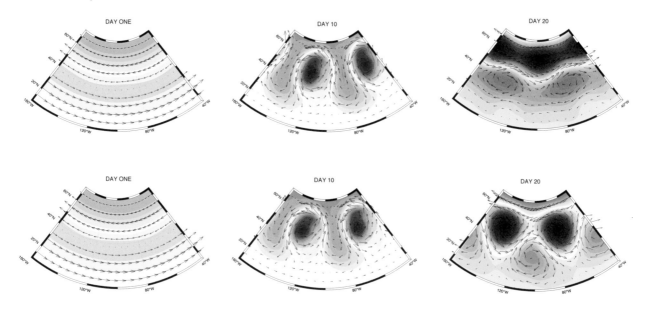

Starting from very similar storm-free quiescent states of the atmosphere, the storms observed on day 10 are much alike. The weather patterns are completely different on day 20: the overall duration of the storms in one simulation is much longer. The chaotic nature of the atmosphere presents challenges to accurate prediction of weather patterns on day 20, only using methods of extrapolation from the weather data on day 10.

As a result, while the atmosphere is fundamentally governed by deterministic Newtonian laws, the forecast of the atmosphere is generally expressed in terms of probability or chance. For instance, National Weather Service may announce that the thunderstorm "probability" tomorrow is 10 percent, or the IPCC Fourth Assessment Report concludes that global warming in the past few decades is "very likely" caused by humans.

In practice, multiple weather forecast experiments are carried out to estimate the effect of small errors in initial conditions (e.g., the flapping of a butterfly's wing) on the forecast results, and the predicted weather is expressed in probability of future weather patterns. On a larger scale, a mean climate is calculated from a collection of chaotic weather events. We know with certainty, for instance, that the summer in year 2050 will be warmer than the winter of that year, and this is because the summer hemisphere receives more solar radiation than the winter hemisphere. As such, a change in atmospheric radiation due to increased greenhouse gases will alter the energy balance in the Earth's climate, allowing atmospheric scientists to forecast future climate change in spite of the chaotic nature of the atmosphere. The errors in the parameterized processes, such as the geographic distribution of clouds, affect the accuracy of the Earth's future climate, simulated in a model in a chaotic way. For example, a bias in the global cloud coverage can affect the albedo (i.e., the fraction of incident radiation that is reflected by a surface) of the planet Earth. The resultant radiative balance in the Earth's climate affects the weather systems that transport the energy that balances the differential radiative heating from the sun, from the low latitudes to the polar region.

**Improved resolution of computer models shows more detailed information for small-scale atmospheric features**. Courtesy of the author.

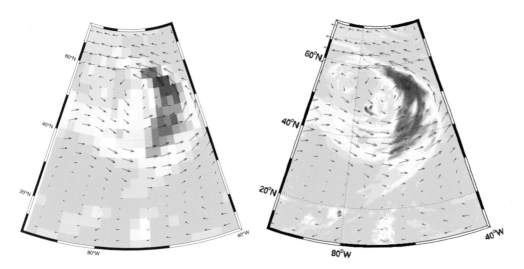

The primary challenge in predicting weather and climate lies in the uncertainties in the parameterized processes and the propagation of the uncertainties in a chaotic atmosphere over time. These uncertainties arise not only because we cannot observe the atmospheric conditions exactly due to lack of instrumental precision, but also because the atmospheric phenomena of interest range from the planetary scale to the size of a cloud water-droplet, which is impossible to resolve exactly in a computer model. These inaccuracies may compound in a nonlinear system, leading to different states in a few weeks. However, a mean climate can be obtained during a time average due to the dominant control of the radiative balance of the climate system rather than individual random events.

The accuracy of the computer model has improved dramatically over the past few decades, thanks to the exponential increase of computing power. One immediate consequence of increased realism is that more small-scale atmospheric features can be resolved in a higher-resolution model with a smaller size of grid box.

It is expected that extreme weather events, such as winter blizzards, hurricanes, or heat waves, will be better represented in a computer model with finer resolution. Representing these events is a major challenge to the current generation of computer models. However, as it is generally agreed among meteorologists that extreme weather will be more likely to occur as a consequence of climate warming, the enhanced computer models will need to continue improving our ability to predict weather patterns in order to overcome the inevitable increasing uncertainty of the weather.

**Endnotes**

1  Peter Lynch, "Margules' Tendency Equation and Richardson's Forecast," *Weather* 58, (May 2003): 186–193.
2  Edward N. Lorenz, "Deterministic Nonperiodic Flow," *Journal of the Atmospheric Sciences* 20, no. 2 (March 1963): 130–141.

## R&Sie(n)/François Roche

*R&Sie(n) is an architectural practice founded in 1989 by François
Roche and Stéphanie Lavaux. R&Sie(n) unfold their protocols through
the restaging of different kinds of contemporary relationships: aesthetic,
machinist, computational, organics, biological, and even artificial.
They consider architectural identity as emanating from principles of
uncertainty defined through provisional processes and forms in which
animism, vitalism, and mechanism become vectors of dynamic mutations.
François Roche is currently a research professor at Columbia University
(since 2005). In 2010, he was a visiting critic at Cornell University and
co-taught a studio titled Mutations, with Caroline O'Donnell.*

# Experimentation on Human Park [1]

Looking beyond a strictly scientific and architectural horizon, and reading beyond the usual philosophical benchmarks, it is tempting, and indeed enlightening, to envisage a modus operandi from a metaphorical and strategic angle when exploring the "chemistry of bodies," often envisaged as an element liable to disturb and alter linear, authoritarian logics, to reach what we might call *swarm intelligence* aggregations.[2] Similarly tempted, we look at the relationship of the body to space, and even more so, of bodies in their social relation: not just their interrelation, within a given cell, but also their intrarelation as part of an osmosis with others. This results in an architecture that plays with conformism and conventions: all bywords of the "undisciplined" conception of production, in its articulation of the collective and the political.

The research *An Architecture des "Humeurs"* constitutes the second leg (after *I've Heard About*, in 2005) of an architectural voyage (in the spirit of Thomas More's Utopia) federating the skills of scientists from a host of disciplines (mathematics, physics, neurobiology, computations, scripts,[3] nanotechnologies,[4] robotic, etc.). This exploration is an attempt to articulate the real and/or fictional link between geographical situations and the narrative structures capable of transforming them. Specifically, the focus here is on using nanotechnology to collect physiological data from all participants to prepare and model, by means of these "moods"—a (post)modern translation of Hippocrates's humors—the foundations of an architecture in permanent mutation, modeled (and modulated) by our unconscious. It is an investigation into an architecture of uncertainty and non-determination.

While this is not a sequel to the "I've Heard About" show held by the MAM (Paris Municipal Modern Art Museum) in 2005, that first research did explore the relationship between physiology, computation, and indeterminism, in the sense of its genesis. "I've Heard About" sought to understand and write (in the sense of writing code) biological geometries that mimic natural ones. The predominant figure was that of coral and its growth. This second piece goes beyond that representation, since we have already studied the factors that condition the emergence of such a geometry. These factors are the principles of exchange—dynamic principles based on a system's immanent forces, to capture the chemistry of the body as an element that can disturb and alter linear logics. Thus, the logics of authorities replace a top-down approach with a bottom-up one.

The *Architecture of Humors*—a double-entendre, meaning both mood and fluid—is an interrogation of the confused region of the psyche that lies between pleasure/desire and need/want, by detecting physiological signals based on neuro-biological secretions and thus realize a "chemistry of humors," treating future property buyers as inputs, who generate a range of diverse, inhabitable morphologies and the relationships between them. The groundwork comes from a rereading of the "Malentendus" inherent in the expression of human desire. Those who traverse public space through the ability to express a choice by means of language, on the surface of things, and those who are underlying and perhaps more disturbing, but just as valid. By means of the latter, we can appraise the body as a desiring machine with its own chemistry: dopamine, hydrocortisone, melatonin, adrenaline, and other molecules secreted by the body itself that are imperceptibly anterior to the consciousness these substances generate. Thus, the making of architecture is inflected by another reality, another complexity, breaking and entering into language's mechanism of dissimulation in order to physically construct its Malentendus: including the data that the acephalous body collects—that can tell us about its adaptation, its sympathy and empathy—in the face of specific situations and environments.

The *Humors* collection is organized on the basis of interviews that make visible the conflict, and even schizophrenic qualities of desire, between those secreted (biochemical and neurobiological) and those expressed through the interface of language (free will). Mathematical tools taken from set theory (belonging, inclusion, intersection, difference, etc.) are used so that these "misunderstandings" produce a morphological potential (attraction, exclusion, touching, repulsion, indifference, etc.) as a negotiation of "distances" between humans who constitute these collective aggregates.

These relational modes are simultaneously elaborated within the residential cell, and on its periphery, in relation to the neighboring colonies. The multiplicity of possible physio-morphological layouts based on mathematical formulations offer a variety of habitable patterns in terms of the transfer of the self to the Other and to others as well.

A construction protocol is necessitated that can deal with complex, nonstandard geometries through a process of secretion, extrusion, and agglutination. This frees the construction procedure from the usual frameworks that are incompatible with a geometry constituted by a series of anomalies and singularities.[5]

The data obtained from the physiological interview with Nanoparticles concerns the following issues: familial socialization (distance and relationship between residential areas within a single unit), neighborhood socialization (distance and relationship between residential units), modes of relations to externalities (biotope, light, air, environment, and also seeing, being seen and hiding, modes of relating to access (receiving and/or escaping, even self-exclusion), and the nature of the interstices (from closely spaced to panoptic)).

We use formulae taken from set theory to define these relationships. This branch of mathematics was founded by the German mathematician Georg Cantor in the late 19th century. Its aim is to define the concepts of sets and belonging. This theory can be used to describe the structure of each situation as a kind of collective defining the relationships between the parts and the whole, while taking into consideration that the latter is not reducible to the sum of its parts (or even to the ensemble of relationships between the parts). It allows for the definition of all the properties of a given situation in relational modes, both the relationships between the elements themselves (residential areas) and those between the elements and the ensemble or ensembles they fit into.

$$\begin{cases} \dfrac{\partial \psi}{\partial t} + V|\nabla \psi| = 0 \\[2ex] \dfrac{\partial J}{\partial \omega}(\omega) \cdot \theta = -\displaystyle\int_{\partial \omega} (Ae(u) \cdot e(u)) \, \theta \cdot n \, ds \end{cases} \longrightarrow \quad V(x) = Ae(u) \cdot e(u)(x) \quad \forall x \in \partial\omega.$$

The operators of belonging, union, inclusion, intersection, and disjunction describe morphologies characterized by their dimensions and position and above all, by the negotiations of distance they carry out with the other parts. This produces relational protocols: protocols of attraction, repulsion, contiguity, dependence, sharing, indifference, exclusion, etcetera. Thus, before the morphology of a habitat is reduced to a functional typology, it is first structured as an area of exchange.

Mathematical formulae[6] aid the development of these combinations and thus become the matrix for the relational structure on which an inhabitable space is based.

In contrast to the standardized-model formatting of habitats, this tool offers the potential to negotiate with the ambiguities of one's own humors and desires. It enables the mixing of contradictory compulsions (appearances) and even some "malentendus," which could be translated both as misunderstandings and mishearings: "I'd like that but at the same time/maybe/not/and the opposite." These malentendus are directly influenced by the pathologies generated by collective living oscillating between -phobia and -philia.

The secondary goal of the research, in terms of mathematical development, is about structural optimization: about defining the structural sustainability of the system as a postproduction.

Not so far from the mimesis (not mimicry) of nature, which is made up of indetermination protocols, algorithms can simulate the growth of a tree in terms of understanding the vitalism of its geometry. Its intrinsic life forces articulate its geometry-photosynthesis-equilibrium-entropy, calculating through iterations. Simultaneously, its incremental generational branches grow and its tendency for recursive re-adaptation (volume and orientation of the trunk) strives for permanent global re-equilibrium, though the generative branching and forking entropy and the re-calculation of the previous morphologies to be loaded by the evolution

The possibility of structure as a postproduction element, emerging a posteriori to become inhabitable morphologies, calls into question the traditional client-relationship and offers an alternative way of generating form. Emancipated from the conceptual logic where the structure is the starting point, the spatial contract takes the place of the social contract. Since it is conceived a posteriori, the structure is reactive, adaptive to multiplicity, as the permanent discovery of new agencies, of entities, and of singularities.

François Jouve developed in the format of this research a mathematical process for "empirically" seeking optimization,[7] by creating forms out of constraints and not vice-versa. The structural optimization algorithm differs from directly calculated structural methods such as calculating the load-bearing structure of a building after it has been designed. In contrast, the algorithm allows the architectural form to emerge from the trajectories of the transmission of forces simultaneously with the calculation that generates them. The algorithm is based on (among other things) two mathematical strategies, one taken from the derivative initiated by the research of Jacques Hadamard (to modify a shape by successive infinitesimal step, to improve the criteria we want to optimize, as a permanent variation of frontier) and the other from the protocol of the representation of complex shapes by Cartesian meshing through level set (to understand locally what could be the line of the highest or lowest resulting point, if we project the local incremental iterative calculus onto a 2D diagram, to extract the $X,Y$ position in the space as data to reinject in the next step of the calculation).

$\partial$ = Frontier
Ext = Exterior
Int = Interior

Frontier of a Group inside Family:

Interior of Group { IntG: {c ⊂ F, G ⊂ F}
Exterior of Group { ExtG: {c ⊂ F, G' ⊂ F}
Frontier of Group { $\partial$G: {c ⊂ F, c ⊄ IntG, c ⊄ ExtG}}

Therefore a Family is: { F: { IntG ∪ $\partial$G ∪ ExtG}}

Frontier of Family:

Interior of Family { IntF: {G ⊂ N, F ⊂ N}
Exterior of Family { ExtF: {G ⊂ N, F' ⊂ N}
Frontier of Family { $\partial$F: {F ⊂ N, G ⊄ IntF, G ⊄ ExtF}}

Therefore a Neighbourhood is: { N: { IntF ∪ $\partial$F ∪ ExtF}}

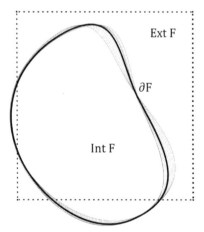

Ext F

$\partial$F

Int F

IntF ∩ $\partial$F = ExtF ∩ $\partial$F = ExtF ∩ IntF = ∅

This secondary goal of these matematical processes is achieved by an incremental and recursive optimization (ex-local, local, and hyper-local) that simultaneously calculates and design's support structures for the physio-morphologies. Following the non-deterministic aggregation of the unpredictable overstacking of desires, the structural branching and coagulating are generated by successive iterations of calculations that physically link the interstices between morphologies so that they can support each other locally and globally. The calculations satisfy precise inputs, including the constraints and characteristics of the materials used, initial conditions, dead load, transfer of forces, intensity, and vectorization of these forces, and so forth.[8]

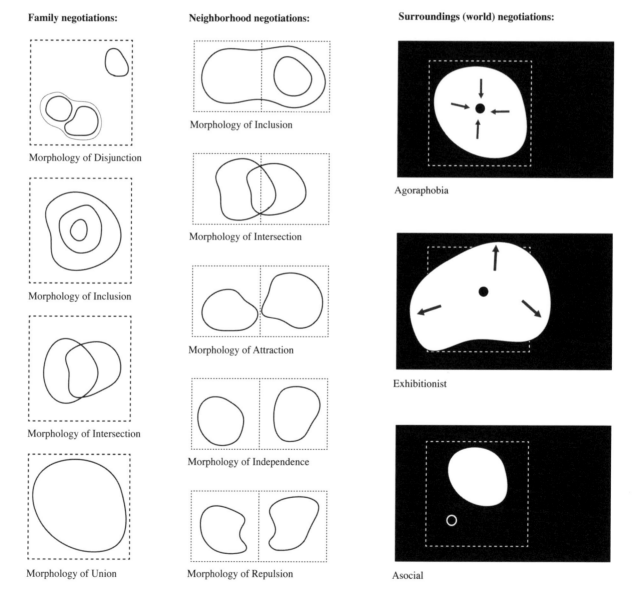

**Family negotiations:**

Morphology of Disjunction

Morphology of Inclusion

Morphology of Intersection

Morphology of Union

**Neighborhood negotiations:**

Morphology of Inclusion

Morphology of Intersection

Morphology of Attraction

Morphology of Independence

Morphology of Repulsion

**Surroundings (world) negotiations:**

Agoraphobia

Exhibitionist

Asocial

The mathematical process of empirical optimization makes it possible for the architectural design to react and adapt to previously established constraints, instead of the opposite.

Through the use of these computational, mathematical, and mechanization procedures, the urban structure engenders successive, improbable, and uncertain aggregations that constantly rearticulate the relationship between the individual and the collective, between top-down and bottom-up, and that reactivate the potential for self-organization, and for the creativity of the Multitude, in the pursuit of the *Metabolism* developed by Constant and Debord.[9] Through the technologies and procedures that exist at present, we can "unachieve" what we could call computed-slums: we can re-question and refresh the democratic delegation of power and its collateral effect: the obligation of resistance to the way in which architects are abused or self-abused to pretend to have any expertise on master city planning.

*This research is being carried out with François Jouve, the mathematician in charge of working out dynamic structural strategies; with the architect and robotics designer Stephan Henrich, with Winston Hampel and Natanael Elfassy on the computational development, including some specific works of Marc Fornes; and Gaetan Robillard and Fréderic Mauclere on the physiological data collection station, following a nanotechnologies scenario by R&Sie(n)–Berdaguer & Pejus.*

*Text by R&Sie(n)/François Roche with assistance from David Sanson and Caroline Naphegyi. All images by R&Sie(n)/François Roche*

**Endnotes**

1   In reference to "Rules for Human ZOO," Peter Sloterdijk (Regeln für den Menschenpark, 1997.

2   Antonio Negri in *Multitudes* reactivated this notion, in its political and social organizational sense, but he never tried to define the tooling, the protocols which could be applied to this physiological and ideological approach in a human social contract and organization. We know that the human pheromones (vectors of sharing knowledge) are missing or are so weak that we cannot distribute an instantaneous and collective informational network so easily. On the other hand, we could suspect the language and the notion of "libre arbitre" (free will) to be too easily influenced and manipulated as a unique channel of information (Spinoza has shown us how this notion could ironically become a self-imposed form of slavery). To start a protocol of swarm intelligences, we have to first develop the factors and vectors of exchanges from something which could be shared by analyzing the multiple disorders of human secretions, in a balance between the body and the language, as the expression of our personal contradictions between the way to negotiate speech in public space and the intimacy of our neuro-biological emission ... Some things between consciousness and pre-consciousness ... negotiating the schizophrenia between 'libre arbitre' and the bio-chemical secretion of "le corps acéphale" (body acephala), "du corps chimique, neurobiologique" (by the rereading of the concentration of Cortisol, Dopamine, Adrenaline, and Melatonin). This mishearing and/or misunderstanding of these schizoid and nonhierarchical inputs is able to inject unpredictability, un-achievement, and indeterminacy between a degree of shamanism and mathematic protocols. At the opposite of a system of survey, of a panoptical anticipation and "masterplan-ication," the computation could absorb and articulate stochastic processes, artifacts rereading, works in progresses, with parameterizing the potential of losing control, of unknown with a latitude of self-organization transmitted by and through the multitude, in the sense of Toni Negri (see below fragment of *Empire*, which Negri coauthored with Michael Hardt, published in 2004):

> *The Communards defending their revolutionary Paris against the government forces attacking from Versailles roam about the city like ants in Rimbaud's poetry and their barricades bustle with activity like anthill. Why would Rimbaud describe the Communards whom he loves and admires as swarming ants? When we look more closely we can see that all of Rimbaud's poetry is full of insects, particularly the sounds of insects, buzzing, swarming, and teeming. "Insect-verse" is how one reader describes Rimbaud's poetry, "music of the swarm." The reawakening and reinvention of the senses in the youthful body—the centerpiece of Rimbaud's poetic world—takes place in the buzzing and swarming of the flesh. This is a new kind of intelligence, a collective intelligence, a swarm intelligence, that Rimbaud and the Communards anticipated.*

3   How to caress this permanent equilibrium-disequilibrium, far away from positivism articulated by a too much mysticism in science, in the pursuit of Auguste Conte, when geometry in architecture is mainly used as a propaganda of control, carrying again and again a magister of control, in a system of surveillance described by Michel Foucault. Paradoxically, because of the way in which architects confuse mathematics and trigonometry, it is not innocent and not anecdotic that Alan Turing and Lewis Carroll were both mathematicians: the first committed suicide in the same way that Snow White did, with the well-known missing part of Steve Job's Apple; the second described how the schizo-paranoia of Alice was able to alter her own reality to the tangible construction of a parallel universe. Mathematics is a science, certainly, with protocols of knowledge, but it is developed with and within a speculative approach which feeds on and pushes its boundaries until pataphysic scenarios and alchemist protocols used to decode and recode the unknown, with logic and illogic, induction and deduction, a field which produced both Descartes and Leibnitz, as a permanent dispute between French Cartesianism, which confused the origin of a phenomenon with its scientific explanation, in a proto-positivistic illusion to decode and unfold the nature of everything, and Leibnitz, with his differential equations asymptotically flirting with the unknown, without pretending to touch or reformulate its unreachable (un)reality.

4   Nanoreceptors, n. (physics, from Nanos, 1 nm $= 1.0 \times 10 - 9$ meters) nanoparticles (NP) used to capture and detect the presence of a chemical substance in a particular atmosphere. Nanoreceptors can be inhaled, making it possible to "sniff" the chemical state of the human body. Functioning: Like pollens, they are concentrated in the bronchia and attach themselves to the blood vessels. This location makes it possible to detect traces of stress hormones (hydrocortisone) carried by the hemoglobin. As soon as they come into contact with this substance, the phospholipidic membrane of the NP dissolves and releases several molecules, including formaldehyde ($H_2CO$) in a gaseous state. The molecules rejected by the respiratory tract are detected using cavity ring-down spectroscopy (CRDS). This is a method of optical analysis using laser beams programmed to a particular frequency, making it possible to measure the density of air-borne molecules. The wavelength used for the detection of formaldehyde is around 350 nanometer. Consequently, the nanoreceptors are becoming the pheromonal re-reading of the chemical body, as one of the vectors of the negotiation between neighbourhoods. This chemical data collected in real time, could work as a substitute for the missing human pheromone....

5   A secretion and weaving machine that can generate a vertical structure by means of extrusion and sintering (full-size 3D printing) using a hybrid raw material (a bio-plastic-cement) that

chemically agglomerates to physically constitute the computational trajectories is in development. This structural calligraphy works like a machinist stereotomy comprised of successive geometrics according to a strategy based on a repetitive protocol. This machine is both additive and formative. It is called Viab02.

6 Calculus parameters (inputs received via a text file of the morphology (from Rhino to Linux)):
– Position and diameter of the inhabitable spaces (the optimization calculation should go around them but touch them so as to produce structural bonding). They are made up of clusters with a minimum inhabitable volume three meters in diameter.
– Position of the vertical distributions (to be stuck into and absorbed by the structural calculation).
– Position of the areas of contact between local and overall calculations, that is, between the inhabitable morphologies and the overall structure (dead zones).

7 Shape optimization (C++ on Linux, developed by François Jouve).

8 Forces and constraints taken as system inputs:
1. The parameters for the positioning of forces are defined by their contact coordinates (given in $x, y,$ and $z$) on the surface of each "base cube" volume (overall and local forces).
2. The parameters for the intensity of forces are defined by the length of the vector.
3. The parameters for the orientation of forces are defined by the original position of the vector (given in $x, y,$ and $z$).
4. Parameterization of avoidance and convergence zones around the habitable clusters.
5. Parameterization of the contact areas between the local and overall calculations so as to produce structural continuity.
6. Parameterization of the g-force directly induced by the addition of volumes and the accretion of mass through successive stacking.
7. Horizontal forces (including wind).
8. Vertical forces (inhabitant load, etc.).
*Search and approximation* of the volume resulting from the structural material surrounding the trajectories (percentage full/empty) based on the density and mechanical characteristics of the construction material. *Strategies for binding heterogeneous* morphologies and occupation chronologies (bottom-up). *Position and definition* of each cell based on the interweaving of four "family" morphologies.

9 "Mood zones" or "Emotional Realities" by Guy Debord, for the New Babylonians residents.

## Archie B. Mackenzie

*is associate professor of architecture in Cornell University Department of Architecture. He teaches, builds, and researches architectural games.*

# ARCH-Games, MATH-Games

*It has long been said that architecture is a game played with clear objectives, but no guiding set of rules. Mathematics, on the other hand, has forever been described by its believers as a form of knowledge best understood as a game with lots of rules but no clear objectives.*[1]

The following piece has been developed as a language-game that plays upon three quotations. The first of these, which appears above, by Brett Steele in his preface to *The New Mathematics of Architecture* (NMA), sets up a reciprocal relationship between MATH and ARCH (architecture) by suggesting that they share the common metaphor of games: MATH, a game of many rules, as it awaits problems to solve; or, in the case of ARCH, forms to produce. The book contains an exceptional range of mathematically generated architectural forms and a very intriguing array of MATH-to-ARCH applications. How apt, however, is the aphorism?

In order to examine it, two boxes have been designated to hold the constituents of MATH on one side and of ARCH on the other. It is easy enough to insert a short list of concepts, representing Steele's "rules" into the MATH box. These clearly belong to MATH and are on loan—as MATH is to any donor of "objectives"—to ARCH. Almost immediately, however, there is a sense of imbalance between the two sides. How does architecture, stripped of its multitude of historical failed attempts to claim architectural Truth, provide "objectives" that are comparable with the immutability of mathematical language?

In the second quotation representing the MATH side, David Hilbert forcefully adds to the unequal equation.

*We are not speaking here of arbitrariness in any sense. Mathematics is not like a game whose tasks are determined by arbitrarily stipulated rules. Rather, it is a conceptual system possessing internal necessity that can only be so and by no means otherwise.*[2]

This does not invalidate the game metaphor for MATH; it simply validates the integrity of MATH-languages that bear Steele's rules.

The third quotation is from Ludwig Wittgenstein, whose later works refuted "essence" in language, preferring to move away from what he calls, and I para-phrase, the frictionless ice of the logical, to the rough ground of common language that he states clearly does not refer to the natural world. He does embrace the notion that fungible languages may occur in the works of humankind, not simply in its verbal transactions. He considers in the following "the Ideal":

> *We misunderstand the role of the ideal in our language. That is to say: we too should call it a game, only we are dazzled by the ideal and therefore fail to see the actual use of the word 'game' clearly.*[3]

The purpose of the essay is to redress the perceived imbalance between the MATH-side and the ARCH-side of the equation by demonstrating that game-building/game-play enables the dialogue between the two sides.

### Move 1.0 EMPTYING OUT the ARCH and MATH BOXES

Move 1.1 NATURE as MATH'S Ultimate AUTHORITY
As Nature is the ultimate authority for MATH, sanctioning the premise that it is "a form of knowledge … with lots of [immutable] rules" (from Steele quote, above), then ARCH, as the other side of the equation should be possessed of immutable "objectives." The opposite seems true, that Architecture has been progressively emptied out and is now either void or awaiting the new contents. What role does MATH now have in determining, warranting, and delimiting these objectives?

Move 1.2 ARCH and MATH Boxes
To look more closely at Steele's conjoined aphorisms, two receptacles are provided—an ARCH Box and a MATH Box—into which items from the lists may be placed and dumped out, like dice in backgammon cups. There are two lists, one of mathematical concepts (from NMA) and one a short-list of "rejected polemics." The arrow to the right in the "MATH Box" loads up the container with a sampling of mathematical procedures, or "rules," from NMA. The arrow to the left shows a sampling of the many polemics from the last century that was rejected by theorists. These acts are mimicked here—by removing the same from the ARCH Box—as an expression of the imbalance between the unchanging rules of MATH and the conditional "objectives" of ARCH.

**Architectural Polemics/Math Procedures**.
Image by Heriberto Rodríguez Valenzuela

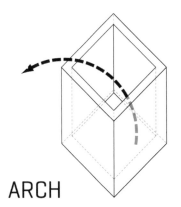
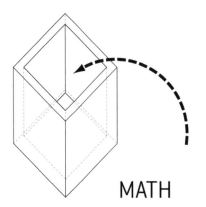

... Rejected Polemics

**no** Form fallows function
**no** Firmness commodity
+ delight
**no** [3] typologies
**no** Program authority
**no** True modernity
**no** Allegory
**no** Phenomenology
**no** Social project
**no** Archetypal taste
**no** Consumption
**no** Validity of plan
**no** ARCH space

ARCH

MATH

Math Procedures ...

Amman tiling
Aperiodic tiling
Arup optimizer
Catenary models
Cellular automation
Danzer packing
Embedding
Homolgy
Immersion
Nurbs
Ruled surfaces
Topology models
Voronoi diagram

Move 1.2.1 REMOVING POLEMICS FROM ARCHITECTURE

Nothing occupies the ARCH Box. It has been emptied out. Not only is it without a guiding set of rules, but also there are no "Objectives" cards in it. This makes sense because at the level of generality attributed to MATH—comprising its immutable languages of symbols and rules—there are no equivalent archetypal objectives left in ARCH. Its baseline has come into question. It has no "form follows function," no firmness, commodity, and delight, no first, second, and third typologies, no program as authority, no true modernity, no allegory, no acceptable phenomenology, no perpetual social project, no such thing as archetypal taste. And it is vulnerable to consumption. Moreover, even the validity of "plan" has been removed; likewise "architectural space." As traditional constituents of ARCH leak away, it begins to appear that ARCH has no immutable principles on a par with the rules of MATH.

## Move 2.0 THE GAME FOR FORMULATING A DEFINITION OF "GAMES"

### Move 2.1 DEFINING "GAME"

Wittgenstein's notion of the "ideal" derives from the philosophical project to use language to define the *essence* of things—and ultimately the essence of *being*. In Philosophical Investigations, he denies the efficacy of this endeavor in favor of an alternate activity, which he calls "language-games." To define the ideal, to calculate the essential, is not to discover immutable Truth but is itself a language-game woven into the culture and methodology of philosophy. The following considers how the author's of *Rules of Play* researched and crafted a definition of "game," a process that is both paradoxical and pragmatic: paradoxical, because profound definitions must maintain engagement with their exclusions; pragmatic because academic fields of inquiry must have boundaries, even if these are incessantly gamed by competing ideas.

As game-builders themselves, the authors of *Rules of Play* were motivated "by the feeling that despite the breathtaking pace of recent technical and commercial advancement, games have remained creatively stunted,"[4] to build a critical discourse for game design. Not to be confused with Game Theory, the mathematical method often employed in economic theory, their work intends to construct a conceptual framework for serious research into the nature of game-building/game-play. They felt the necessity to not only bring conceptual order to the burgeoning not-quite-yet-field of game design but to ask what is holding it back from what it could become.

The formulation that follows is the product of their efforts:

*A Game Is a System in Which Players Engage in on Artificial Conflict, Defined by Rules That Results in a Quantifiable Outcome.*[5]

A full discussion of their terminology is beyond the scope of this piece; instead, the meaning of the terms is exemplified by what is usually called "circular" but more recently would be regarded as "recursive" thinking—that is, to accept the formulation of a definition for "game" as a language game in its own right. Or, more directly: to consider the work of the authors of *Rules* (Salen and Zimmerman) as an academic game to define a critical terminology needed to enable the field itself to coalesce.

Move 2.2 APPLYING THE TERMS OF THE AUTHOR'S DEFINITION OF "GAME" TO DESCRIBE THE GAME THEY PLAYED TO FORMULATE IT

One might employ their terms to describe their game-to-define-games. Firstly, the *Rules'* game system could reasonably be identified as the book itself, the covers of which act as a symbolic boundary to the game-space. (To construct this space, of course, the authors had to explore an even larger one; still, the book has digested that search into a focused presentation.) Secondly, the players are the authors, specific supporters and potential antagonists, the members of the field in general, commercial game-building professionals, and a broader public to which the field may appeal. Thirdly, the desired outcomes of the definition-game are echoed in the evocative fragments: *breathtaking pace, creatively stunted, build a critical discourse*, and *focusing the burgeoning field*. Fourthly, the artificial conflict is variously: the competing ideas of the players, the anarchy of the field, which hitherto had resisted conceptualization, and the difficulty of finding a potent yet durable terminology. Fifthly, the resulting definition must both engender debate yet persist against its inevitable challenges. And, finally, the outcome is not purely quantifiable but rather must be judged by the quality of its survival or demise.

Perhaps the most defining term here is *game system*, because in many ways *Rules* embodies a field and is achieved by a design process. In this language-game to define "game," the words *game* and *design* are nearly synonymous. Similarly, game-building is a design process; and designing is, in many but not all ways, a game. The authors of *Rules* built a (re) search space to create—to design—the core "rule" of the field: the definition of "game."

## Move 3.0 LEAKY CONCEPTS, ASSOCIATIVE PATHWAYS

### Move 3.1 Still Rules CONSTRUCTING a WEB of INTRA- and EXTRA-MURAL OBJECTS

In *Rules*, the authors researched the work of seven prominent writers on the nature of games; selecting critical features from the definition search gave for "games." They then plotted game features* to authors** in a table, in order to compare the seven definitions to each other and to their own formulation. Finally, they extracted a definition they believed was sufficiently broad and concise to both stand up to academic scrutiny and yet to include a significant range of exemplary games. Their final definition is paired below with a version cobbling together fragments from five numbered features—from the original 15 that they determined relevant to their conception of "game." The second version reflects upon the parsimony of the first,

---

\* List from table, p. 79, 15 possible features for the definition of games: A game (1) proceeds according to rules that limit players; (2) engages in conflict or contest; (3) is goal-oriented /outcome oriented; (4) is an activity, process, or event; (5) involves decision making; (6) is not serious or absorbing; (7) is never associated with material gain; (8) is an artificial/safe/outside normal life; (9) creates special social groups; (10) is voluntary; (11) is uncertain; (12) engages in make-believe and the representational; (13) is inherently inefficient; (14) is a system of parts/tokens; and (15) is a form of art. Katie Salen and Eric Zimmerman, *Rules of Play* (Cambridge, MA; London, UK: The MIT Press, 2004), 79.

\*\* List from table, p. 79, eight game theorists: A. Parlett, B. Abt, C. Huizinga, D. Caillois, E. Suits, F. Crawford, G. Costikyan, H. Avedon/Sutton-Smith, and I. K. Salen and E. Zimmerman.

both suggesting the author's struggle to posit a core terminology for a new field and yet hinting at exclusions: for example, "quantifiable outcomes" as opposed to "goal-oriented" play. The diagram following immediately restores the 10 rejected features, not in an attempt to undermine the *Rules* definition but rather to suggest a rhizome-like relationship between the core and the creative, if marginal, potential of the satellite concepts engendered by the *language-game* to define "games."

> *A Game Is a System in Which Players Engage in on Artificial Conflict, Defined by Rules That Results in a Quantifiable Outcome. (See Move 2.1)*

A game is (14) a system in which players (2) engage in conflict or contest that is (8) artificial (and) outside normal life, that (1) proceeds according to rules that limit players and that is directed towards (3) a goal-oriented/outcome oriented result. (See note *.)

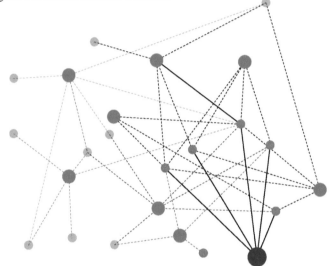

**Family resemblances**. The diagram shows a network of the game theorists (red nodes) and possible game features (blue nodes). The purple node represents Salen and Zimmerman's definition; the five solid lines emanating from a single node indicate those features that are consistent with their definition. The red nodes show dashed black lines connecting to many but not all of the same features. This cluster bears substantial agreement between authors but with differences. The lighter lines of varying colors designate connections of game definitions and features substantially at odds with the main group — the former, immediate family of similarities; the latter, distant relatives. Image by Heriberto Rodríguez Valenzuela

## Move 4.0 A WEB OF RELATIONSHIPS

The network (above) is biased toward its dominant object, which is the final definition of "game." In other words, the network is rooted in its most successful element. Like a banyan tree, however, the diagram of relationships may be thought of as growing outward from its trunk—while all of the tendrils of previous researchers' definitions are cross-linked one to another by features they share. This makes a network of relationships that grows the way banyan trees grow, whose branches project aerial roots that drop to the ground and later become accessory trunks. The central trunk is equivalent to a key concept, or dominant methodology; sustaining the trunk even while it fails is not calamitous to the tree, if accessory elements can take over growth. Such a shift in conceptual loading to an accessory truck system is similar to the gestalt structural heuristic called re-centering. Linear, cumulative design procedures are committed to successive moves, previous ones becoming the foundation for subsequent ones. Unlike re-centering (above), such processes are inherently brittle, as they are not rooted in fields of competing ideas in the way games are.

Move 4.1 RECENTERING upon EXCLUDED FEATURES
The following statements exemplify what the definition of "game" from *Rules of Play* would exclude from game-building if it were employed as a way of designing. Each statement has two parts: excluded activities (EXCL), i.e., design modes not considered game features, and included ones (INCL), or how those same modes might usefully serve game-building and game-play.

*EXCL. Purely cooperative games: activities without conflict are not games. INCL. Cooperation may occur between certain players to gain advantage over others; when the game pits the "designer" against the "problem," team members may sometimes compete to have an idea accepted or cooperate to develop various aspects of a scheme.*

*EXCL. Qualitative games: a true game must have a quantifiable outcome. INCL. ARCH-games "always" have conditional features that require qualitative judgment.*

*EXCL. Games in search of rules: a game must be a game throughout play. INCL. Searching for rules is a form of structural play.*

*EXCL. Games that produce surpluses without use: non-engageable elements do not make elegant games. INCL. Auxiliary elements, like this excluded feature, may be used later in the game, just as they may in design.*

Move 4.2 WITTGENSTEIN'S MULTIPLICITY
The critical ingredient in Wittgenstein's aphorism on "multiplicity" is the emphasis on the activities into which language is woven. He illustrates common language-games as everyday activities in which the task and the context of language usage allow words to "mean" specifically something. He imagines such common practices as games, because we make "moves" in situations and are limited and directed by the grammars of the activity. In this regard, ARCH-design may be seen as innumerable language-games played within the evolving milieu of the project. Below, Wittgenstein lists common tasks-as-games to stress the ubiquity of game-like procedures in everyday life.

*Review the multiplicity of language-game in the following examples, and in others: Giving orders, and obeying them—Describing the appearance of an object, or giving its measurements—Constructing an object from a description (a drawing)—Reporting an event—Speculating about an event—Forming and testing a hypothesis—Presenting the results of an experiment in tables and diagrams—Making up a story; and reading it—Play-acting—Singing catches—Guessing riddles—Making a joke; telling it—Solving a problem in practical arithmetic—Translating from one language into another—Asking, thanking, cursing, greeting, praying ... It is interesting to compare the multiplicity of the tools in language and of the ways they are used, the multiplicity of kinds of word and sentence, with what logicians have said about the structure of language. (Inducing the author of the Tractatus Logico-Philosophicus.)* [L.W.'s parentheses]

While Wittgenstein's examples are not specifically about ARCH design, they suggest the myriad activities that comprise architectural projects—like the "rejected" heuristics above that nonetheless play roles in design games.

Move 4.3. THE WEB AS A LATTICE OF COMBINATIONS
Wittgenstein understood the body of all games as "a complicated network of similarities overlapping and criss-crossing...." Instead of a common thread that all others obey, they are more like "family resemblances:" what we might refer to today as the consequent similarities and differences resulting from genetic combinations. Siblings, for example, will have some unique mix of the pool of eye and hair color, facial features, build, or left or right-handedness.

This, of course, is very much like the network described above; moreover, it identifies a set of morphological language-games that account for various historical architectures.

### Move 5.0 GAMES that BRIDGE ARCH and MATH

The history of architecture is replete with games, whether Renaissance gardens or postmodern "French Hotels," that play with narrative or precedent. While scores of examples have been produced in the many years that this thinking has been the subject of studio investigations at Cornell, a single example will suffice to demonstrate the potential trajectory into an ARCH-game future.

Move 5.1 THE DENSITY GAME
The Density Game (below) is both system of production and rhetorical language that focuses an ARCH problem and offers a rule-based system for describing a MATH task should it be needed. Rather than beginning a priori with the assumption of MATH modeling, it nonetheless requires the formulation of a game appropriate to the emerging problem. This stresses the importance of the uniqueness of the problem rather than one defined by an exploration of a MATH procedure. If efficiency and optimization are key issues, then these might be built into the game —but without preempting the search for an appropriate language.

The image—showing blocks stacked in a pattern that barely remains stable— is not even, not yet, perhaps not ever, a building. It is, however, a kind of tipping point in a design project that poses interesting questions about the MATH-side and the ARCH-side of the discussion so far. Has it reached the state where a designer might ask, "Can this game be modeled and so manipulated by an algorithm?" In other words, has it reached that point where it is so well articulated as an OBJECTIVE that the mathematician can *calculate* it?

The sides of the basic diagram, MATH and ARCH, might be renamed temporarily as the activities LANGUAGE CALCULATIONS and LANGUAGE GAMES to reflect Wittgenstein's move from his seminal study of the logic of language in *Tractatus*[6] to language games in *Philosophical Investigations*.[7] From the perspective of the former, one's task would be to create a generative grammar of forms that could account for the pile of blocks and its textual relationships. From the latter, we would consider what sort of *form game(s)* might do the same. Clearly, the latter strategy would be easier and more flexible, but would presumably lack the capacity to automatically generate the block pile. Similarly, George Stiny has long sought to subsume architectural production through logical operations of his "shape grammars," his version of the MATH-side of this discussion. However, he has recently published a competing argument in a book called *Shape*.[8] Citing Wittgenstein in references to both *Tractatus* and *Philosophical Investigations*, he appears to be retracing the philosopher's own repudiation of "logical philosophy" in favor of systems of meaning embedded in the activities of usage. At the same time he searches for "ways of counting" and "calculating" with shapes.

With Stiny's *shape grammars* in mind, that is, a formal, mathematically driven object language, we might take the pile as an OBJECT to be modeled as a grammar. Unfortunately, without further development, this would not only be an impossible task—we would know neither the meaning of all placements nor be able to review multiple variations that would reveal the pile's conditional logic—but would miss the process, the game, that created it. The discussion that follows, on the other hand, speculates on such further development of the ARCH-pile's language to bring it to a point at which MATH modeling would be feasible.

Move 5.2 A GAME SIMULATION

While one cannot do justice to this design process in the space left in the essay, a great deal comes into focus even when the game is briefly described. The imperative that preceded the studio exercise, for example, was to discover scales and patterns in a small town that would suggest any addition to the town fabric. In this case, the designer initially chose the party wall texture and the massing of its buildings along a main commercial street. The buildings forming that pattern, while dominant, were undistinguished and when appropriated for her design, merely reproduced the pattern. She invented her game, not because she understood the logic of the site but because she did not. What she did have, on the other hand, was the conviction that some grain, some mixture of scales, was needed to set her building apart even while embedding it in the urban fabric. To her "density" meant all these things.

To shorten the story: she created an inventory of many small blocks and, placing these in a Plexiglas container, experimented with producing a "natural" pattern. The strategy, in retrospect, was to search for a mix of scales relevant to the artifacts of the town—its porches, rooms, windows, furniture, even paintings, rugs, and the like—rather than its urban fabric. For the tourist town, the pile-of-blocks would become cabinets of wonder, inventorying town fragments and breaking through the party wall obstacle. Openings in the pile would give access to a new lateral, day/night, summer/winter, and tourist/citizen street cutting through perpendicular to the party wall rhythm.

Gradually, using gravity and the dynamics of collision and settling as a "natural" way to order the pieces, she devised means for influencing the process. By mixing blocks of different sizes and proportions and by coaxing "architectural order" with formworks of rods, wedges, channels, planes, and so on, she imparted indirect control to the "natural phenomenon." Interestingly, this indirect manipulation of behavior is similar to cellular automata: the blocks are simple passive "cells" governed by gravity and the shaking of the box. The rules were also passive in the sense that they were strictly physical conditions. The designer intervened by determining starting patterns, by progressively introducing formworks, and by analyzing multiple outcomes to determine behaviors. Like cellular automata, the design was evolutionary, in which good starting patterns, formwork tactics, shaking schemes, and updated ratios and densities of aggregate blocks were monitored. As the process evolved, additional conditions and artifacts were identified and included: block size-to-usage; groupings of blocks to ARCH function; space-to-mass for occupancy; movement, light, and air; density/scarcity; and structural latency in block arrangement versus separate systems.

The accompanying image captures the density-game as it approaches a plausible balance between natural and architectural orders. The process of defining an emergent architectural language has just begun. It is a moment of confidence and a branching point for the way forward. Because game-building develops rule systems for ARCH languages in whatever representational mode, it provides a way to manage methodological decisions dependent on time, resources, and knowledge. The Density Game described above may by-pass sophisticated methods for small projects or low budgets. It can be ramped-up to create a MATH-driven simulation, or proceed as a to-and-fro process of alternating algorithm-driven and manual operations.

**An Architectural Pile**. This is the last of three-steps, in which the pile-of-blocks becomes a plausible basis for a study for an urban Architectural Cabinet of Wonders.

**A Gravily Game**. This the first of three-steps, in which a gravity game—comprising random blocks shaken in a game-box—challenges the player to achieve architectural order within a "natural" procedure.

**Gravity Game Box**. Cut-away of a plexi Gravity Game Box, into which rods, wedges, channels, etc. are inserted in order to herd "natural" behavior into architectural order. All models by Camille Vélez (B. Arch. '14).

### Concluding remarks

Although Steele's paired aphorisms have ARCH presenting OBJECTIVES to MATH, the last century saw most polemics stripped away from architectural discourse. MATH, in its guises of morphogenics, biomimetics, cellular automata, and so on, has become a surrogate for the authority of Nature. As such, mathematical procedure sets ideological OBJECTIVES, not architecture. Hence the dis-balance in Steele's pairing.

The thrust of this essay has been to introduce and demonstrate the validity of a way of working called the Architectural Game and to redress the imbalance perceived in Steele's aphorism about the relationship between architecture and mathematics. The essay asserts that game-building/game-play is a natural mediator between the language games of architectural design and the *"conceptual system possessing internal necessity"*[9] that is mathematics. ARCH-games—because of their inherent rule-building capacity, their propensity to become language games, and their characteristics as systems that are bounded, interactive, structured, and flexible—are suited for gathering, mixing, and resolving the exigencies of ARCH and MATH.

### Closing note

While the central topic, *Mathematics: From the Ideal to the Uncertain*, has been subordinated in the essay to the ARCH/MATH dialog, the spirit of the IDEAL and of the UNCERTAIN is captured in the image of the Density Game, in which a randomness is herded, by successive moves, into a relative order. The player must abide by the rules of the game, even as its ingredients are nudged toward a balance between a NATURAL and an ARTIFICIAL order. Simulated Nature provides the host phenomenon; artifice intervenes. By cosmological analogy, the IDEAL is a consequent, not a predetermined form; it is a consequence of a universe structured in ways that depending on celestial activity perfect limits are approached. The argument here is that the ideal is MADE, or more accurately, achieved as a limit; that it may also be felt, because the sensorial subject is also MADE—possibly to be harmonic.

**Endnotes**

1 Brett Steele, "War of the Gods," in Jane Burry and Mark Burry, *The New Mathematics of Architecture* (New York: Thames & Hudson, 2010), 6–7.

2 David Hilbert; Paul Bernays, *Grundlagen der Mathematik (Foundations of Mathematics)* (Berlin; Heidelberg; New York: Springer, 1968).

3 Lois Sawver, *Commentary on Wittgenstein's Philosophical Investigations* (Internet: Rhizomeway.com, November 2011), Aphorism 100.

4 Frank Lantz, from the Foreword to *Rules of Play*, Katie Salen and Eric Zimmerman (Cambridge, MA;, London, UK: The MIT Press, 2004).

5 Lois Sawver, *Commentary on Wittgenstein's Philosophical Investigations* (Internet: Rhizomeway.com, November 2011), Aphorism 23.

6 Ludwig Wittgenstein, *Tractatus Logico Philosophicus* (Germany: Annalen der Naturphilosophie, 1922). English translation published by Kegan Paul, 1922.

7 Ludwig Wittgenstein; G. E. M. Anscombe; Elizabeth Anscombe, *Philosophical Investigations* (New York: Wiley-Blackwell, 1991). The German Text and a Revised English (US) Translation.

8 George Stiny, *Shape* (The MIT Press: Cambridge, MA, 2008).

9 David Hilbert; Paul Bernays, *Grundlagen der Mathematik (Foundations of Mathematics)* (Berlin; Heidelberg; New York: Springer, 1968).

## Anthony Vidler

*is a historian and critic of modern and contemporary architecture. He is Dean of the Irwin S. Chanin School of Architecture, The Cooper Union. From 1965 to 1997 he taught in the School of Architecture, Princeton, where he chaired the PhD program and Directed the European Cultural Studies Program. He served as professor and Chair of the Department of Art History at UCLA, with a joint appointment in the School of Architecture, and as Dean of AAP at Cornell University. He has published widely—his study of James Stirling was published by Yale University press in 2010, and his latest book* Scenes of the Street and Other Essays *was released in 2011.*

# A Strategy of Posing Questions

In conversation with Carly Dean, Le Luo, Alison Nash, and Ishita Sitwala

**Ishita**

You studied in Cambridge with Colin Rowe in the early 1960s: what is your view of the "mathematics" he espoused in his 1947 essay "The Mathematics of the Ideal Villa?"

**Anthony**

This essay was, in fact, hardly concerned with mathematics, but rather with the ordering device identified by his teacher Rudolf Wittkower in the Palladian villa plan. Rowe took this A-B-A-B-A rhythm that was allied either to the square of the Villa Rotonda or the rectangle of the Villa Malcontenta as a strategy for the analysis of Le Corbusier's two paradigmatic villas, Poissy and Garches. The only time that geometry came into question was the sense that underlying all these plans was some version of the Golden Section rectangle—Rowe was taken by the newly translated book by Matila Ghyka, *Le Nombre D'or* [The Geometry of Art and Life] and illustrated one of his diagrams. The question of proportion was widely discussed in Britain after the war—from about 1946 to 1949—inspired by Le Corbusier's publication of the first volume of *Le Modulor*, and Wittkower's *Architectural Principles in the Age of Humanism* [1949]. This led to what Banham described as a "Palladian revival" although Peter Smithson, whose Hunstanton School and entry for the Coventry Cathedral rebuilding subscribed to geometrical principles, announced that this revival was already over by 1948. Colin was, however, always fascinated by the properties of the "Palladian" grid, and used to try it out at all scales when drawing at the desk. For him, geometry was never a rigorous ordering system but rather a visual mnemonic. I remember his critique of Peter Eisenman's doctoral thesis, that it was all too "systematic."

**Le**

I am intrigued by Palladio and Palladian ordering principles. I would like to ask about a derivative of that system: the nine-square design problem that has been very

important pedagogically at Cornell and also at the Cooper Union, begun by
John Hejduk there. Do you believe that the exercise is still relevant in today's
architectural education and that it is a satisfactory method for teaching the basics
of architecture?

**Anthony**

There is a vast range of different pedagogical techniques used for students to
understand formal relationships. Paul Klee's pedagogical sketch books demonstrate the curriculum that he developed for teaching his techniques in the Bauhaus,
following his inquiries into the psychology of perception. *Gestalt* theory, as
explored by Kohler and Arnheim, was a central interest of Colin Rowe's, allowing
him to identify figure-ground relationships, and thence to draw the connection
with the ambiguities of Mannerism. Eisenman's first exploration of the formal
principles of modern architecture was also based partially on the *Gestalt* theory
of vision, embedded as it was in the active qualities of form in itself.

Certain pedagogical devices are extremely important as introductions for
students to manipulate the distribution of volumes and masses. Hejduk's abstraction of the nine-square problem, in two and three dimensions, proved a powerful
teaching vehicle for the exploration of themes and variations. The moment he
realized that this exercise was becoming too formulaic, he switched to other
strategies, such as the three dimensional analysis of two-dimensional paintings.
Pedagogical techniques have continually to be renewed.

**Alison**

Are ordering systems still relevant as a device for integrating contemporary
mathematics into architecture?

**Anthony**

That, of course, depends on what ordering systems you are deploying—geometrical,
topological, parametric and so on. The A-B-A-B-A structure is less of a mathematical system than a spatial device for the organization of a *parti*. Such devices were
very common in the Renaissance, and continued to be used throughout the Beaux
Arts in the 19th century.

**Ishita**

Do algorithms have the potential to create a new architecture that goes beyond the
failed objectives of modernism? Could this potentially implement social change
and be closer to its social obligations?

**Anthony**

First, there is no "new" architecture, in the same sense that Bruno Latour claims
that "we have never been modern." Parametricism is one of a wide range of
numerical controls that have been applied to architectural solutions. Mario Carpo has
made the point that even Alberti was "parametric" in his approach. While there are
those who claim that parametricism has produced a new "style," and it is certainly
true that it has produced a proliferation of curvilinear schemes, its "newness" seems
relative when compared, for example, with the work of a pre-digital architect like
Hans Scharoun.

Second, architecture has only a responsive relationship to social and political production. It cannot form society. Architecture can develop spatial organizations that are more or less inhibiting or accommodating to certain social operations, and it is clear that the so-called Deleuzian school has appealed to the flows and networks envisaged by post-Fordist managerial theory. Absent advanced technology, however, the demands of habitat do not necessarily fit into folded envelopes.

### Ishita
New techniques incorporating numbers and data, in your opinion, do not implement any social relationship of the architecture?

### Anthony
Of course new technologies of testing and evaluating, and new technologies of construction, allow for a greater sophistication in the calculation of the environmental characteristics of a building. But that is only a part of the equation in social terms. The selection of materials, their appropriateness to context, the compositional strategies relating to use, and a host of other concerns make up the social relations of architecture.

### Carly
Perhaps the way that we start to think about mathematics in this new global climate has more to do with urban density, numbers, and data.

### Anthony
Data is data. It is the interpretation of data and its translation into spatial terms that is important. When John McHale, who worked with Bucky Fuller for many years, wrote his masterpiece *The Ecological Context* in 1971, he collected and used data in such a way that he was able to analyze in each chapter, according to different perspectives, a different weighting of the data, to talk about the limited resources of the world for supporting human life. In that book, his four pages on global warming reads as potently now as it did then.

A simple diagram of the data can sometimes produce an interesting if not a radical re-shaping of a problem—that is Koolhaas's brilliance. But all his emphasis on research does not get over the fact that he is first and foremost a designer, using his design of the data to produce programmatic transformations of traditional typologies. Beneath the semblance of the data forming a tabula rasa for architecture, there is a calculated and subtle re-working of modern types whether taken from the "standard" versions, from his preferred masters Mies and Corbu, or from hidden sources from Constant to Amancio Williams. In this sense, he frames himself as *the* new Mies-Corb. Colin Rowe claimed that Corbusier took the Palladian villa and re-worked it for modernism, so Rem takes the Corbusian villa and upends it in the Bordeaux house. No data in the world can take away from him his architectural imagination, or his design skills.

### Carly
We watched the lecture "The Crisis of Modernism: James Stirling Out of the Archive" that you gave at the Architectural Association in 2010. You mentioned using James Stirling's drawings as an example and means of instruction for your

own thesis students because of the transparency of his iterative thought process evident in his drawing.

**Anthony**

I show his thesis to my thesis students because of the completeness of the project: program, plan, city center, individual buildings, resolved in the detailed elaboration of a single building. I also advance Stirling's design method, in its developed iteration of scheme after scheme, drawn at the smallest and largest scale, as a model of process. Nevertheless, these remain examples of process not of form or style. Students should learn to analyze, interpret, and abstract from precedent, composition, distribution, and organization of architectural ideas, rather than emulate a particular style.

**Carly**

Considering the importance of James Stirling's iterative thought-process demonstrated through his drawing, do you think that a parametric design process detracts from one's ability to iterate like this? Or can new digital techniques together with a traditional iterative thought process produce transformative architecture?

**Anthony**

I think it is very important to be able to draw. I think drawing actually trains you to judge distance, to measure scale, to form detail, and to control design. There is something about the relationship of the hand to the eye and thence to thought that still embodies form and space in a human dimension. Iteration in two and three dimensions is at the root of a thoughtful design process. Certainly, digital iteration if carefully controlled can extend our knowledge of a hand-drawn sketch, can develop technical information, and present alternatives—always as long as it is not seen as an end or an authority in itself. Iteration for me is a way for understanding your own thought process. It's a way of thinking through a design. Every drawing is a thought about architecture and every drawing leads to another drawing. What I privilege is the idea, the concept of the building itself: its relationship to its culture, its cultural context and its lineage, where architecture stands at a particular time and place, its role and its material being in the world is. If you can control that in thought and design, you control the work. In the process of elaboration, technologies, spatial organization, and contextual questions all have to be worked out, sometimes in sequence, sometimes in reverse.

**Alison**

In an era of increasing unpredictability and uncertainty in terms of climate, economy, and government, is it possible for architecture to express power and control?

**Anthony**

We have never *not* lived in a period of uncertainty. All periods, in the present, have been uncertain. Accidents are uncertain. The notion of chaos is uncertain. The problem at the moment is that we are in a period where too many people are too certain. Opinion rules politics, as it does crucial debates over climate change and economic development.

But in what way should architecture need to *express control*? Why should architecture demonstrate any form of power? Should not architecture be accommodating? Fascist architecture certainly wanted to demonstrate power. I think that neo-liberalist capitalism in its corporate forms wants to assert iconic power. But, in the end, the inhabited forms of the CCTV building are just office floors. The office is cloaked in an iconic shape but it doesn't do anything different than a standard office building.

### Ishita

The Baroque period tells a similar tale of uncertainty, of tension, of a sense of dissatisfaction. Do you think we are revisiting the Baroque in contemporary practice?

### Anthony

"Baroque" can mean many different things. It can mean religious revival, it can mean using architecture as propaganda [*propoganda fide*]. "Baroque" is also a stylistic and formal concept developed by art historians. Colin, in his article from 1950, "Modern Architecture and Mannerism," tried to demonstrate that modern architecture had a "Mannerist," component. Indeed, seeing "Mannerism" everywhere and in everything in the 1930s and 40s was very fashionable—a way of speaking of uncertainty in the wake of the loss of Enlightenment certitude. Similarly, attributing the curvilinear forms of a Guggenheim Bilbao to a "new" Baroque is a merely stylistic comparison—"stylistic" in the terms established by art-history in the 1900s.

### Ishita

Your forthcoming book *Utopian Transcripts*, explores a subject that has always been fascinating to architects and urbanists. How was your book conceptualized and why is utopia important today?

### Anthony

I have been interested in the concept of utopia from the very beginning of my life in architecture. My tutor at Cambridge, Colin Rowe, was obsessed with the idea—one of his first and best essays was for the Cambridge journal *Granta* in the 1950s, where he accurately characterized Modern Movement urbanism as utopian, and traced the intertwined histories of utopia (a literary mode invented by Thomas More) and the ideal city (an architectural mode invented by Filarete) and critiques the way in which they have influenced each other. Later he took up the idea of piece-meal utopia from the philosopher Karl Popper, and developed it as a basis for Collage City. My own work started with the study of Enlightenment utopia, and Ledoux of course. The new book traces the intellectual roots of More's utopia in classical philosophy, and thence the history of ideal cities, not so much as a critique but as a re-reading that tries to de-monumentalize the diagrams and see them as so many instances of a dialogue—much in the way that Plato's descriptions of Socrates's search for the just city play out.

For Plato's ideal republic was not one single, fixed ideal or a *polis*, but it was a series of dialectical discussions about the *possible* forms of an ideal state, of a city of truth, of beauty, each of which had its own deep dialectical disadvantages so that when you read the Platonic dialogues, you are reading a series of questions and answers which are a continuous process which never end: always that next question is emerging. Similarly, Thomas More's conversations in letters with Erasmus, looked ironically at the conditions of life in Europe and England at that particular moment and dialectically posed counter-positions in order to critique his present. More's *Utopia* is a playful critique, not a positivist solution. My understanding of the role utopia is very similar to that of Frederic Jameson in his recent book, *Archaeologies of the Future: The Desire Called Utopia and Other Science Fictions (Poetics of Social Forms)*. There he argues that one of the most important aspects of utopian thought is to keep the possibility of change, and the possibility of critical thought alive in moments of the greatest despair.

### Alison

So, utopia is an unreachable goal, simply a process?

### Anthony

I would say it is a strategy of posing questions as opposed to a fixed ideal city. I am trying to undermine the idea of a fixed, ideal city by a strategic idea of critical questioning.

### Ishita

How is this idea similar to Le Corbusier's conception of Chandigarh? Can utopia be physically built in this way, or do you believe that utopia can be achieved through incremental change over time or even through informal means?

### Anthony

I think the master-stroke of Chandigarh was to leave the building of the city to itself. All that was established was a network, communication, and then a group of symbolic buildings at the top. Corbusier did not build the entire city as a monument, but rather established a planned network to be filled in by developed growth. I am for a certain sense of incremental change, strategies that can, at the smallest scale of intervention, as opposed to the largest, physically transform a society's life. In a sense it is a strategy of architectural micro-investment. Architecture has to be at the scale of transformation as opposed to the scale of the transformed.

### Carly

Speaking of cities, scale, and numbers, what are the psychological ramifications of increasing density in cities in terms of claustrophobia, agoraphobia, and placelessness?

### Anthony

In *Warped Space*, I was interested in looking at how the rise of psychology, and its transformation into psychoanalysis, was contemporaneous with the rise of the metropolis. Cities of half a million to a million turned into cities of three million, like Berlin, over a period of a few decades. This was accompanied by a series of social shocks, when rural populations moved to cities for industrial jobs and met head-on a rather comfortable bourgeois society. The individual, confronted by that strange, heterogeneous, and apparently unformed and threatening mass—a mass that seemed threatening—turned to psychology as a way of explaining the phenomena of urban alienation. I don't have the social or historical knowledge to examine the massive social ramifications of the rapid urbanization of Asia or the Americas, and certainly not to analyze the role of psychoanalysis in cultures that are very different from that of turn of the century Vienna.

### Alison
You mentioned how the Radiant City undermined the idea of utopia: that it is a mis-interpretation of the genre of utopia. Is perhaps one of the reasons you wrote the book today because of all the "ideal" building that is happening in the Far East right now; physical manifestations of the Radiant City?

### Anthony
I don't feel that a little book on utopia will have any influence on any of the great building campaigns of the next 50 years. It would be nice for architectural students to realize the limits of the discipline and to also understand the dialectical relationships of the discipline in relation to thinking about society. Like the Occupy Movement, people's ability to self-organize into small communities seems much more the scale of desired architectural development in the future than control by large scale hedge fund investment. One, buildings made with huge investments face almost immediate obsolescence at the moment when they are built. Two, no amount of building at the scale that is it being built is going to ever deal or will ever serve a population that is growing at such a rate. Mike Davis pointed out, by 2040 80% of the world population will be living in cities. And 40% of that population will be living in slums. That is huge. What is clear, though, is that we have look on what we often call "informal settlements" in a totally different way. Architecture in the traditional sense has little role to play in this context. Very few of the experiments of the 60s and 70s were successful in re-building the favelas. One that has survived and prospered was the experimental *siedlung* of PREVI near Lima, Peru, and, to return to Stirling, his expandable house prototypes—what he called "climbing frames"—have remained favored among the twenty or so other houses proposed by the team of international and national architects in 1974. Interestingly enough, Stirling's project is planned on a nine-square grid!

## Joseph Choma

*is an architect and designer, and founder of Design Topology Lab,*
*a research platform dedicated to the ontology of space defined by*
*mathematics. He is writing the first pedagogical guide into trigonometric*
*transformations. Choma completed his graduate studies in design and*
*computation at Massachusetts Institute of Technology, and is currently*
*an assistant professor at Southern Polytechnic State University, where he*
*directs the Digital Fabrication Lab.*

# T-h-i-c-k-e-n-i-n-g

Two seemingly identical lines—each defined by a unique parametric equation—are different, because the location of an object in space is part of a shape's mathematical DNA: the $x$ and $y$ values define the location of points in a two-dimensional Cartesian coordinate system.

$x = u$
$y = \pi/3$

*for all*
$u \in [0, 2\pi]$

$x = u$
$y = -\pi/3$

*for all*
$u \in [0, 2\pi]$

If we imagine that this is a section cut through two surfaces in space, this shape acquires thickness. If this example were to be a three-dimensional shape, each surface would be defined by the parameters: $u$ and $v$. Within digital software, the distance or thickness between two surfaces is considered to be a separate parameter: $w$. However, $w$ does not always operate separately. For example, a sphere with an offset thickness would require two parametric equations, defining two different spheres in space. Although the parameter $w$ is oriented perpendicular to the surface normal, it is not used to define the inherent geometry or "DNA" of either shape.

Within typical digital software environments, we do not have a means to manipulate the *w* parameter—that which is not part of the shape's "DNA." However, if we begin to reconsider *w* as part of the inherent DNA of the shape, the possibility of creating a "thick shape" with one parametric equation arises.

A simple sine curve mediates between two boundary conditions. Based on our new definition, this could be considered a "thick shape," although the curve still reads as a single line. It is only after the sine curve's frequency increases to a certain threshold that a zero-thickness shape begins to have the illusion of thickness. Eventually the undulations visually read as a solid "thick" black rectangle: a thick shape.

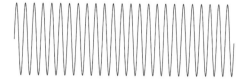

$x = u$
$y = sin(25u)$

*for all:*     $u \in [0, 2\pi]$

Accepting this, a question arises: Is it possible to define more than one boundary condition with a single parametric equation? In the example below, a curve is embedded inside another curve, such that the curve modulates between four boundaries. Mathematically, it is possible to combine parts of shapes to create a different singular shape. This type of trigonometric transformation might be called *texturing*: shapes of different frequencies combine; the lower-frequency shape becomes the receiver for the higher-frequency shape. Here, the curve of frequency 25 is "textured" by the curve of frequency 50, which is placed inside it.[1]

Like constructive interference in sound waves, as waves combine the increase in amplitude is determined by the collision of the apexes.[2]

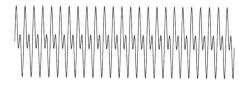

$x = u$
$y = (sin(50u) + sin(25u))/1.75$

*for all:*     $u \in [0, 2\pi]$

By introducing an additional parameter to the parametric equation, we are able to see the shape grow in another manner. In this simplified two-dimensional example, by adding the parameter, $v$, the previous curve transforms into a surface.

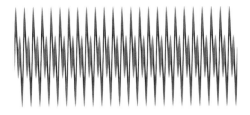

$x = u$
$y = v+(sin(50u)+sin(25u))/1.75$

*for all:*   $u \in [0, 2\pi]$
　　　　　$v \in [-\pi/8, \pi/8]$

In some ways, this is similar to the three-dimensional example in the pages that follow. However, in the those examples, where parameter $w$ is introduced, the parametric equation needs to be defined by a second subset of $x$, $y$, and $z$. This subset allows a single geometry to modulate infinitely between multiple three-dimensional boundary conditions. The depth at which the geometry modulates between these boundaries is controlled by the parameter $w$. This type of trigonometric transformation could be called *thickening*.

After a shape has been defined by the second subset of $x$, $y$, and $z$, a whole new range of geometric freedom is introduced. In a more complex trigonometric transformation (called *containing*), the boundary of one three-dimensional shape can be placed inside the boundary of another three-dimensional shape. Finally, the complete geometric hierarchy of a shape can be altered in a single transformation, within one parametric equation. As the sphere thickens over a series of recursions, its geometry begins to mediate between multiple envelopes. The sphere no longer has one boundary but rather multiple boundaries, while the drawing on its surface is perceived as a thickening; from an object state to that of an atmosphere.

*All images by Joseph Choma, 2012.*

**Endnotes**

1   Note that these two parts in $y$ are scaled by 1.75.
2   The scaling function in this example is used to keep the amplitude (or thickness) consistent with the examples above.